Dr Wang Yang is a professor in Preventive Medicine and Public Health in China. He was a graduate from the world-famous West-China Medical University in 1983 and a postgraduate from the University of Liverpool in the UK in 2000. He is currently a consultant to international bodies such as World Bank, and DFID (Dep. International Development, UK).

His clients and students include politicians, eminent scholars, millionaires, and celebrities. The field of his prediction covers very wide areas such as the stock market, health, policy and strategy development, careers, avoiding accidents and so on.

He is one of the best-selling authors in China with 20 books and over 100 papers published in various magazines and newspapers, both in China and abroad.

Jon Sandifer studied at the Michio Kushi Institute in London and Boston from 1977 to 1980. Shortly afterwards he began to teach oriental face diagnosis, shiatsu massage, macrobiotic philosophy, Zen cookery, yin & yang, Chinese astrology and the I Ching. He later directed the Kushi Institute of London until 1993 and has since become the author of seven books, including *Feng Shui for Life*, *Feng Shui Astrology* and *Zen & the Art of Cooking*.

In 1981 he was a co-founder of the Shiatsu Society, in 1995 he founded the Macrobiotic Association of Great Britain and is curre͏   n of the Feng Shui Society (GB). He writes regularly for t   ide publication on feng shui – *Feng Shui for Modern Living*

For my mother, Professor Tan Zhiping, a scholar of
Chinese classical literature and a poet

Wang Yang

THE AUTHENTIC
I CHING

The Three Classic Methods of Prediction

Dr Wang Yang and Jon Sandifer

Watkins Publishing
London

This edition published in the UK in 2003 by
Watkins Publishing, 20 Bloomsbury Street, London, WC1B 3QA

Cover design by Echelon Design
Designed by Jerry Goldie
Typeset by WestKey Ltd, Falmouth, Cornwall
Printed and bound in Great Britain

British Library Cataloguing in Publication data available

Library of Congress Cataloging in Publication data available

ISBN 1 84293 052 4

www.watkinspublishing.com

Contents

Acknowledgements

The author and editor wish to acknowledge the following people who have contributed to the publication of this book.

Michael Mann of Watkins, who commissioned us to write this book, for his encouragement and support throughout the project.

Florence Hamilton for the excellent feedback and diligent editing of the final manuscript which was very much appreciated by us both.

Derek Walters, one of the world's greatest scholars on the I Ching and Chinese astrology, for providing us with the formula used in chapter 4, The Chinese Calendar.

Justin Sandifer for creating the tables for the Chinese calendar.

Nicola Savage and Mary Sandifer for typing the manuscript.

Drew McNaughton for all his technical assistance, editing and troubleshooting the final manuscript.

Thank you all very much indeed for your help and contributions.

Editor's Introduction

In July 2000 I received a fascinating e-mail from Professor Wang Yang of China who was then a Research Fellow at the University of Liverpool. He enclosed his CV which immediately caught my attention. Here was a man I had been longing to meet for many, many years. Not only was he qualified in traditional Chinese medicine but he was also a professor of preventive medicine in China, with a strong lineage in traditional Chinese studies. In his initial communication with me he wrote about his interest in feng shui and how in his opinion the subject was largely being misrepresented in the West. His argument was that feng shui was intended to improve people's health and not their wealth, and he went on to congratulate me on my latest book *Feng Shui Journey* which emphasised health and the prevention of disease. Since he was only in the UK for a couple of months, I warmly invited him to my home to discuss feng shui, Chinese astrology and the I Ching.

We met a couple of weeks later and set aside the day to share our knowledge and experience. The man is a gem. He is very kind, thoughtful, considerate, remarkably humble and yet is willing to argue any points. Over the years I have studied with and met several masters from China, Japan, Taiwan, Hong Kong and Malaysia, and in initial discussions they often remain guarded and like to parry by asking questions to test your knowledge. Within a few minutes, we were discussing Chinese horoscopes – known as the Four Pillars – and I asked him whether he considered that people born in the southern hemisphere should have their charts examined differently. I pointed out that I was born just south of the equator (Mombasa, Kenya) and rather than dismissing the question, he said 'why don't we test the system now?' He asked for my year, month, day and hour of birth and in return gave me his birth data. Chinese masters rarely if ever give out this information! He then suggested that we do each other's charts and open up the Fate Pillars and see if there was any common ground that we could discuss or observe.

It usually takes me about an hour to formulate a chart and open up the Four Pillars and the Fate. I use the thousand-year calendar and make all the calculations using Chinese characters and numbers and elements. My desk is usually a sprawling mass of papers and tables and almanacs when I get involved in doing a horoscope.

Professor Wang Yang sat in his chair with no desk and produced a small piece of paper and a tiny thousand-year calendar. He appeared to be making calculations on his palm and on his fingertips as well. He glanced up occasionally and was very impressed that I was using Chinese characters. Ten minutes later he asked how I was getting on as he had completed my chart and was ready to analyse it for me.

Since he was returning to China after his research at Liverpool University in September 2000 and had no plans to return, I asked if he would be willing to spend a day sharing his knowledge and insights with a number of my colleagues and top students. He was delighted by the prospect. Over the next few weeks we worked on an outline and the event went ahead at the end of September just prior to his return to China. All of us present had either a passion or a professional interest in feng shui, Chinese astrology, tai chi, chi kung, acupuncture or the I Ching itself. All of us were aware of the I Ching and what is known as the Classic method of consulting this fascinating oracle and now Professor Wang Yang was going to share two new methods – the Na Jia method and the Mei Hua method. In order to benefit from this, we needed a basic understanding of Chinese astrology. What impressed all of us was how he was able to present the Four Pillars in 90 minutes and achieve what many of us had struggled to learn in not just hours but often weeks of intensive seminar studies.

Stephen Skinner, the publisher of *Feng Shui for Modern Living*, the international magazine on feng shui, was present at the seminar and is one of my western colleagues who has studied this subject in depth. He was greatly impressed by Professor Wang Yang's knowledge and skill. The other western expert for whom I have immense respect is Derek Walters and two days later, on the eve of Professor Wang Yang's return to China, I was able to get these two great minds to meet. Again, Derek, like Stephen, was greatly impressed with Professor Wang Yang.

Having had seven of my own books published in the West by four different publishers, I was eager to see what interest there lay in the work of Professor Wang Yang and his knowledge of the I Ching, especially these two almost unknown methods that he was presenting. I sent out outlines and had several meetings with publishers and eventually Michael Mann of Watkins realised that here was a genius at work.

The I Ching is only one area of Professor Wang Yang's knowledge, and I look forward to his writing on Chinese medicine, Taoism, oriental diagnosis and more. Professor Wang Yang is not only a great teacher, but also a scholar. It has been the challenge of both Watkins and myself as an editor not to dilute his work, but to make it accessible to any reader. Whether like me you have been familiar with the I Ching for over 25 years, or if this is the first time you have picked up a book on this subject, either way you will find this book a delight. For the beginners, so that there is no need to buy a copy of the I Ching, I have summarised each of the hexagrams and the meaning of the moving lines for your benefit. For the old timers, please delve into your own great book.

The biggest challenge was to bring all the relevant and necessary background material into one book, including a thousand-year calendar. To this end I'm deeply grateful to Derek Walters who supplied me with simple sheets and handouts that he uses in his lectures and seminars. Together with various tables in chapter 4, this will enable you to compute the year, month, day and hour in relation to questions you may have using the Mei Hua method.

I sincerely hope that the I Ching will become an integral part of your life, both now and in the future. Its timeless wisdom and clarity can help us all when we are looking for guidance, insight or confirmation of our own intuition. Please enjoy it!

Editor's Background

At the age of 23 I arrived in the UK from Mombasa, Kenya, having spent the previous six years working and travelling my way around the world. I'd been born and raised in Kenya, but my parents were looking to sell up and return to the UK. When I arrived in the UK I had all my worldly possessions strapped on my back and £20 in my pocket. After several weeks of travelling around Scotland, England and Wales, I was flat broke and found myself hitch-hiking from northern Wales toward London in search of employment and somewhere to live. A young Canadian theology student gave me a ride in his battered Volkswagen and I told him my tale. He said that since I was at a turning point in my life, now was the time to consult the great book. I thought to myself this was not the time to be trapped in a car with some kind of religious fundamentalist!

He pulled the car into a lay-by and produced a copy of the I Ching wrapped in a black seamless cloth in the glove compartment of his car. Using three of my own coins (I was literally down to almost these!) he told me how to cast the coins, create a hexagram and look up the response in the great book. It was a magical moment and the oracle, as I understood it then, suggested that I travelled south, but did not cross the great water. For some reason I took this to mean that I should head for the south coast and by that evening I was in Brighton. The following day I found a job and accommodation and within a week discovered a copy of the I Ching on the landlady's bookshelf.

Since then I have devoted my time to the study, and later the professional practice of shiatsu massage, Zen cooking, macrobiotics, oriental astrology and feng shui. The I Ching for me confirms that there is an Order in the Universe. In times of crisis, or self-doubt, or when a new direction is opening up, I find the I Ching can provide fascinating insights that I would not normally have been aware of. Having used only the Classical method over the years, I find that Professor Wang Yang's Na Jia method and Mei Hua method simply bring more depth, flexibility and possibility to this timeless oracle.

Author's Introduction

Why I Wrote This Book

We are all aware that we are living in a changing world and that change is occurring at a faster rate than ever. Events may suddenly happen and have a great impact on us in a positive or negative way. On the plus side, you may land a fantastic job, gain promotion, find a loving partner, have great success with your career, or make a lot of money unexpectedly from an investment. On the down side, you may suddenly suffer from serious disease, have an unexpected accident, lose your job or have your credibility undermined.

What can we do to cope and help us to understand the future or the unseen world? Clearly, we can have a choice of attitude. Firstly, in a passive way, we can just wait for something to happen and do nothing. Secondly, we can take a more active or positive stance to seek new opportunities, develop our luck, and prevent, or at least reduce, the impact of a bad turn of fortune. How, on a practical level, can we actively take a stand? As a professor of preventive medicine who has studied the accepted western model of prevention, I have been concerned with this issue as it relates to patients' health, happiness and well-being. Over the years, I have collected many useful case histories where I had consulted the I Ching regarding the potential outcome for my patients, family and friends. The subjects that interest me and that I have researched include:

- The outcome of a patient's health
- Predicting the future for children
- How to prevent accidents

- Strategy and timing for promotion, investment, study and success
- Improving relationships
- How to use feng shui remedies correctly

Personally I have benefited immensely from my long-term study and application of the I Ching and the various prediction methods. I have always wanted to share my experience and joy with my friends, students and colleagues. My frustration has been that too few people know of the applications and implications of this ancient study. My aim in writing this book, based on my years of experience and research, is to provide you with information on three areas:

- To introduce you to new and practical methods of I Ching prediction step by step. By becoming familiar with these methods you will be able to use this ancient oriental wisdom in your daily life and improve the quality of your life. For many, the I Ching has been a lifelong study but I will share with you the formulae, the case studies and my own stories to make the material interesting and easily accessible. With practice, you will be able to look at events in your own life and compare the outcome based on any of the methods presented here.
- Throughout the book I will provide you with examples which essentially prove and demonstrate why it is possible to justify that the I Ching is a very useful prediction tool.
- The I Ching is essentially the world's oldest and most exciting brain-teaser! How can the I Ching predict the future? In the text and in the case histories supplied here you will find many useful clues and explanations as to why prediction is possible and how to use your intuition and judgement to unravel the truth.

Why This Book Is Different

There are literally hundreds of editions of the I Ching circulating not only in China, but throughout the western world as well. Mainly they focus on the Classical method of prediction which involves devising a hexagram and interpreting the outcome. In my research of this fascinating subject, I have become aware that few people in the West know about the other methods of prediction using the I Ching that are commonly used and practised in China. It is vital not to dismiss the Classical method, but to cover it in sufficient depth so that you can refer to its methodology and even combine it with any of the other methods that I present in this book.

The Mei Hua method is a relatively simple and effective use of prediction based on analysing the top and bottom trigrams of any hexagram. In essence, the upper trigram relates to the questioner, and the lower trigram represents the event or question concerned. It is a very simple, practical and quick method of prediction that is extremely popular in China.

The Na Jia method will undoubtedly appeal to the mathematical, scientific and logical minds of western readers. It not only combines the trigrams and hexagrams of the I Ching, but introduces another layer – the Chinese calendar. Here, the influences of the various elements relative to time bring far more precision and accuracy to the prediction.

If you are familiar with, or work with, the skill of feng shui, then Form School can be compared to the Mei Hua method, and the more intricate calculation-orientated Compass School of feng shui is more similar to the Na Jia method. Ultimately, as in feng shui, it is the combined overview of different systems, schools, and interpretations that can give a more accurate reading.

The integrated method that I present in this book does precisely this. By combining the more intuitive Classical method, together with the basic building blocks of the trigrams using the Mei Hua method, and the precise use of time and elements in the Na Jia method it can give you a fascinating insight into any potential outcome.

To my knowledge, there is no other book available that can give you all of this! Whether you are a complete novice with the I Ching or have been studying and reading it all your life, I am confident that you will enjoy the new discoveries to be found by practising the Mei Hua, the Na Jia and integrated methods as well. There is sufficient material, evidence and formulae within this book for you to practice and use the book on a regular basis. As you progress with your practice, I encourage you to acquire or read more on the I Ching and the symbolism of the trigrams, the hexagrams, each individual line and especially the changing lines.

The I Ching And Prediction

If you are a newcomer to the I Ching, let me explain how prediction is possible using this wonderful book. In early Chinese mythical prehistory there was an understanding that humanity was influenced, or governed, by the forces of heaven (Yang) and the energy that emanated below their feet and homes – the earth (Yin). Sandwiched between these two potent forces are human beings. The earliest attempts to graphically express this symbolism was the formation of three horizontal lines stacked one above the other. Effectively, the top line was heaven, the middle line humanity, the lower line earth. These horizontal lines could either be represented in a complete form (yang) or with a gap in the centre (yin). The full range of these three broken or unbroken lines is eight in total and they are known as trigrams. Stack two of these trigrams one on top of the other to form six lines, and these are collectively known as hexagrams.

When making a prediction with the I Ching, the questioner, using a variety of different methods – many explained in this book – builds up a hexagram line by line from the bottom towards the top while considering the question. It is as if the subconscious mind gets involved with not just the question, but the whole procedure of creating the hexagram. The next stage is to analyse the hexagram (there are 64 permutations) and to look at the significance of each line as well. By reading the appropriate text associated with the hexagram in combination with the question that has been raised about the future, it is possible, with a combination of intuition and reading the significance of the hexagram, for the questioner to come up with a prediction or an answer.

For thousands of years the Chinese have regarded every aspect of their world, their lives, health and destiny, as intertwined somehow. They have a unique perspective that there is a microcosm within the macrocosm. This basic underlying aspect of Chinese culture, through the influence no doubt of the I Ching, underpins their medicine, astrology, philosophy and agriculture. For the Chinese, the I Ching is equivalent to the Christian Bible or the Islamic Koran. It is a guidebook for living. Over the centuries many famous scholars have examined the text and written their own commentaries. Around the sixth century BC, the Chinese sage Lao Tsu was most certainly influenced by the I Ching in his development of Taoism. Confucius himself wrote lengthy commentaries on the I Ching at this time and is said to have declared as an elderly man that if he had another twenty years to live he would dedicate all of them to further study of the I Ching.

Among the great influences of the I Ching on Chinese culture, science and technology in the past has been its contribution to Traditional Chinese Medicine (TCM). The famous treatise on TCM is known as the Neiching. The translation of this great book is known as 'The Yellow Emperor's Classic Of Internal Medicine' and draws directly from the I Ching the principles for diagnosis and treatment of patients using acupuncture, herbs and moxabustion. Many of the yin/yang theories and concepts of the Five Elements form the basis of TCM. The Neiching emphasises seeing human beings as an inherent part of the universe and their health as dependent on their connection with their immediate environment and the chi of the heavens. The Yellow Emperor believed that health is a result of harmony between human beings and nature, whereas illness is caused by conflict and imbalance of yin and yang or the Five Elements, both internally and externally. The famous TCM doctor, Sun Simiao, once said, 'A doctor who doesn't understand the I Ching is not a qualified doctor.'

The only way to find out whether the I Ching actually works is to try it out for yourself. Carl Jung believed the reason why the predictions could be accurate was through synchronicity and what he calls 'the acausal connecting principle'. In the 1990s, researcher Mike Hayes studied the DNA code at Leicester University in the UK. DNA appears to be a spiral interconnection of living cells which for a human being can determine everything about us, from the colour of our eyes to the size of our ears or feet. Within its spiral molecule there are four chemical bases which can explain, for example, why some people have blue eyes or brown eyes. Whilst continuing his studies, Hayes discovered that these four chemical bases make up 64 'triplets'. As he pondered on this figure of 64, he wondered where he'd come across this figure before – it was the I Ching! The more he looked into the structure of DNA from a mathematical perspective, the more he realised that it matched the I Ching, with all the possibilities built up from eight basic core blocks known as trigrams.

Perhaps this is why the I Ching works as a predictive tool. The Chinese sages who created and studied this centuries ago must have known intuitively about life and destiny. Perhaps they also knew that the universe that we inhabit is set up like a random computer database. All that is needed to find the relevant information is to send out the right signals (the aura that charges us as we formulate our question) and wait for the reply that the I Ching provides us with through the formation of two trigrams (the hexagram).

It is pleasing to note that so many rational and scientific minds have been drawn to the I Ching in recent centuries. In the early eighteenth century the French missionary Joachim Bouvet studied the I Ching and discussed his findings with his close friend G. W. Leibniz, the German philosopher and mathematician widely acknowledged as the founder of modern calculus. Leibniz also discovered the binary system on which computer science is now based. Carl Jung studied the I Ching for years and found it a source of enormous wisdom. The Nobel Prize-winning physicist Niels Bohr recognised parallels between the concepts of modern atomic science and the I Ching. He actually used the yin/yang symbol as a basis for his own personal coat of arms. More recently Martin Schonberger in his book *The Hidden Key To Life* compares the structure of the 64 hexagrams of the I Ching with the 64 DNA codons of the genetic code. The I Ching is only just beginning to unravel its truth!

In *I Ching: The No. 1 Success Formula* the scholar Christopher Market states: 'I found that the I Ching does not reveal the truth in objective terms, but that it triggers subjective mental associations which are relevant to our particular situation at a particular time. It follows from this that only you can interpret your hexagram. Nobody else can do it for you and neither can you interpret for anyone else.' He continues: 'Neither did I find any evidence of a mysterious law of synchronicity at work, which connects the event of questioning the I Ching with other simultaneous events around us or within us. Instead, it is our own conscious and unconscious minds that interact with the text to produce relevant answers. When consulting the I Ching, sudden flashes of intuition let us see how the pieces of our puzzle fit together.'

Many modern Chinese scholars believe that the essential key to the I Ching method of prediction can be associated with holographic theory. Based on this theory, any detail, event or matter in the universe can be accurately represented by an extremely small piece of that event or matter. This is also the basis of the modern biological technique of cloning.

My View Of The I Ching

Firstly, I strongly believe that there must be a law which governs all movements and developments of every event or phenomenon in the universe. If we could understand this law then we could predict the outcome for all events in the universe. It could be on the same level as scientists who can forecast the weather, the tides, volcanic activity and earthquakes with appropriate modern technology and instruments. Secondly, we need to understand how all events and phenomena are interconnected within this universe. I think the holographic theory is the best explanation so far. It is widely acknowledged that the human being is the most complex and advanced life form on the planet. The ancient Chinese believed that the human being is a condensed microcosm of the universe itself. They saw the human being as an inherent part of the universe, merged with nature and the cosmos, and from this assumption they believed that any small sign or signal within a human being can reflect everything around us. Just as the ancient sage Fu Hsi is reported to state in the I Ching, 'Anciently, when Fu Hsi had come to the rule of all under heaven, looking up, he contemplated the brilliant forms exhibited in the sky, and looking down he surveyed the patterns shown on the earth. He contemplated the ornamental appearances of birds and beasts and the different suitabilities of the soil. Near at hand, in his own person, he found things for consideration, and the same at a distance, in things in general. On this he devised the eight trigrams, to show fully the attributes of the spirit-like and intelligent and to classify the qualities of the myriads of things.'

Thirdly, prediction using the I Ching is by no means associated with using only our subconscious or unconscious or intuition. This is an important part of the prediction, but I believe that there are other factors. I believe that prediction is not only subjective, but also objective. You will find strong evidence for this in the prediction about the age of a young girl's brother (see page 93). In this case, using three different methods separately conducted by three individuals, each came up with the same accurate answer simultaneously. I provide more evidence in the study of the two satellites (see page 179). On this particular occasion according to the time of launch, everybody will find their own unique answer.

Finally, I am very inspired by Christopher Market's wonderful metaphor: 'The I Ching functions like a great memory bank that is packed with the wisdom of the ages. But the most amazing computer is your own brain with its conscious and unconscious mind. When you connect your brain to the software contained in your hexagram, it automatically selects the relevant clues out of millions of possible combinations. Your own mind becomes universal when it is inspired by a great teacher like the I Ching.'

Chapter 1

The Different Methods of I Ching Prediction

'To explore what is complex, search out what is hidden, to look up what lies deep, and reach to what is distant, thereby determining the issues for good or ill of all events under the sky, there is nothing greater than the I Ching. It exhibits the past and teaches us to discriminate the issues of the future. It manifests what is still small and brings to light what is obscure.'

Christopher Market, *The I Ching: The No. 1 Success Formula*

A Brief Summary Of The Five Popular Prediction Methods

1. The Classical Method

This is undoubtedly the most popular method of prediction using the I Ching and most westerners are familiar with the approach. The questioner needs to create a relevant hexagram, either by randomly opening the I Ching or by the coin-casting method (see page 57). The procedure is fairly simple:

- Create a specific hexagram
- Read the attached text from the I Ching and try to understand its metaphor
- Look at the imagery of the two trigrams and contemplate the wider meaning of their symbolism

- Note where there are any moving lines (or line) and recreate the hexagram by substituting any moving line with its opposite (see page 59). This will give the questioner a new hexagram which represents the future or the outcome.

The procedure for analysis using this method is very flexible and the questioner can be left with a conclusion that might be interpreted in many different ways. Ideally, with this method of prediction, you need to have a sound knowledge of the hexagrams, the trigrams and their relevant meaning. The great value of this method is that it allows you to trust and develop your own intuition. If you happen to have in your possession a weighty copy of the I Ching, then this method allows you to delve into more detail and enjoy the profound Chinese philosophy including the Taoism and Confucianism that accompanies the texts and the commentaries in the original I Ching. The weakness of the Classical method is that, as with any new tool, it takes a little practice to get used to. The procedure for creating the trigrams takes a little time and the meaning of the hexagram is wide open for interpretation. That is why when the same question is asked by different individuals using the same method they often obtain completely opposite answers.

2. The Mei Hua Method

In the Mei Hua method the hexagram is created not by casting coins but by using the Chinese calendar. Working with precise dates and times it is possible to build an entire hexagram in a very logical way. Using this approach it is possible to get a clear and direct prediction very quickly. Essentially the questioner needs to compare and analyse the relationship between the upper and lower trigram, or the Subject trigram and Object trigram, of the given hexagram. In the Mei Hua method the Subject trigram represents yourself, the questioner or the client who has consulted the I Ching for guidance or advice, while the Object trigram represents the specific event or person that is of concern to the questioner. After combining these trigrams the questioner can also read the image of the hexagram from the I Ching. The Mei Hua method is very simple and easy to learn. Sometimes the prediction can give very precise answers such as a definitive yes or no. This is one of the most popular divination methods in China. Creating the hexagrams by time data calculation is very objective and less influenced by subjective factors or distractions than the Classical method. It can be especially useful when you need to make a decision urgently or in an emergency. It is, however, quite a flexible system and, like the Classical method, it takes time and practice to develop the true understanding of the hexagrams.

3. The Na Jia Method

This approach to prediction can deduce the development of an event and its final outcome through precise logical step-by-step calculation. To begin with it is necessary to identify what I call the Self line and Response line from the hexagram. In some ways it is similar to the Mei Hua method. The Self line represents the questioner or the client who is consulting the I Ching for guidance or advice. The Response line represents the specific event or person concerning the questioner or client. It is then necessary to match each line of the hexagram with the Earthly Branch – one of the twelve Chinese animals in astrology. The name Na Jia means literally 'matching lines'. It is possible with this method not to refer to the I Ching text at all and so it differs from the first two methods in this respect.

The Na Jia method is easy to apply and put into practice. It can be compared with the procedure involved in a mathematical exercise. It has remained one of the most popular methods of I Ching prediction used by the Chinese people for over 2000 years. It is especially popular in the scientific and academic community or for those individuals who like rational methodology. It is known in China as the 'orthodox school's great method'.

Its strengths are that it is relatively rational and easy to understand. The outcome of the question is easily uncovered and the answer and advice are always definite and unchangeable, e.g. yes or no. Also the trend and the development of the event can often be described in detail and often in a very realistic fashion. This is an excellent method of using the I Ching prediction for western people who are less familiar with traditional Chinese culture. Its weakness is that the procedure takes a little time and patience. It takes longer than the Mei Hua method to complete a prediction as you need to match the Earthly Branches with the lines very carefully. However, with experience half an hour is enough to complete an accurate prediction.

4. The Integrated Method

This approach to prediction combines all the methods. By adopting their strengths and setting aside their weaknesses, this integrated method can become a very useful new tool. It is simple, flexible, easy to understand and practical. The process involves creating a hexagram, using the Mei Hua method, the coin-casting method, or any other method that you may have learnt already. It is vital to carefully consider the question and how the outcome can evolve. For this method we need to study the Self line and the Response line of the hexagram using the Na Jia method. In terms of understanding the strength of the possible outcome you can analyse the Five Elements of each relevant line and the interaction between them. Other factors to consider are the elements of the Four Pillars for the specific date. To help understand the trend that lies behind the final outcome it is possible to refer to the complete hexagram and gain some insight from the metaphoric symbolism that the Classical method lends to prediction.

Finally, by interpreting the symbolism of the hexagram and combining all the details on a checklist you will be able to identify the outcome clearly and easily.

5. Forest of I Ching by Jiao

This method of early prediction was created by Jiao Gan who was the teacher of Jin Fang (77–37 BC). Master Jiao set up 4,096 possible answers according to the different changing lines of the 64 hexagrams. Historically, this is known as the very first example of the oracle method. Jin Fang was himself the founder of the Na Jia method that I cover in this book.

The Forest of I Ching makes predictions by the use of metaphor in the shape of a very short oracle poem that is usually about ten words long. For my own personal use and study I refer to this book when conducting a complex prediction or when completing the integrated method. I will quote from this wonderful book in some of the case histories on pages 126 and 183.

Before looking at the different ways to use the I Ching it will be helpful to understand the basis of yin and yang and the Five Elements.

Chapter Two

Yin and Yang and The Five Elements

Yin and Yang

The complementary yet antagonistic qualities of yin and yang energy form the basis of most Chinese philosophy and culture. The mythical sage Fu Hsi, who is believed to be the source of the I Ching, suggests that the Tao refers to yin and yang, 'Therefore in the I Ching, there is the Tai Chi, which produced the Two Elementary Forms (yin and yang). These forces produced the Four Emblematic Symbols (the cardinal points of North, South, East and West), which in turn produced the Eight Trigrams.'

Figure 1 Yin Yang Symbol

From this perspective, at the beginning of the universe there was nothing and this was known as Wu Chi followed by tai chi (chaos), yin and yang, the Four Emblematic Symbols, the eight trigrams, 64 hexagrams and everything in the world.

Figure 2 Progression of Creation

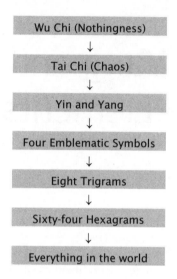

Wu Chi (Nothingness)
↓
Tai Chi (Chaos)
↓
Yin and Yang
↓
Four Emblematic Symbols
↓
Eight Trigrams
↓
Sixty-four Hexagrams
↓
Everything in the world

When you look at the yin yang symbol the dark aspect represents the yin (the night-time, stillness) and the white portion represents yang energy (activity and daylight). The 'tail' of the yang portion of the yin yang symbol sits low down and represents the birth of yang. Moving clockwise the energy or chi becomes more active until it is at its fullest expression at the top of the symbol. At this point the chi reverses and the thin narrow tail of yin starts to evolve, culminating in its full expression in the lower portion of the symbol. The cycle can represent a 24-hour phase of time where midnight is at the lowest point and the peak of yang at noon is at the top of the cycle. Since nothing in the universe is totally yin or yang, the small portion of the opposite quality is represented by a small dot in each half of the symbol. Within the yin portion there is a presence of yang, and within the yang sector there is a presence of yin.

There are four main principles in yin yang theory.

- Every phenomenon possesses two kinds of energy represented as yin and yang. For example the upper part of the body can be seen as yin and the lower part yang, the surface as yin and the interior yang. The roots of plants can be represented as yang, their leaves and branches as a manifestation of yin.

- Yin and yang are complementary and integrated with each other. Both are mutually indispensable and feed each other while at the same time they cannot be separated. In terms of Traditional Chinese Medicine, the chi of a human is regarded as yang while the blood is yin, and both coexist.
- Yin and yang transform each other. At their extreme, yin converts into its opposite and yang will also become yin. This can be seen in terms of the cycles in nature when the chi of deep winter (yin) gives way to the new fresh strong active chi of yang in the spring. At the high point of summer yang is at its strongest and yin at its weakest, and conversely in deep winter yin is dominant whereas the yang is weakest.
- Yin and yang continually interact and create change. We do not live in a static world or universe and the polarity of yin and yang and its relative charge brings about change. Excessive yang or excessive yin can bring conflict, imbalance and intolerance.

The Five Elements

The Five Element theory is effectively a slightly more sophisticated version of the yin yang model of change. As with the yin yang cycle, where yang's energy is at its peak at the top of the cycle and yin at its lowest, the Five Elements represent five different stages, or phases, of change within this cycle. It is sometimes known as the Five Transformations. Try to think of the Five Elements (fire, earth, metal, water and wood) not as static, but more as phases within the cycle of change.

Low down in the cycle when energy is quiet and still – such as at midnight or midwinter – the phase is known as water. At this stage energy is still and floating, but ready to give birth to, or produce, the next element. As dawn or spring approaches, the rapid growth and fresh new chi of wood appears. Plants and trees are supported by water. This phase in turn fuels the peak of energy represented by midday or the summer which is known as fire. Fire is fuelled by wood and as it burns itself through the residue of ashes fuels the next phase known as earth.

Late summer and the early afternoon have a mellowing settled quality of chi. The ashes from the fire, rather like the richness from the ash of a volcano, create excellent soil and compost. As this earth phase begins to experience the condensing downward force of the late afternoon, early evening or autumn, this gathering solidifies the earth into rocks and minerals known as metal. In traditional times, the autumn was a time of harvest, of gathering, of storing and even acquiring money from the sale of the harvest.

As with the yin yang theory, one extreme leads to the birth of its opposite. This holds true at the lower end of this phase as energy condenses to the point where it needs to melt. Ultimately metal melts and this fluid plasmic phase is known as water. This cycle is commonly known as the Birth or Support Cycle.

- Water gives birth to wood
- Wood gives birth to fire
- Fire gives birth to earth
- Earth gives birth to metal
- Metal gives birth to water

The Control Cycle

The second aspect of the Five Element theory is the relationship of control that one element may have to its opposite. Cutting across the interior of the cycle, each element both controls another element and is controlled by another element. These relationships are fundamental to getting the most out of the prediction methods in this book, and also are used widely in Chinese astrology, Traditional Chinese Medicine and feng shui.

The main controlling factors are:

- Fire controls metal (fire melts metal)
- Earth controls water (earth absorbs or dams the flow of water)
- Metal controls wood (an axe chops wood)
- Water controls fire (water extinguishes fire)
- Wood controls earth (the roots of vegetation break up the soil)

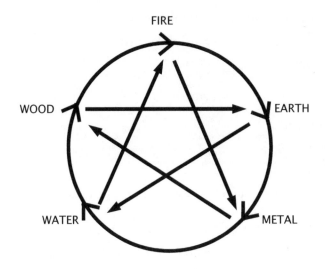

Figure 3 The Five Element Cycle

Each of the Five Elements is drawn from the natural world. The wood element represents plants, trees and vegetables; the water element rain, lakes and rivers; the fire element sunlight, or actual fire; the earth element fields, the soil; the metal element gold or iron.

The Five Elements In Different Seasons

Each of the four seasons is covered by a specific element: spring with wood, summer with fire, autumn with metal and winter with water. In Chinese astrology, each season is assigned three months. The first two months of any given season always represent the season's element, e.g. in spring the first two months belong to the wood element. However, the third month in any given season is always represented by the earth element. This earth phase or season is seen as the natural buffer between the seasons as they change. If we live in a four-season climate, we are aware of this phase as winter, for example, attempts to break through into spring. For several weeks the weather and climate can swing between the two seasons. This is known as the earth stage.

Figure 4 The Elements in Different Seasons

	Wood	Fire	Earth	Metal	Water
Spring	Prosperous	Second Prosperous	Dead	Sick	Retired
Summer	Retired	Prosperous	Second Prosperous	Dead	Sick
Autumn	Dead	Sick	Retired	Prosperous	Second Prosperous
Winter	Second Prosperous	Dead	Sick	Retired	Prosperous

Each element goes through five stages of change in accordance with each season.

- Prosperous. This stage represents the element being positioned in its own season, e.g. fire is prosperous during the summer.
- Second Prosperous. This is a strong phase and is the season after the birth of the particular element, e.g. water is second prosperous during the autumn.
- Retired. This is not a strong phase and is going towards becoming weaker. It is always the season prior to the season of the element that you are looking at, e.g. the element water is retired in the wood phase associated with the spring.
- Sick. This phase is always represented by the season which is the controlling element of the phase that you are looking at, e.g. with the wood element (born in spring) the sick phase is autumn (metal).
- Dead. This is the lowest ebb of the entire cycle and is seen as the season and element that is controlled by the element in question, e.g. fire is controlled by water, therefore during the winter the fire element is dead.

Spring/Wood Season

During springtime plants, trees, vegetables and new shoots appear very quickly and the wood element is prosperous. Because wood is the mother of fire, this child, the fire element is second prosperous during the spring. When wood is strong it will naturally destroy earth and therefore this element is dead. The metal element is the child of earth and when the mother is dead, the child will be sick. The water element is the mother of wood and when her child grows and becomes strong, she retires.

Summer/Fire Season

This is the strongest phase for the fire element, making it prosperous. Because fire is the mother of earth this child is second prosperous during the summer. In turn, fire when it is powerful will destroy metal and as an element during the summer it is dead. The water element represents the child of metal, and when the mother is dead the child is sick. The wood element is the mother of fire and when her child (fire) matures and becomes strong the element wood retires.

Autumn/Metal Season

This season represents harvest and its traditional tools were made of metal. The process of gathering is also the metal phase associated with autumn. This makes metal prosperous during this season. Since metal is the mother of the water element, this child is second prosperous during the autumn (water). Since the metal is very strong during this season it will destroy wood and this element is dead. The fire element, as the child of wood, will become sick because its mother is dead. The earth element is the mother of metal and as this child becomes strong, the earth retires.

Winter/Water Season

The cold, still nature of winter creates the most prosperous phase for the water element. Since water is the mother of wood, this child (wood) is second prosperous during the winter. With very strong water during the winter it will destroy the fire, therefore this element is dead. The earth element is the child of fire and since its mother is dead, the child is sick. The metal element is the mother of water and as her child matures and becomes strong, the mother retires.

The Earth Season

The twelve months in the Chinese calendar are all assigned a particular element and Chinese animal. The element and animal are known as the Earthly Branch.

Of the three months of any given season, the first two months are associated with the animal and element that match the element of the particular season. E.g. the first months of the water season are dominated by the Pig and the Rat. However, the third and final month of each season always has an earth element and animal associated with it.

- The Ox month is the third month of winter
- The Dragon month is the third month of spring
- The Sheep month is the third month of summer
- The Dog month is the third month of autumn

Winter/<u>Water</u> = the Rat and the Pig	+ Ox (<u>Earth</u>)
Spring/<u>Wood</u> = the Tiger and the Rabbit	+ Dragon (<u>Earth</u>)
Summer/<u>Fire</u> = the Snake and the Horse	+ Sheep (<u>Earth</u>)
Autumn/<u>Metal</u> = the Monkey and the Rooster	+ Dog (<u>Earth</u>)

Chapter Three

The Lines, Trigrams and Hexagrams of the I Ching

Whichever method of prediction you choose to employ using the I Ching, you will need to work from a hexagram. In this chapter I will take you through the mechanics and construction and symbolism of the hexagrams. The more familiar you become with the construction of hexagrams from the trigrams and individual lines, the more freedom, flexibility and pleasure can be derived from the prediction methods outlined in chapters 5, 6, 7 and 8.

Yin Yang Lines

The core of any hexagram is the lines involved and these are very simple and versatile as they completely represent yin and yang. Represented in simple linear form, the Chinese always referred to a line as Yao and these are the smallest unit of a hexagram.

Yang/Solid Line

—— Yang lines represent male, positive, strong, creative. Its numbers are 7 or 9.

Yin/Broken Line

− −   Yin lines represent female, negative, receptive, weaker. Yin line numbers are 6 or 8.

The Eight Trigrams

Any combination of yin or yang lines creates a basic trigram (Gua). Each of these trigrams has: a name, symbolism, an attribute, an element, an image, an associated family member, a direction and a number. (See figure 5, The Eight Trigrams)

The first step in the analysis of any trigram is to assess whether it is yin or yang. A trigram made up of three solid lines represents full yang (father) and a trigram made up of three broken lines represents complete yin (mother). For the remaining six trigrams, it is the one single line that is different from the other two that dominates the trigram, e.g. one broken line (yin) together with two solid lines (yang) represents a yin trigram.

One of the easiest ways to familiarise yourself with the trigrams of the I Ching initially is to regard them as a family. The family is made up of a father and a mother and six children. These children are the eldest, middle and youngest sons, and the eldest, middle and youngest daughters. The trigram Ch'ien with three solid yang lines represents father. The trigram K'un with three broken yin lines represents the ultimate feminine chi – mother. Solid yang is father, complete yin is the mother.

An easy way to remember the children is:

- Remember that the trigrams begin from the bottom upwards
- The one solitary yin or yang line within the trigram represents its gender
- Look for the position of this line within the trigram

Chen
The eldest son – the first solitary yang line

K'an
The second son where the middle line of the trigram is solid

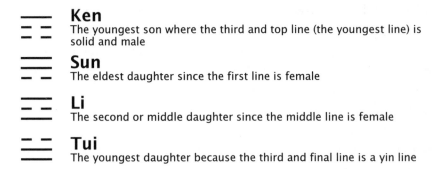

Ken
The youngest son where the third and top line (the youngest line) is solid and male

Sun
The eldest daughter since the first line is female

Li
The second or middle daughter since the middle line is female

Tui
The youngest daughter because the third and final line is a yin line

Figure 5 The Eight Trigrams

Symbol	Name	Attribute	Element	Image	Direction*	Number**	Family Member
	Ch'ien (Creative)	Strong	Metal	Heaven	NW	1	Father
	K'un (Receptive)	Devoted Yielding	Earth	Earth	SW	8	Mother
	Chen (Arousing)	Inciting Movement	Earth	Thunder	E	4	Eldest son
	K'an (Abysmal)	Dangerous	Water	Water	N	6	Second son
	Ken (Keeping Still)	Resting	Earth	Mountain	NE	7	Youngest son
	Sun (Gentle)	Penetrating	Wood	Wind, Wood	SE	5	Eldest daughter
	Li (Clinging)	Light-giving	Fire	Fire	S	3	Second daughter
	Tui (Joyous)	Joyful	Metal	Lake	W	2	Youngest daughter

* The direction is based on the Later Heaven Eight Trigram Sequence Chart

** The number is based on the Early Heaven Eight Trigram Sequence Chart

Numbers And Directions Of The Trigrams

Each of the eight trigrams represents a different cardinal or intercardinal direction. These directions being: north, north-east, north-west, south, south-east, south-west, east and west. The way traditional Chinese scholars and experts on the I Ching and feng shui depicted these directions was born out of the Five Elements rather than magnetic compass readings. That is why it is often confusing in feng shui to always see south at the top of any map or plan! Keeping the Five Elements in mind, it is easy to see why this makes sense. At the top of the cycle - or the map - is the element fire, representing the sun or south. The lowest point of chi in the Five Element cycle is water, representing the cold, winter and the north. This represents north and is always at the bottom of the map. Rising on the left of the cycle is the energy of spring and dawn, which represents the east. Whereas the settling, gathering early evening or autumnal chi is on the right side of the plan - the west. It is good to mention this point now in case you choose to study further the fascinating skill of Feng Shui.

There are two ways of arranging these trigrams according to compass direction. Both arrangements or sequences will become apparent in later chapters when I present different prediction methods, and you can refer back to figure 6 and figure 7, the Early and Later Heaven Sequence Charts.

The Earl Heaven Sequence Chart

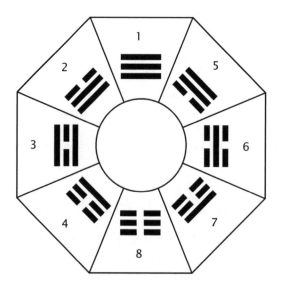

Figure 6 Earl Heaven Sequence

You may already be familiar with this octagonal chart where the arrangements of trigrams appear in the Early Heaven Sequence. This is known as the Pa Kua. You may have seen this painted on five-inch octagonal boards with a reflective mirror in the centre, often hung above a door of a Chinese home, business or restaurant. Never placed inside the home, they are used to guard or ward off negative chi. The Early Heaven Sequence represents the fast-moving chi of the universe, the direct influence of heaven and how chi is circulating outside of the property. An easy way to spot this trigram is to notice that the trigram Ch'ien is always at the top, or the south aspect of this arrangement.

The Later Heaven Sequence Chart

With this arrangement it is possible to see a closer association with the Five Elements. For example, in the south at the top of this Pa Kua is the fire trigram and at the bottom of the Pa Kua, in the north, is the water trigram. The east and south-east both have wood element trigrams and the west and north-west metal element trigrams.

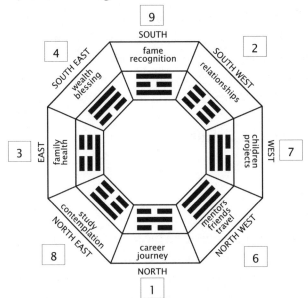

Figure 7 The Later Heaven Sequence

The Later Heaven Sequence represents how chi manifests within the home or in the present time. This sequence of trigrams also forms the foundation of what is known as the Lo Shu Magic Square.

Please note that you read the trigrams in both of these illustrations from the centre towards the outside. In other words, the first or lower line is drawn out toward the centre of these two Pa Kua.

The 64 Hexagrams

A hexagram is built up of two trigrams giving a total of six lines. These two halves of a hexagram can be called the upper or external trigram, and the lower or internal trigram.

Figure 8 T'ai No. 11 Peace

The above image is the T'ai hexagram, number 11, symbolising Peace. It is built up from the lower trigram of Ch'ien which has three solid yang lines, and the upper trigram of K'un which is built of three broken yin lines.

When you look at the hexagram P'i, number 12, Standstill, there is a completely opposite construction yet the same two trigrams are involved.

Figure 9 P'i No. 12 Standstill

Although this hexagram is built with the same two identical trigrams as that in the T'ai hexagram, the arrangement and interpretation are different. Since the position of the two trigrams is reversed, the image is also different. The imagery of T'ai shows the perfect combination or meeting of heaven and earth, yin and yang, male and female. Heaven is now on earth, bringing peace (T'ai) in

Pi, although the trigrams of heaven and earth appear in their correct position, the downward energy of heaven prevents the upward creative yin energy of earth from flourishing. Hence the symbolism of Standstill.

There are 64 versions of these combinations of trigrams and figure 10 will help you quickly construct and locate them for future reference.

Figure 10 The 64 Hexagrams

Upper Trigram / Lower Trigram	Ch'ien	Chen	K'an	Ken	K'un	Sun	Li	Tui
Ch'ien	1	34	5	26	11	9	14	43
Chen	25	51	3	27	24	42	21	17
K'an	6	40	29	4	7	59	64	47
Ken	33	62	39	52	15	53	56	31
K'un	12	16	8	23	2	20	35	45
Sun	44	32	48	18	46	57	50	28
Li	13	55	63	22	36	37	30	49
Tui	10	54	60	41	19	61	38	58

The Names and Numbers of the 64 Hexagrams

1	Ch'ien	䷀	The Creative
2	K'un	䷁	Receptive
3	Chun	䷂	Initial Difficulty
4	Meng	䷃	Youthful Folly
5	Hsu	䷄	Waiting/Nourishment
6	Sung	䷅	Conflict
7	Shih	䷆	The Army
8	Pi	䷇	Holding Together/Union
9	Hsiao Ch'u	䷈	The Taming Power of the Small
10	Lu	䷉	Treading/Conduct
11	T'ai	䷊	Peace
12	Pi	䷋	Standstill/Stagnation
13	T'ung Jên	䷌	Fellowship with Men

14	Ta Yu		Possession in Great Measure
15	Ch'ien		Modesty
16	Yu		Enthusiasm
17	Sui		Following
18	Ku		Work on what has been spoiled/Decay
19	Lin		Approach
20	Kuan		Contemplation/View
21	Shih Ho		Biting Through
22	Pi		Grace
23	Po		Splitting Apart
24	Fu		Return/The Turning Point
25	Wu Wang		Innocence/Unexpected
26	Ta Ch'u		The Taming Power of the Great
27	I		Corners of the Mouth/Providing Nourishment

28	Ta Kuo		Preponderance of the Great/Excess
29	K'an		The Abysmal/Water
30	Li		The Clinging/Fire
31	Hsien		Influence/Wooing
32	Heng		Duration
33	Tun		Retreat
34	Ta Chuang		The Power of the Great
35	Chin		Progress
36	Ming I		Darkening of the Light
37	Chia Jen		The Family/The Clan
38	K'uei		Opposition/Disunion
39	Chien		Obstruction
40	Hsieh		Deliverance
41	Sun		Decrease

42	I	䷩	Increase
43	Kuai	䷪	Breakthrough/Resoluteness
44	Kou	䷫	Coming to Meet
45	Ts'ui	䷬	Gathering Together/Massing
46	Sheng	䷭	Ascending/Pushing Upward
47	K'un	䷮	Oppression/Exhaustion
48	Ching	䷯	A Well
49	Ko	䷰	Revolution/Moulting
50	Ting	䷱	The Cauldron
51	Chen	䷲	The Arousing/Shock/Thunder
52	Ken	䷳	Keeping Still/Mountain
53	Chien	䷴	Development/Gradual Progress
54	Kuei Mei	䷵	The Marrying Maiden
55	Feng	䷶	Abundance/Fullness

56	Lu	䷷	The Wanderer
57	Sun	䷸	The Gentle/The Penetrating/Wind
58	Tui	䷹	The Joyous/Lake
59	Huan	䷺	Dispersion/Dissolution
60	Chieh	䷻	Limitation
61	Chung Fu	䷼	Inner Truth
62	Hsiao Kuo	䷽	Preponderance of the Small
63	Chi Chi	䷾	After Completion
64	Wei Chi	䷿	Before Completion

The Eight Palaces

This arrangement of the hexagrams was created by the Chinese scholar Jin Fang who was also the founder of the Na Jia method (see chapter 7) and who made an enormous contribution to prediction using the I Ching. The Eight Palaces Chart (see figure 11) is absolutely vital for using the Na Jia prediction method.

In the Eight Palaces Chart, the 64 hexagrams are arranged in a particular pattern that highlights what is known as the Changing or Moving Line. These Eight Palaces govern the associated hexagrams that are born out of them and the family of the element involved.

Figure 11 The Eight Palaces Chart

Original 8 trigrams	1	2	3	4	5	6	7	Element
(1) Ch'ien								Metal
(2) K'an								Water
(3) Ken								Earth
(4) Chen								Wood
(5) Sun								Wood
(6) Li								Fire
(7) K'un								Earth
(8) Tui								Metal

Note: o = Changing/Moving Line

- Chien Palace (metal)

In the left-hand column are two identical trigrams and the following seven columns show the moving line marked with a circle.

- Kan Palace (water)
- Ken Palace (earth)
- Chen Palace (wood)

- Sun Palace (wood)
- Li Palace (fire)
- Kun Palace (earth)
- Tui Palace (metal)

The lines of each hexagram in the right-hand seventh column change with regularity from the bottom line to the fifth line, returning to the fourth and third line.

If you look at the first palace – Chien Palace – the original hexagram on the left, Chien (no. 1 the Creative) is built up of identical Ch'ien trigrams. There are no changing/moving lines in this hexagram, so it is known as the Original hexagram of the Chien Palace. If you then look at the next hexagram (Kou, no. 44) you can see that this originates from the Original hexagram Chien, since the first line is changing. Based on this formula, the hexagram Tun (no. 33) originates from the previous trigram Kou, as the second line has changed. Next the hexagram P'i (no. 12) originates from the previous hexagram Tun (no. 33) as the third line is changing. This pattern progresses through each of the palaces and the changing/moving line is marked with a small circle for your reference.

Chapter Four

The Chinese Calendar

To really benefit from the Na Jia method of prediction (chapter 7), it is vital to have a working knowledge of the Chinese calendar. Given that this calendar does not tie up with the western calendar, it is important to simplify it and make it as accessible as possible. What is exciting about the system is that it is based purely on yin and yang, the Five Elements and the seasons.

Traditionally in China, astrologers would use this system to create a horoscope for a newborn child based on their year, month, day and hour of birth. The imperial courts employed astrologers to select dates and times that were auspicious for various occasions. Perhaps the Emperor needed to travel to a certain province, or declare war on a warlord, or initiate an important project. Even today, feng shui astrologers are highly respected for their skill in being able to select the hour, the day and the month to start the construction of a new building, open a new office, move home or for two people to get married.

The Four Pillars

Bringing in an accurate time dimension to the I Ching prediction methods simply adds a new layer of possibility. To begin with, it is important to understand the fundamental procedures and calculations to work with the Chinese calendar. Unlike traditional Chinese astrologers, you will not need to have a detailed working knowledge of how to calculate a Chinese horoscope and analyse it in detail. However, you will need to understand whether the year, the month, the day or even the hour pertaining to the prediction involved is governed by yin or yang, one of the Five Elements or one of the Chinese animals: the year of the rat, the year of the ox, the year of the tiger, etc.

In this chapter I will take you through, step by step, how to correlate the time, the day, the month and the year of any given event in the western calendar with the Chinese calendar. To aid in this step-by-step process, you may find it useful to work around the given date of: 17 March 1964 at 2.30 p.m. local time.

Chinese astrology is based around what is known as the Four Pillars. Each pillar represents an aspect of time. These are:

- The year in question
- The month in question
- The day in question
- The hour in question

Each of these pillars is further sub-divided into two. Each of the pillars, like a hexagram, has an upper and lower section. The upper half of a pillar is known as a Heavenly Stem, representing the influence of the heavens, with either a yin or yang version of each of the Five Elements. This gives a total of ten Heavenly Stems. These are yin or yang wood, yin or yang earth, yin or yang metal, yin or yang water, yin or yang fire.

Figure 12 The Ten Heavenly Stems

No	Yin/Yang	Five Elements
1	Yang	Wood
2	Yin	Wood
3	Yang	Fire
4	Yin	Fire
5	Yang	Earth
6	Yin	Earth
7	Yang	Metal
8	Yin	Metal
9	Yang	Water
10	Yin	Water

The lower half of each pillar is connected to the energy of the earth and Chinese astrology symbolises this section of the pillar by calling it an Earthly Branch. There are 12 of these – as with the 12 months of the year and the 12 two-hour blocks that make up a full day. Many people are familiar with these Branches in the West, as they are with the Chinese animals. In addition to the Chinese animal concerned, each one is either yin or yang and has an associated Five Element attached to it, e.g. the rabbit is yin wood.

Figure 13 The 12 Earthly Branches

Animal	Yin/Yang	Element
Rat	Yang	Water
Ox	Yin	Earth
Tiger	Yang	Wood
Rabbit	Yin	Wood
Dragon	Yang	Earth
Snake	Yin	Fire
Horse	Yang	Fire
Sheep	Yin	Earth
Monkey	Yang	Metal
Rooster	Yin	Metal
Dog	Yang	Earth
Pig	Yin	Water

When analysing a prediction accurately using the Na Jia method it is important to look at the precise time of the event in question. It is for this purpose that we need to understand the elements of each stem and branch in each of the Four Pillars.

Presenting The Four Pillars

As you progress through the preparation stages of formulating the Four Pillars, you will need to add them to the diagram below (see figure 14, The Four Pillars Chart). Eventually, each of the Four Pillars, sub-divided into the Heavenly Stems and Branches will give you the yin/yang qualities, the Five Elements qualities and, in the case of the branches, the Chinese animal involved. Working on the example of 17 March 1964 at 2.30 p.m. (local time), we will complete the chart for this time, day, month and year by the end of this chapter.

Figure 14 The Four Pillars Chart

	HOUR	DAY	MONTH	YEAR
HEAVENLY STEM				
EARTHLY BRANCH				

Clashes And Combinations

Just to add a little more spice to this fascinating system of astrology, a new dimension is then added using the mechanism of the Five Element concept. Some elements clash (wood and earth, fire and water) and others can combine together to form a completely new element. Getting to grips with all these various permutations makes the richness and accuracy of the Na Jia method even more interesting.

For the purposes of this book, I will be showing you how to use the Chinese calendar to examine and analyse the various elements that were at work at the time in question for the event that you are looking at. It means that you could look at a date in history, in recent times, at a headline news event, or predict the outcome of a future event. The possibilities are endless!

Calculating The Year Pillar

The first step is to calculate the Heavenly Stem and Earthly Branch of the year in question. For this you need to know precisely on what date the year commenced as the Chinese do not use 1 January as New Year's Day. For centuries there have been discussions and debates over which is the correct starting point for the New Year. Briefly, the three arguments are:

Winter Solstice

a) begin the year on the winter solstice, 20 or 21 December annually

Solar Year

b) use the Chinese solar year which normally commences on 4 February every year with the following exceptions:

begins on 3 February in 2017, 2020, 2025, 2028
begins on 5 February in 1902, 1903, 1904, 1906, 1907, 1908, 1910, 1911, 1912, 1915, 1916, 1919, 1920, 1923, 1924, 1927, 1928, 1931, 1932, 1935, 1936, 1939, 1940, 1943, 1944, 1948, 1952, 1956, 1960, 1961, 1964, 1968, 1972, 1976, 1980

Lunar Year

c) the year commences on the date of the popularly recognised Chinese New Year. This always begins with the first new moon after the winter solstice. Unlike the small variation for the winter solstice or even the solar year beginning on 3, 4 or 5 February, Chinese New Year can begin between 22 January and 17 February.

For the purpose of this book, we will be using the Chinese New Year based on the lunar calendar.

The chart in figure 15 gives the date of the Chinese New Year from 1911 to 2030.

It is always very important to remember that if you are dealing with an event or prediction that falls in January or February, you need to establish whether it is after or before the New Year. For example, if the New Year begins on 17 January and you are looking at a date of 10 January of that same year, then the year that you are looking at actually commenced the year before and has not yet finished. Therefore, you are looking at the year before, according to the western calendar.

E.g. 14 January 2004: 2004 commences on 22 January 2004, therefore the year that you are looking at is actually 2003 which began on 1 February 2003 and will end on 21 January 2004.

Taking our working example of 1964 the year begins on 13 February 1964 and ends on 1 February 1965. We can then safely use 1964 as the correct date.

Figure 15 The Lunar Chinese New Year

Year	Month	Day
1911	1	30
1912	2	18
1913	2	6
1914	1	26
1915	2	14
1916	2	3
1917	1	23
1918	2	11
1919	2	1
1920	2	20
1921	2	8
1922	1	28
1923	2	16
1924	2	5
1925	1	25
1926	2	13
1927	2	2
1928	1	23
1929	2	10
1930	1	30

Year	Month	Day
1931	2	17
1932	2	6
1933	1	26
1934	2	14
1935	2	4
1936	1	24
1937	2	11
1938	1	31
1939	2	19
1940	2	8
1941	1	27
1942	2	15
1943	2	5
1944	1	25
1945	2	13
1946	2	2
1947	1	22
1948	2	10
1949	1	29
1950	2	17

Year	Month	Day
1951	2	6
1952	1	27
1953	2	14
1954	2	3
1955	1	24
1956	2	12
1957	1	31
1958	2	18
1959	2	8
1960	1	28
1961	2	15
1962	2	5
1963	1	25
1964	2	13
1965	2	2
1966	1	21
1967	2	9
1968	1	30
1969	2	17
1970	2	6

Year	Month	Day
1971	1	27
1972	2	15
1973	2	3
1974	1	23
1975	2	11
1976	1	31
1977	2	18
1978	2	7
1979	1	28
1980	2	16
1981	2	5
1982	1	25
1983	2	13
1984	2	2
1985	1	20
1986	2	9
1987	1	29
1988	2	17
1989	2	6
1990	1	27

Year	Month	Day
1991	2	15
1992	2	4
1993	1	23
1994	2	10
1995	1	31
1996	2	19
1997	2	7
1998	1	28
1999	2	16
2000	2	5
2001	1	24
2002	2	12
2003	2	1
2004	1	22
2005	2	9
2006	1	29
2007	2	18
2008	2	7
2009	1	26
2010	2	14

Year	Month	Day
2011	2	3
2012	1	23
2013	2	10
2014	1	31
2015	2	13
2016	2	8
2017	1	28
2018	2	16
2019	2	5
2020	1	25
2021	2	12
2022	2	1
2023	1	22
2024	2	10
2025	1	29
2026	2	17
2027	2	6
2028	1	26
2029	2	13
2030	2	2

Calculating The Stems And Branches Of The Year

For the first step in our exercise of establishing the stems and branches for 1964 you will need to refer to figure 16 on page 36. This table sets out clearly a cycle of 60 years which is constantly repeating itself. Since there are 10 Heavenly Stems, they will repeat their own cycle every 10 years, i.e. 10, 20, 30, 40, 50 and 60 years. With the 12 Earthly Branches, their cycle will repeat every 12, 24, 36, 48 and 60 years. The only time that the 10 stems and 12 branches will complete the cycle will therefore be at the 60-year stage.

The Stems and Branches in 60 Pairs

The table in figure 16 will help you to determine the stems and branches during this 60-year cycle. Close beginnings of these 60-year stem and branch cycles are:

- 1924
- 1984
- 2044

Example

To find out the cyclical number for 1999, use the following formula.

The beginning of the most recent cycle would be 1984.

1984 to 1999 spans 15 years. Because the 60-year cycle begins with 1 (not zero), you must now add 1 to this figure. This gives you the cyclical number for 1999 as 16. Now refer to the chart in figure 16 and you will see that the cyclical number 16 represents 6–IV which has the stem of yin earth above the branch of the rabbit.

Example

Find the cyclical number for 1964.

- 1924 to 1964 is 40 years. Add 1 as the cycle begins with 1 and not 0, which gives you 41.

Figure 16 The Stems and Branches in 60 Pairs

Cyclical Number	Heavenly Stem		Earthly Branch
1	1	+ Wood	I Rat
2	2	– Wood	II Ox
3	3	+ Fire	III Tiger
4	4	– Fire	IV Rabbit
5	5	+ Earth	V Dragon
6	6	– Earth	VI Snake
7	7	+ Metal	VII Horse
8	8	– Metal	VIII Sheep
9	9	+ Water	IX Monkey
10	10	– Water	X Rooster
11	1	+ Wood	XI Dog
12	2	– Wood	XII Pig
13	3	+ Fire	I Rat
14	4	– Fire	II Ox
15	5	+ Earth	III Tiger
16	6	– Earth	IV Rabbit
17	7	+ Metal	V Dragon
18	8	– Metal	VI Snake
19	9	+ Water	VII Horse
20	10	– Water	VIII Sheep
21	1	+ Wood	IX Monkey
22	2	– Wood	X Rooster
23	3	+ Fire	XI Dog
24	4	– Fire	XII Pig
25	5	+ Earth	I Rat
26	6	– Earth	II Ox
27	7	+ Metal	III Tiger
28	8	– Metal	IV Rabbit
29	9	+ Water	V Dragon
30	10	– Water	VI Snake
31	1	+ Wood	VII Horse
32	2	– Wood	VIII Sheep
33	3	+ Fire	IX Monkey
34	4	– Fire	X Rooster
35	5	+ Earth	XI Dog
36	6	– Earth	XII Pig
37	7	+ Metal	I Rat
38	8	– Metal	II Ox
39	9	+ Water	III Tiger
40	10	– Water	IV Rabbit
41	1	+ Wood	V Dragon
42	2	– Wood	VI Snake
43	3	+ Fire	VII Horse
44	4	– Fire	VIII Sheep
45	5	+ Earth	IX Monkey
46	6	– Earth	X Rooster
47	7	+ Metal	XI Dog
48	8	– Metal	XII Pig
49	9	+ Water	I Rat
50	10	– Water	II Ox
51	1	+ Wood	III Tiger
52	2	– Wood	IV Rabbit
53	3	+ Fire	V Dragon
54	4	– Fire	VI Snake
55	5	+ Earth	VII Horse
56	6	– Earth	VIII Sheep
57	7	+ Metal	IX Monkey
58	8	– Metal	X Rooster
59	9	+ Water	XI Dog
60	10	– Water	XII Pig

- Therefore the cyclical number for 1964 is 41.
- Refer to the table in figure 16 and you will see that the cyclical number 41 represents 1-V. The Heavenly Stem is yang wood and the Earthly Branch is the dragon.

A Working Example

The date we are working with is 17 March 1964 at 2.30 p.m. local time. You can now start to fill in the stem and branch information for the year in question.

Figure 17

	HOUR	DAY	MONTH	YEAR
HEAVENLY STEM				Yang Wood (+)
EARTHLY BRANCH				Dragon (+Earth)

Calculating The Month Pillar

The next step is to establish the stem and branch of the month that you are looking for. In our working example we are using March but do remember that all the months in the western calendar start later. You need to refer to figure 19 (Stems and Branches of the Month) to establish whether the date you are looking at falls within the month or belongs to the previous month, e.g. if we were looking at 3 March 1964, this date would actually belong to February. In our working example, 17 March is clearly March which is the second month of the Chinese calendar – the Rabbit.

Generally, as far as the Earthly Branches are concerned, the Rat is always regarded as the beginning of the 12-phase cycle. However, with the month this is the exception. Spring always begins on 4 February annually which is the Tiger month and this is always regarded as the first month.

Figure 18 The Chinese Calendar in Comparison with the Western Calendar by Month

Branch Number	Chinese Calendar	Animal	Western Calendar
I	1st month	Tiger	4, 5 Feb–5, 6 Mar
II	2nd month	Rabbit	5, 6 Mar–4, 5 Apr
III	3rd month	Dragon	4, 5 Apr–5, 6 May
IV	4th month	Snake	5, 6 May–5, 6 Jun
V	5th month	Horse	5, 6 Jun–7, 8 Jul
VI	6th month	Sheep	7, 8 Jul–7, 8 Aug
VII	7th month	Monkey	7, 8 Aug–7, 8 Sep
VIII	8th month	Rooster	7, 8 Sep–8, 9 Oct
IX	9th month	Dog	8, 9 Oct–7, 8 Nov
X	10th month	Pig	7, 8 Nov–7, 8 Dec
XI	11th month	Rat	7, 8 Dec–5, 6 Jan
XII	12th month	Ox	5, 6 Jan–4, 5 Feb

To work out the relevant stem and branch of any month within the 60-year cycle, you need to follow these steps:

1. From the previous section remember the year stem of the year in question (1964 is yang wood).
2. Now refer to the chart in figure 19 and find where the yang wood stem appears on the top line of the chart.
3. Look down the left-hand column until you find month 2, March, and the Rabbit.
4. By dropping down from the Heavenly Stem and cutting across from the Earthly Branch of Rabbit, you will find the Heavenly Stem of yin fire and the Earthly Branch of Rabbit.
5. This is the stem and branch of March 1964.

Figure 19 Stems and Branches of the Month

YEAR STEM / MONTHLY BRANCH	YANG EARTH or YIN WATER	YIN FIRE or YANG WATER	YANG FIRE or YIN METAL	YIN WOOD or YANG METAL	YANG WOOD or YIN EARTH	
I	FEBRUARY TIGER	+WOOD TIGER	+WATER TIGER	+METAL TIGER	+EARTH TIGER	+FIRE TIGER
II	MARCH RABBIT	-WOOD RABBIT	-WATER RABBIT	-METAL RABBIT	-EARTH RABBIT	-FIRE RABBIT
III	APRIL DRAGON	+FIRE DRAGON	+WOOD DRAGON	+WATER DRAGON	+METAL DRAGON	+EARTH DRAGON
IV	MAY SNAKE	-FIRE SNAKE	-WOOD SNAKE	-WATER SNAKE	-METAL SNAKE	-EARTH SNAKE
V	JUNE HORSE	+EARTH HORSE	+FIRE HORSE	+WOOD HORSE	+WATER HORSE	+METAL HORSE
VI	JULY SHEEP	-EARTH SHEEP	-FIRE SHEEP	-WOOD SHEEP	-WATER SHEEP	-METAL SHEEP
VII	AUGUST MONKEY	+METAL MONKEY	+EARTH MONKEY	+FIRE MONKEY	+WOOD MONKEY	+WATER MONKEY
VIII	SEPTEMBER ROOSTER	-METAL ROOSTER	-EARTH ROOSTER	-FIRE ROOSTER	-WOOD ROOSTER	-WATER ROOSTER
IX	OCTOBER DOG	+WATER DOG	+METAL DOG	+EARTH DOG	+FIRE DOG	+WOOD DOG
X	NOVEMBER PIG	-WATER PIG	-METAL PIG	-EARTH PIG	-FIRE PIG	-WOOD PIG
XI	DECEMBER RAT	+WOOD RAT	+WATER RAT	+METAL RAT	+EARTH RAT	+FIRE RAT
XII	JANUARY OX	-WOOD OX	-WATER OX	-METAL OX	-EARTH OX	-FIRE OX

You can now add the stem and branch of March 1964 to the working example below.

The Working Example

	HOUR	DAY	MONTH	YEAR
HEAVENLY STEM			Yin Fire (-)	Yang Wood (+)
EARTHLY BRANCH			Rabbit (-Wood)	Dragon (+Earth)

Calculating The Day Pillar

You are now halfway through constructing an accurate Four Pillars chart for 17 March 1964 at 2.30 p.m. The Day Pillar calculation will involve referring to three separate charts in order to make the calculations. You will need figures 20 and 21 below and opposite, and figure 16 on page 36. The following six steps will take you through to discovering the Day Pillar for our working example and can be applied to any day between 1901 and 2010.

Step 1

Take the cyclical number for January for the year in question. Refer to figure 20.

- 1964 = 45

Figure 20 Cyclical Number for January

1901 15	1902 20	1903 25	1904 30	1905 36	1906 41	1907 46	1908 51	1909 57	1910 2
1911 7	1912 12	1913 18	1914 23	1915 28	1916 33	1917 39	1918 44	1919 49	1920 54
1921 0	1922 5	1923 10	1924 15	1925 21	1926 26	1927 31	1928 36	1929 42	1930 47
1931 52	1932 57	1933 3	1934 8	1935 13	1936 18	1937 24	1938 29	1939 34	1940 39
1941 45	1942 50	1943 55	1944 0	1945 6	1946 11	1947 16	1948 21	1949 27	1950 32
1951 37	1952 42	1953 48	1954 53	1955 58	1956 3	1957 9	1958 14	1959 19	1960 24
1961 30	1962 35	1963 40	1964 45	1965 51	1966 56	1967 1	1968 6	1969 12	1970 17
1971 22	1972 27	1973 33	1974 38	1975 43	1976 48	1977 54	1978 59	1979 4	1980 9
1981 15	1982 20	1983 25	1984 30	1985 36	1986 41	1987 46	1988 51	1989 57	1990 2
1991 7	1992 12	1993 18	1994 23	1995 28	1996 33	1997 39	1998 44	1999 49	2000 54
2001 0	2002 5	2003 10	2004 15	2005 21	2006 26	2007 31	2008 36	2009 42	2010 47

Step 2

Add the month factor. Refer to figure 21.

- March = 59

Figure 21 The Month Factor

Jan	Feb	Mar	Apr	May	Jun	Jul	Aug	Sep	Oct	Nov	Dec
0	31	59	30	0	31	1	32	3	33	4	34

The month factors here refer to the western calendar months

Step 3

Add the actual date of the day in question.

- 17

Step 4

If the year in question happens to be a leap year **but only if the date is 1 March or later**, add 1.

- 1964 is a leap year
- 17 March is after 1 March
- Add 1

Step 5

Add up the total.

- 1964 = 45, month = 59, day = 17, leap year = 1
- Total = 122

Step 6

If the total is greater than 60, subtract 60 to give you the cyclical number of the stem and branch pair from figure 16.

If the final figure is greater than 120, subtract 120.

With either method you will be left with a final figure of 60 or less.

- 17 March 1964 = 122
- -120 = 2

Now refer to figure 16 and the cyclical number 2 represents the Heavenly Stem of yin wood and the Earthly Branch of the Ox.

Now you can add this day stem and branch to your working example, as follows:

The Working Example

	HOUR	DAY	MONTH	YEAR
HEAVENLY STEM		Yin Wood (–)	Yin Fire (–)	Yang Wood (+)
EARTHLY BRANCH		Ox (–Earth)	Rabbit (–Wood)	Dragon (+Earth)

The Hour Pillar

The hours used in these calculations are based on local time, unless otherwise stated. If you are aware that the 'real time' has been affected by summer time adjustments to the clocks, then go back to the actual time. E.g. in the spring in the UK clocks move forward an hour until the autumn, so if the date in question falls during this time, simply subtract an hour from your calculation.

To calculate the hour Heavenly Stems and Earthly Branches on any given day, you need to refer to the chart in figure 22.

Step 1

Begin by determining the Heavenly Stem of the day in question from the top line.

- From our example this is yin wood.

Step 2

Drop down the column on the left-hand side of the chart until you come to 13–15 which is where 2.30 p.m. falls.

Figure 22 Hour Stems and Branches

	THE HOURS	YANG EARTH YIN WATER	YIN FIRE YANG WATER	YANG FIRE YIN METAL	YIN WOOD YANG METAL	YANG WOOD YIN EARTH	HEAVENLY STEMS EARTHLY BRANCHES
1	23–01	+WATER RAT	+METAL RAT	+EARTH RAT	+FIRE RAT	+WOOD RAT	RAT
2	01–03	−WATER OX	−METAL OX	−EARTH OX	−FIRE OX	−WOOD OX	OX
3	03–05	+WOOD TIGER	+WATER TIGER	+METAL TIGER	+EARTH TIGER	+FIRE TIGER	TIGER
4	05–07	−WOOD RABBIT	−WATER RABBIT	−METAL RABBIT	−EARTH RABBIT	−FIRE RABBIT	RABBIT/ HARE
5	07–09	+FIRE DRAGON	+WOOD DRAGON	+WATER DRAGON	+METAL DRAGON	+EARTH DRAGON	DRAGON
6	09–11	−FIRE SNAKE	−WOOD SNAKE	−WATER SNAKE	−METAL SNAKE	−EARTH SNAKE	SNAKE
7	11–13	+EARTH HORSE	+FIRE HORSE	+WOOD HORSE	+WATER HORSE	+METAL HORSE	HORSE
8	13–15	−EARTH SHEEP	−FIRE SHEEP	−WOOD SHEEP	−WATER SHEEP	−METAL SHEEP	SHEEP
9	15–17	+METAL MONKEY	+EARTH MONKEY	+FIRE MONKEY	+WOOD MONKEY	+WATER MONKEY	MONKEY
10	17–19	−METAL ROOSTER	−EARTH ROOSTER	−FIRE ROOSTER	−WOOD ROOSTER	−WATER ROOSTER	ROOSTER
11	19–21	+WATER DOG	+METAL DOG	+EARTH DOG	+FIRE DOG	+WOOD DOG	DOG
12	21–23	−WATER PIG	−METAL PIG	−EARTH PIG	−FIRE PIG	−WOOD PIG	PIG

Step 3

Check whether there needs to be any adjustment to real local time. No.

- Therefore the hour in question is still 2.30 p.m.

Step 4

Drop down the column from the top where yin wood is situated until you meet the horizontal column coming from hour 8 (13–15), the Sheep hour.

Step 5

Read off the stems and branches.

• For this example, the Heavenly Stem is yin water and the Earthly Branch is the Sheep.

Now you can complete the entire data for the chart for 2.30 p.m. on 17 March 1964.

The Working Example

Figure 23

	HOUR	DAY	MONTH	YEAR
HEAVENLY STEM	Yin Water (−)	Yin Wood (−)	Yin Fire (−)	Yang Wood (+)
EARTHLY BRANCH	Sheep (−Earth)	Ox (−Earth)	Rabbit (−Wood)	Dragon (+Earth)

Adding the Time Numbers from the Chinese Calendar

The final calculation that you need to make, which is vital for the Mei Hua and Na Jia methods of prediction, is to add in the number of the day from the Chinese calendar. The days of the month in the Chinese calendar commence from the new moon every month. Firstly, you need to know when the new moon was in the month that you are looking at and simply count forward the days until you meet the day that you are looking at from the western calendar. Do remember though that a lunar month is 28 days and western calendar months vary from 28 to 31 days. As a result every two and a half to three years an extra month comes into the Chinese Calendar, known as an intercalary month. The stems and branches of these months are the same as the preceding month.

The table in figure 24 is designed to help you find the Chinese calendar day for the date in question.

Each year, month, hour and day has an associated number. All of these relate to the Earthly Branches. For example, when you refer to figure 16 regarding 1964 it will have the Roman numeral V next to the year. This gives the year number of 5.

The number óf the month branch can be found in figure 19. The branch for March 1964 is a Rabbit-2.

The hour number can be found in figure 22 and in the example we are currently using the time is 14.30. In the left-hand column you will see the number 8.

17 March in 1964 can be found in figure 24 below. Begin by noticing that March begins on the 14th in 1964. This makes 17 March the fourth day of the month giving it the number 4.

To complete the full calculation here is the working example with additional space to add the relevant number of each of the branches.

	HOUR	DAY	MONTH	YEAR
HEAVENLY STEM	Yin Water (–)	Yin Wood (–)	Yin Fire (–)	Yang Wood (+)
EARTHLY BRANCH	Sheep (–Earth)	Ox (–Earth)	Rabbit (–Wood)	Dragon (+Earth)
TIME NUMBER	8	4	2	5

Figure 24 Chinese Lunar Calendar

	i	ii	iii	iv	v	vi	vii	viii	ix	x	xi	xii
	TIGER	RABBIT	DRAGON	SNAKE	HORSE	SHEEP	MONKEY	ROOSTER	DOG	PIG	RAT	OX
	Feb.	March	April	May	June	July	August	Sept.	Oct.	Nov.	Dec.	January
1908	2/2	3/3	4/1	4/30	5/30	6/29	7/28	8/27	9/25	10/25	11/24	12/23
1909	1/22	2/20 3/22	4/20	5/19	6/18	7/17	8/16	9/14	10/14	11/13	12/13	1/11
1910	2/10	3/11	4/10	5/9	6/7	7/7	8/5	9/4	10/3	11/2	12/2	1/1
1911	1/30	3/1	3/30	4/29	5/28	6/26 7/26	8/24	9/22	10/22	11/21	12/20	1/19
1912	2/18	3/19	4/17	5/17	6/15	7/14	8/13	9/11	10/10	11/9	12/9	1/7
1913	2/6	3/8	4/7	5/6	6/5	7/4	8/2	9/1	9/30	10/29	11/28	12/27
1914	1/26	2/25	3/27	4/25	5/25 6/23	7/23	8/21	9/20	10/19	11/17	12/17	1/15
1915	2/14	3/16	4/14	5/14	6/13	7/12	8/11	9/9	10/9	11/7	12/7	1/5
1916	2/3	3/4	4/3	5/2	6/1	6/30	7/30	8/29	9/27	10/27	11/25	12/25
1917	1/23	2/22 3/23	4/21	5/21	6/19	7/19	8/18	9/16	10/16	11/15	12/14	1/13
1918	2/11	3/13	4/11	5/10	6/9	7/8	8/7	9/5	10/6	11/4	12/3	1/2
1919	2/1	3/2	4/1	4/30	5/29	6/28	7/27 8/25	9/24	10/24	11/22	12/22	1/21
1920	2/20	3/20	4/19	5/18	6/16	7/16	8/14	9/12	10/12	11/10	12/10	1/9
1921	2/8	3/10	4/8	5/8	6/6	7/5	8/4	9/2	10/1	10/31	11/29	12/29

	i	ii	iii	iv	v	vi	vii	viii	ix	x	xi	xii
	TIGER	RABBIT	DRAGON	SNAKE	HORSE	SHEEP	MONKEY	ROOSTER	DOG	PIG	RAT	OX
	Feb.	March	April	May	June	July	August	Sept.	Oct.	Nov.	Dec.	January
1922	1/28	2/27	3/28	4/27	5/27 6/25	7/24	8/23	9/21	10/20	11/19	12/18	1/17
1923	2/16	3/17	4/16	5/16	6/14	7/14	8/12	9/11	10/10	11/8	12/8	1/6
1924	2/5	3/5	4/4	5/4	6/2	7/2	8/1	8/30	9/29	10/28	11/27	12/26
1925	1/24	2/23	3/24	4/23 5/22	6/21	7/21	8/19	9/18	10/18	11/16	12/16	1/14
1926	2/13	3/14	4/12	5/12	6/10	7/10	8/8	9/7	10/7	11/5	12/5	1/4
1927	2/2	3/4	4/2	5/1	5/31	6/29	7/29	8/27	9/26	10/25	11/24	12/24
1928	1/23	2/21 3/22	4/20	5/19	6/18	7/17	8/15	9/14	10/13	11/12	12/12	1/11
1929	2/10	3/11	4/10	5/9	6/7	7/7	8/5	9/3	10/3	11/1	12/1	12/31
1930	1/30	2/28	3/30	4/29	5/28	6/26 7/26	8/24	9/22	10/22	11/20	12/20	1/19
1931	2/17	3/19	4/18	5/17	6/16	7/15	8/14	9/12	10/11	11/10	12/9	1/8
1932	2/6	3/7	4/6	5/6	6/4	7/4	8/2	9/1	9/30	10/29	11/28	12/27
1933	1/26	2/24	3/26	4/25	5/24 6/23	7/22	8/21	9/20	10/19	11/18	12/17	1/15
1934	2/14	3/15	4/14	5/13	6/12	7/12	8/10	9/9	10/8	11/7	12/7	1/5
1935	2/4	3/5	4/3	5/3	6/1	7/1	7/30	8/29	9/28	10/27	11/26	12/26
1936	1/24	2/23	3/23 4/21	5/21	6/19	7/18	8/17	9/16	10/15	11/14	12/14	1/13
1937	2/11	3/13	4/11	5/10	6/9	7/8	8/6	9/5	10/4	11/3	12/3	1/2
1938	1/31	3/2	4/1	4/30	5/29	6/28	7/27 8/25	9/24	10/23	11/22	12/22	1/20
1939	12/19	3/21	4/20	5/19	6/17	7/17	8/15	9/13	10/13	11/11	12/11	1/9
1940	2/8	3/9	4/8	5/7	6/6	7/5	8/4	9/2	10/1	10/31	11/29	12/29
1941	1/27	2/26	3/28	4/26	5/26	6/25 7/24	8/23	9/21	10/20	11/19	12/18	1/17
1942	2/15	3/17	4/15	5/15	6/14	7/13	8/12	9/10	10/10	11/8	12/8	1/6
1943	2/5	3/6	4/5	5/4	6/3	7/2	8/1	8/31	9/29	10/29	11/27	12/27
1944	1/25	2/24	3/24	4/23 5/22	6/21	7/20	8/19	9/17	10/17	11/16	12/15	1/14
1945	2/13	3/14	4/12	5/12	6/10	7/9	8/8	9/6	10/6	11/5	12/5	1/3
1946	2/2	3/4	4/2	5/1	5/31	6/29	7/28	8/27	9/25	10/25	11/24	12/23
1947	1/22	2/21 3/23	4/21	5/20	6/19	7/18	8/16	9/15	10/14	11/13	12/12	1/11
1948	2/10	3/11	4/9	5/9	6/7	7/7	8/5	9/3	10/3	11/1	12/1	12/30
1949	1/29	2/28	3/29	4/28	5/28	6/26	7/26 8/24	9/22	10/22	11/20	12/20	1/18
1950	2/17	3/18	4/17	5/17	6/15	7/15	8/14	9/12	10/11	11/10	12/9	1/8
1951	2/6	3/8	4/6	5/6	6/5	7/4	8/3	9/1	10/1	10/30	11/29	12/28
1952	1/27	2/25	3/26	4/24	5/24 6/22	7/22	8/20	9/19	10/19	11/17	12/17	1/15
1953	2/14	3/15	4/14	5/13	6/11	7/11	8/10	9/8	10/8	11/7	12/6	1/5
1954	2/3	3/5	4/3	5/3	6/1	6/30	7/30	8/28	9/27	10/27	11/25	12/25
1955	1/24	2/22	3/24 4/22	5/22	6/20	7/19	8/18	9/16	10/16	11/14	12/14	1/13
1956	2/12	3/12	4/11	5/10	6/9	7/8	8/6	9/5	10/4	11/3	12/2	1/1

	i	ii	iii	iv	v	vi	vii	viii	ix	x	xi	xii
	TIGER	RABBIT	DRAGON	SNAKE	HORSE	SHEEP	MONKEY	ROOSTER	DOG	PIG	RAT	OX
	Feb.	March	April	May	June	July	August	Sept.	Oct.	Nov.	Dec.	January
1957	1/31	3/2	3/31	4/30	5/29	6/28	7/27	8/25 9/24	10/23	11/22	12/21	1/20
1958	2/18	3/20	4/19	5/19	6/17	7/17	8/15	9/13	10/13	11/11	12/11	1/9
1959	2/8	3/9	4/8	5/8	6/6	7/6	8/4	9/3	10/2	11/1	11/30	12/30
1960	1/28	2/27	3/27	4/26	5/25	6/24 7/24	8/22	9/21	10/20	11/19	12/18	1/17
1961	2/15	3/17	4/15	5/15	6/13	7/13	8/11	9/10	10/10	11/8	12/8	1/6
1962	2/5	3/6	4/5	5/4	6/2	7/2	7/31	8/30	9/29	10/28	11/27	12/27
1963	1/25	2/24	3/25	4/24 5/23	6/21	7/21	8/19	9/18	10/17	11/16	12/16	1/15
1964	12/13	3/14	4/12	5/12	6/10	7/9	8/8	9/6	10/6	11/4	12/4	1/3
1965	2/2	3/3	4/2	5/1	5/31	6/29	7/28	8/27	9/25	10/24	11/23	12/23
1966	1/21	2/20	3/22 4/21	5/20	6/19	7/18	8/16	9/15	10/14	11/12	12/12	1/11
1967	2/9	3/11	4/10	5/9	6/8	7/8	8/6	9/4	10/4	11/2	12/2	12/31
1968	1/30	2/28	3/29	4/27	5/27	6/26	7/25 8/24	9/22	10/22	11/20	12/20	1/18
1969	2/17	3/18	4/17	5/16	6/15	7/14	8/13	9/12	10/11	11/10	12/9	1/8
1970	2/6	3/8	4/6	5/5	6/4	7/3	8/2	9/1	9/30	10/30	11/29	12/28
1971	1/27	2/25	3/27	4/25	5/24 6/23	7/22	8/21	9/19	10/19	11/18	12/18	1/16
1972	2/15	3/15	4/14	5/13	6/11	7/11	8/9	9/8	10/7	11/6	12/6	1/4
1973	2/3	3/5	4/3	5/3	6/1	6/30	7/30	8/28	9/26	10/26	11/25	12/24
1974	1/23	2/22	3/24	4/22 5/22	6/20	7/19	8/18	9/16	10/15	11/14	12/14	1/12
1975	2/11	3/13	4/12	5/11	6/10	7/9	8/7	9/6	10/5	11/3	12/3	1/1
1976	1/31	3/1	3/31	4/29	5/29	6/27	7/27	8/25 9/24	10/23	11/21	12/21	1/19
1977	2/18	3/20	4/18	5/18	6/17	7/16	8/15	9/13	10/13	11/11	12/11	1/9
1978	2/7	3/9	4/7	5/7	6/6	7/5	8/4	9/3	10/2	11/1	11/30	12/30
1979	1/28	2/27	3/28	4/26	5/26	6/24 7/24	8/23	9/21	10/21	11/20	12/19	1/18
1980	2/16	3/17	4/15	5/14	6/13	7/12	8/11	9/9	10/9	11/8	12/7	1/6
1981	2/5	3/6	4/5	5/4	6/2	7/2	7/31	8/29	9/28	10/28	11/26	12/26
1982	1/25	2/24	3/25	4/24 5/23	6/21	7/21	8/19	9/17	10/17	11/15	12/15	1/14
1983	2/13	3/15	4/13	5/13	6/11	7/10	8/9	9/7	10/6	11/5	12/4	1/3
1984	2/2	3/3	4/1	5/1	5/31	6/29	7/28	8/27	9/25	10/24 11/23	12/22	1/21
1985	2/20	3/21	4/20	5/20	6/18	7/18	8/16	9/15	10/14	11/12	12/12	1/10
1986	2/9	3/10	4/9	5/9	6/7	7/7	8/6	9/4	10/4	2/11	12/2	12/31
1987	1/29	2/28	3/29	4/28	5/27	6/26 7/26	8/24	9/23	10/23	11/21	12/21	1/19
1988	2/17	3/18	4/16	5/16	6/14	7/14	8/12	9/11	10/11	11/9	12/9	1/8
1989	2/6	3/8	4/6	5/5	6/4	7/3	8/1	8/31	9/30	10/29	11/28	12/28
1990	1/27	2/25	3/27	4/25	5/24 6/23	7/22	8/20	9/19	10/18	11/17	12/17	1/16

	i	ii	iii	iv	v	vi	vii	viii	ix	x	xi	xii
	TIGER	RABBIT	DRAGON	SNAKE	HORSE	SHEEP	MONKEY	ROOSTER	DOG	PIG	RAT	OX
	Feb.	March	April	May	June	July	August	Sept.	Oct.	Nov.	Dec.	January
1991	2/15	3/16	4/15	5/14	9/12	7/12	8/10	9/8	10/8	11/6	12/6	1/5
1992	2/4	3/4	4/3	5/3	6/1	6/30	7/30	8/28	9/26	10/26	11/24	12/24
1993	1/23	2/21	3/23 4/22	5/21	6/20	7/19	8/18	9/16	10/15	11/14	12/13	1/12
1994	2/10	3/12	4/11	5/11	6/9	7/9	8/7	9/6	10/5	11/3	12/3	1/1
1995	1/31	3/1	3/31	4/30	5/29	6/28	7/27	8/26 9/25	10/24	11/22	12/22	1/20
1996	2/19	3/19	4/18	5/17	6/16	7/16	8/14	9/13	10/12	11/11	12/11	1/9
1997	2/7	3/9	4/9	5/7	6/5	7/5	8/3	9/2	10/2	10/31	11/30	12/30
1998	1/28	2/27	3/28	4/26	5/26 6/24	7/23	8/22	9/21	10/20	11/19	12/19	1/17
1999	2/16	3/18	4/16	5/15	6/14	7/13	8/11	9/10	10/9	11/8	12/8	1/7
2000	2/5	3/6	4/5	5/4	6/2	7/2	7/31	8/29	9/28	10/27	11/26	12/26
2001	1/24	2/23	3/25	4/23 5/23	6/21	7/21	8/19	9/17	10/17	11/15	12/15	1/13
2002	2/12	3/14	4/13	5/12	6/11	7/10	8/9	9/7	10/6	11/5	12/4	1/3
2003	2/1	3/3	4/2	5/1	5/31	6/30	7/29	8/28	9/26	10/25	11/24	12/23
2004	1/22	2/20 3/21	4/19	5/19	6/18	7/17	8/16	9/14	10/14	11/12	12/12	1/10
2005	2/9	3/10	4/9	5/8	6/7	7/6	8/5	9/4	10/3	11/2	12/1	12/31
2006	1/29	2/28	3/29	4/28	5/27	6/26	7/25 8/24	9/22	10/22	11/21	12/20	1/19
2007	2/18	3/19	4/17	5/17	6/15	7/14	8/13	9/11	10/11	11/10	12/10	1/8
2008	2/7	3/8	4/6	5/5	6/4	7/3	8/1	8/31	9/29	10/29	11/28	12/27
2009	1/26	2/25	3/27	4/25	5/24 6/23	7/22	8/20	9/19	10/18	11/17	12/16	1/15
2010	2/14	3/16	4/14	5/14	6/12	7/12	8/10	9/8	10/8	11/6	12/6	1/4
2011	2/3	3/5	4/3	5/3	6/2	7/1	7/31	8/29	9/27	10/27	11/25	12/25
2012	1/23	2/22	3/22	4/21 5/21	6/19	7/19	8/17	6/19	10/15	11/14	12/13	1/12
2013	2/10	3/12	4/10	5/10	6/9	7/8	8/7	9/5	10/5	11/3	12/3	1/1
2014	1/31	3/1	3/31	4/29	5/29	6/27	7/27	8/25	9/24 10/24	11/22	12/22	7/19
2015	2/19	3/20	4/19	5/18	6/16	7/16	8/14	9/13	10/13	6/12	12/11	1/10
2016	2/18	3/9	4/7	5/7	6/5	7/4	8/3	9/1	10/1	10/31	11/29	12/29
2017	1/28	2/26	3/28	4/26	5/26	6/24 7/23	8/22	9/20	10/20	11/18	12/18	1/17
2018	2/16	3/17	4/16	5/15	6/14	7/13	8/11	9/10	10/9	11/8	12/7	1/6
2019	2/5	3/6	4/5	5/5	6/3	7/3	8/1	8/30	9/29	10/28	11/26	12/26
2020	1/25	2/23	3/24	4/23 5/23	6/21	7/21	8/19	9/17	10/17	1/15	12/15	1/13
2021	2/12	3/13	4/12	5/12	6/10	7/10	8/8	9/7	10/6	11/5	12/4	1/3
2022	2/1	3/3	4/1	5/1	5/30	6/29	7/29	8/27	9/26	10/25	11/24	12/23
2023	1/22	2/20 3/22	4/20	5/20	6/18	7/18	8/16	9/16	10/15	11/13	12/13	1/11
2024	2/10	3/10	4/9	5/8	6/6	7/6	8/4	9/3	10/3	11/1	12/1	12/31

The Analysis Of The Heavenly Stems And Earthly Branches

Now that you are able to construct and understand the Four Pillars from the previous section, it would be wise to familiarise you with some of the subtle interactions of the stems, the branches and the elements, so that you can gain more insights from the Na Jia method of prediction in chapter 7. Constructing and analysing the Four Pillars – whether it is for an individual's chart or a specific date or event – is not unlike the analysis needed for an accurate I Ching prediction. Always try to keep in the back of your mind: yin and yang and the Five Elements.

The Ten Heavenly Stems

By now you are familiar with these stems and their associated elements. Now add to them the directions and note that there are subtle differences between the yin yang qualities of the different elements.

- Yang wood is like the hard wood of the trunk of a tree
- Yin wood can represent the grasses and shoots and more flexible plant life
- Yang fire represents the sun itself
- Yin fire can be a candle, a flame or the stove
- Yang earth is dry and hard and solid
- Yin earth is soft, light and fertile
- Yang metal is hard and sharp like an axe or a weapon
- Yin metal is smaller like a kitchen knife or a pair of scissors
- Yang water is like the ocean or a sea or rain
- Yin water represents a small stream, a brook or water from a spring

Figure 25 The Ten Heavenly Stems

No	Chinese Name	Yin/Yang	Five Elements	Direction
1	Chia	Yang	Wood	East
2	Yi	Yin	Wood	East
3	Ping	Yang	Fire	South
4	Ting	Yin	Fire	South
5	Wu	Yang	Earth	Centre
6	Chi	Yin	Earth	Centre
7	Keng	Yang	Metal	West
8	Hsin	Yin	Metal	West
9	Jen	Yang	Water	North
10	Kuei	Yin	Water	North

The 12 Earthly Branches

Each of the 12 Earthly Branches represents an element, a yin yang quality, a year, an hour number, an animal and a different month number. Remember from the previous section that the first month is always the Tiger.

Note that with the four earth animals, the Ox, the Dragon, the Sheep and the Dog, each one has a store or a reservoir hidden within it of a particular element. These are all noted in brackets in the central column.

The Relationships Between The Heavenly Stems And Earthly Branches

The elements of the stems and branches are naturally dynamic and are constantly interacting and reacting with one another throughout time. These relationships are born purely out of yin and yang dynamics and the Five Element theory. To gain the most from your interpretation of I Ching predictions, particularly with the Na Jia method, it is well worth examining the two main kinds of relationship that exist: the Combination Relationship and the Clash Relationship.

Figure 26 The 12 Earthly Branches

Chinese Name	Animal	Yin/Yang	Element	No. yr	Month	Hour	Direction
Tzu	Rat	Yang	Water	1	11th	1st (23-01)	North
Ch'ou	Ox	Yin	Earth (Metal)	2	12th	2nd (01-03)	North
Yin	Tiger	Yang	Wood	3	1st	3rd (03-05)	East
Mao	Rabbit	Yin	Wood	4	2nd	4th (05-07)	East
Ch'en	Dragon	Yang	Earth (Water)	5	3rd	5th (07-09)	East
Ssu	Snake	Yin	Fire	6	4th	6th (09-11)	South
Wu	Horse	Yang	Fire	7	5th	7th (11-13)	South
Wei	Sheep	Yin	Earth (Wood)	8	6th	8th (13-15)	South
Shen	Monkey	Yang	Metal	9	7th	9th (15-17)	West
Yu	Rooster	Yin	Metal	10	8th	10th (17-19)	West
Hsu	Dog	Yang	Earth (Fire)	11	9th	11th (19-21)	West
Hai	Pig	Yin	Water	12	10th	12th (21-23)	North

The Combination Relationship Of Heavenly Stems

When two Heavenly Stems meet there are occasions when their elements interact with each other and combine to produce a new element. The following table lists these combinations and they need to be considered first in any analysis. For example, when yin wood combines with yang metal a new element appears – metal, rather than the old elements of wood and metal alone.

Figure 27 The Combinations of the 10 Heavenly Stems

Yang Wood	+	Yin Earth	=	Earth
Yin Wood	+	Yang Metal	=	Metal
Yang Fire	+	Yin Metal	=	Water
Yin Fire	+	Yang Water	=	Wood
Yang Earth	+	Yin Water	=	Fire

The Earthly Branch Combinations

As with the Heavenly Stems, when certain Earthly Branches meet their elements interact and combine to produce a new element. There are six different combinations of these relationships and they are listed below in figure 28. For example, when the Earthly Branch of Rat (water element) combines with the Earthly Branch of Ox (earth element) a new element is produced which is earth.

Figure 28

Rat/Water	+	Ox/Earth	=	Earth
Tiger/Wood	+	Pig/Earth	=	Wood
Rabbit/Wood	+	Dog/Earth	=	Fire
Dragon/Earth	+	Rooster/Metal	=	Metal
Snake/Fire	+	Monkey/Metal	=	Water
Horse/Fire	+	Sheep/Earth	=	Fire

The Four Clashes Of The Heavenly Stems

Next it is important to consider the clashes and begin by noting those that occur within the Heavenly Stems. They are:

- Yang wood clashes with yang metal. The imagery here is that an axe can do serious damage to the trunk of a tree.
- Yin metal clashes with yin wood. A small knife or a pair of scissors or shears can do immense damage to young shoots and leaves. Imagine taking an axe to do some light pruning on one of your plants.
- Yang fire clashes with yang water. Here the sun can boil and evaporate the rain or the sea or a large lake.
- Yin fire clashes with yin water. A flame or stove can boil water while at the same time a bucket of water can extinguish a small fire.

The Six Clashes Of The Earthly Branches

This is a contrary situation to the Six Combination Relationship of the Earthly Branches. When two Earthly Branches meet it is possible that their elements will interact with each other and cause conflict. These clashes generally occur because of the elements involved. For example, the Rat (water element) can clash with the Horse (fire element). In more subtle situations, because the Horse is much stronger than the Rat, the control cycle can feed the opposite direction.

Figure 29 The Six Clashes of the Earthly Branches

Rat (Water)	–	Horse (Fire)
Tiger (Wood)	–	Monkey (Metal)
Rabbit (Wood)	–	Rooster (Metal)
Dragon (Earth)	–	Dog (Earth)
Snake (Fire)	–	Pig (Wood)
Ox (Earth)	–	Sheep (Earth)

The only exception regarding the control or clash of the Five Elements is represented with the Dragon (earth) and the Dog (earth). How can they clash when they are the same element? The reason for this clash is that the Dragon is located in the east and the Dog is located in the west, completely opposite each other. In addition, the west is metal and the east is wood, forming a further clash. The Ox and the Sheep are also located opposite each other – the Ox in the north and the Sheep in the South. Again, being diametrically opposed, they clash and the elements of water from the north and fire from the south also clash.

The Six Injury Relationship Of The Earthly Branches

This is a milder form of clash, but it is well worth noting. There are six injuries and they are as follows:

- Rat – Sheep
- Tiger – Snake
- Rabbit – Dragon
- Dog – Rooster
- Pig – Monkey
- Horse – Ox

The Great Combination Of Three Elements In The Earthly Branches

This is another special combination which is very powerful and together three elements can produce a new stronger element. In each of these four combinations, you will note that each one of them has an Earthly Branch of earth present. Also, the central Earthly Branch and its natural element is actually the element that these three combinations create.

Figure 30 The Great Combination of the Earthly Branches

• Monkey (Metal)	–	Rat (Water)	–	Dragon (Earth)	produces	**Water**
• Tiger (Wood)	–	Horse (Fire)	–	Dog (Earth)	produces	**Fire**
• Pig (Water)	–	Rabbit (Wood)	–	Sheep (Earth)	produces	**Wood**
• Snake (Fire)	–	Rooster (Metal)	–	Ox (Earth)	produces	**Metal**

As a general rule, note that the new element produced by this combination of three Earthly Branches is always the same as the Earthly Branch located in the middle of the three combination. For example, in the first group, the combination of Monkey, Rat and Dragon, the new element is water, which is the same as the Rat.

Also, the first Earthly Branch in each group is always giving birth to the second or central Earthly Branch within the group. The last or the third of the Earthly Branches within any of these four combinations is always the earth element originally. At the same time, it is one of the four stores or reservoirs of a particular element. You can see these again in figure 26 on page 51.

There is also great beauty and simplicity in this particular model. If you look, for example, at the first group of the Monkey, Rat and Dragon, the Monkey represents metal, which in turn gives birth to the Rat which is water, and the last branch Dragon which in essence is earth, is also the reservoir of water. In a way this group is like a river – the first Earthly Branch is like the spring which gives birth to the next branch, which can be compared to a river, and the last branch is like the end of a river where it enters into a reservoir.

Example

To give you a practical example of combinations and clashes when examining the Four Pillars, have a look at the following table.

Figure 31 24 September 2000 at 10.30 a.m.

	HOUR	DAY	MONTH	YEAR
HEAVENLY STEM	Yin Metal (–)	Yin Wood (–)	Yin Wood (–)	Yang Metal (+)
EARTHLY BRANCH	Snake (–Fire)	Rooster (–Metal)	Rooster (–Metal)	Dragon (+Earth)
TIME NUMBER	6	27	8	5

This is the precise hour, day, month and year that I taught my seminar on the I Ching in London for Jon Sandifer and his colleagues.

Beginning with the relationship of the Heavenly Stems, there is a combination of the year and the month (yang metal and yin wood). There is also a combination of the Earthly Branches from the year and the month – the Dragon and the Rooster combine together.

This is an excellent combination as two stems and their two branches combine together respectively at the same time. The imagery is that it is similar to two trees closely embraced from the top of the tree right down through to their roots. Its other name is Combination of Heaven and Earth, or Combination of the Two Happiest Couples. It is the closest combination relationship and symbolises the best collaboration and partnership. In addition, on this date, there is a Half Great Combination of the Three Elements (this refers to two of the three elements combining together). This is the combination of the Rooster and the Snake Earthly Branch of the day and the hour. Because there are so many combination relationships at that time and on that day, it means that plenty of cooperation would exist. I will share more about the outcome of this combination in a case history later in the book.

Half Great Combination Of Three Elements

Sometimes it is not possible to get a full combination of the Monkey, the Rat and the Dragon to form water, or the Tiger, the Horse and the Dog to form fire. If any two of these elements combine, e.g. Pig (water) and Rabbit (wood), it is known as a Half Great Combination. Naturally it is not as powerful as a Three Great Combination, but is well worth noting.

Chapter Five

The Classical Method

Creating The Hexagram

The original method of creating a hexagram, the yarrow stalk method, was initiated over 3000 years ago. Because the procedure was too complex to be learnt and difficult to put into practice, the great master, Jin Fang, reformed it by devising the coin-casting method about 2000 years ago. Few people use the yarrow stalk method in China today and for this reason I introduce only the coin method here.

Preparing to Consult the I Ching

To begin with, you will need three coins of the same denomination that are clearly visible in terms of heads and tails. It is wise to select and keep three coins specifically for when you use the I Ching. In order that the coins are 'neutral' and more capable of reflecting your intention with the question, wash them first and allow them to dry if possible in the sunshine for a few hours. Always keep these coins separate and perhaps store them in a special box or purse with your own version of the I Ching. Some people like to use antique Chinese coins from the Qing dynasty but you need to identify which side you consider is heads and which is tails.

Preparing the Question

You need a quiet space to sit and formulate the question. You will need either this book or your own treasured version of the I Ching, your three coins and paper and pen for jotting down the lines of the hexagram.

The Procedure

What you are trying to accomplish in this exercise is to create the six lines of a hexagram. You will also need to note if any lines in the hexagram are changing lines and if so you will need to create a second hexagram which reveals the longer range answer to your question, and is known as the Final hexagram.

The Lines

Each line is formed by casting the three coins simultaneously and noting the combination of heads or tails that is produced. The two values are:

3 equals heads
2 equals tails

There are four possible permutations:

3 heads = 9	——
2 heads + 1 tail = 8	— —
2 tails + 1 head = 7	——
3 tails = 6	— —

Changing Lines

In addition to these four possibilities you need to check whether you have cast any changing lines. The changing lines are 6 and 9 and are denoted as follows:

$$— X — \quad = \quad 6$$
$$—— X —— \quad = \quad 9$$

Step 1
Begin by holding the coins in your hands or one fist and consider the question you want to ask. Cast the coins six times, noting the total value of each cast, i.e. 6, 7, 8 or 9.

Step 2
Construct the lines based on their value from each of the six casts from the bottom towards the top. As a working example, your first cast produced 9,

the second made 7, the third made 7, the fourth made 8, the fifth cast produced 6 and finally the sixth cast made 8.

Step 3

Write down the order, numerical value and whether the line is broken or solid.

6th cast/line	8	-- --
5th cast/line	6	-- --
4th cast/line	8	-- --
3rd cast/line	7	——
2nd cast/line	7	——
1st cast/line	9	——

Step 4

Notice if any changing lines appear in your Original hexagram. There are two in this example. You now need to create a second hexagram, called the Final hexagram by turning any changing lines into their opposite.

e.g. Solid yang (9) becomes a broken yin line

——   to   -- --

Broken yin line (6) becomes a solid yang line

-- --   to   ——

Original Hexagram	Final Hexagram
-- --	-- --
– X –	——
-- --	-- --
——	——
——	——
– X –	-- --

Step 5 Identifying the Hexagram(s)

Each hexagram is subdivided into two trigrams. The upper trigram (lines 4, 5, 6) sits above the lower trigram (lines 1, 2, 3).

Refer to figure 10 on page 21 to identify the hexagram.

Find the lower trigram in the left-hand column and upper trigram on the top line of the chart. Read down and across to identify the hexagram.

Original Hexagram	Final Hexagram
– –	– –
– X –	——
– –	– –
——	——
——	——
– X –	– –
11	48

Step 6

- Read the text for the original hexagram, including any changing lines.
- Read the text only for the Final hexagram which will infer the longer term outcome of the question.

Analysing The Hexagram

There are two ways of analysing the hexagram. The first way is to look at the image of the hexagram and consider the wider meaning contained in it. The second way is to read and study the text on the hexagrams and relevant lines from the I Ching. When you conduct the classical method, you may use the two ways together, or sometimes only use one of them, whichever you prefer. You may wonder and ask me: 'When should I use both ways and when should I use only one of them?' My answer is 'It is up to you.' There is a well-known old saying in China: 'The way of divination is by no means a fixed way,' which infers that this is a relatively flexible method. Unfortunately many people, not only westerners but also many Chinese people, simply check the text of the hexagram and the line and totally ignore the image of the hexagram. Perhaps they are not aware how important it is to look at the image of the hexagram. This is the main reason why people sometimes find it difficult to get a right answer and useful guidance when they employ this method. Of course, it is possible to get very clear guidance from reading the text of the I Ching without looking at the image.

Looking At The Image Of The Hexagram And Its Wider Significance

The main considerations in looking at the image of the hexagram include: a) hexagram place, b) hexagram image, c) line image, d) line place.

a) The hexagram place refers to the specific location of the two trigrams in the hexagram. For example in the T'ai hexagram, Peace, the trigram Kun is located above and the trigram Chien is located below. Different locations of the two trigrams in the hexagram have different meanings.

b) The hexagram image refers to the symbol of the hexagram and its wider meaning. The symbol of one hexagram may have many meanings, and you need to use your intuition when looking at it and understanding it. E.g the hexagram Chien symbolises heaven, the male, the father, the figure 1, or the west ... There are so many possibilities, but which one is the appropriate symbol for your specific question? It depends on your intuition and experience relative to the question. The essential symbols of the eight basic trigrams are listed in the table in figure 32 (page 63).

c) Line image refers to the symbol of the line. There are only two kinds of line: a yin or yang line (broken or solid). The main symbol of the yang line is male, king, strong and any events or matters in the universe with a yang nature. The main symbol of the yin line is female, common people, gentle and any events and matters in the universe with a yin nature.

d) Line place refers to the location of the line in the hexagram. This concept is open to many interpretations, however there are some general principles as follows:

- The order of the lines is from bottom to top. The line at the bottom is the first line and the line on the top is the sixth line.
- The first line, third line, and fifth line are at the place of yang; the second line, fourth line and sixth line are at the place of yin.
- The fifth line and sixth line are at the place of heaven; the first line and second line are at the place of earth; the third line and fourth line are at the place of humanity.
- In the trigram, the first line is in the lower position, the second line is in the middle and the third line is in the upper position. Because there are two trigrams in a hexagram, the first line and fourth line are in the lower position, the second line and fifth line are in the middle, and the third line and sixth line are in the upper position.
- The fifth line is known as the place of heaven, or place of king. The second line is the place of earth, or place of minister/wife. The third line is the place of humans.

Reading And Studying The Text Of The I Ching

There are several different situations with hexagrams, which necessitate different ways of reading the text. They are: a) no line changed in the hexagram, b) only one line changed in the hexagram, c) two lines changed in the hexagram, d) three lines changed in the hexagram, e) four lines changed in the hexagram, f) five lines changed in the hexagram and g) all 6 lines changed in the hexagram.

- When no line changes, look at the Original hexagram and read the text on this hexagram.
- When one line changes, look at and read the text on the changing line.
- When two lines change, look at and read the text on the upper one among the two changing lines in the Original hexagram.
- When three lines change, look at and read the text on both hexagrams or the Original hexagram and the Final hexagram, regardless of the text on the line.

- When four lines change, look at and read the text on the lower one among the two non-changing lines in the Final hexagram.
- When five lines change, look at and read the text on the non-changing line in the Final hexagram.
- When six lines change, look at and read the text on the Final hexagram.

Below is an interesting table that lists the various attributes of the eight trigrams used in the I Ching. Their properties and qualities are useful to know or refer to when either making a prediction or trying to unravel a particular interpretation. Several of these qualities will be referred to in case histories throughout the book.

Figure 32 The Main Symbols of the Eight Basic Trigrams

Symbols in different area	Ch'ien	Tui	Li	Chen	Sun	K'an	Ken	K'un
Nature	Heaven	Lake	Fire	Thunder	Wind	Water	Mountain	Earth
Weather	Snow	Rain	Sunny	Thunder	Windy	Rain	Cloudy	Cloudy
Geography	Capital	Lake, well	Dry land	Forest	Garden	Lake, river	Hill	Field
People	King, father	Youngest daughter	Second daughter	Eldest son	Eldest daughter	Second son	Youngest son	Mother, farmer
Body	Head, lung	Tongue, mouth	Eye, heart	Foot	Buttocks	Ear, kidney	Finger, nose	Abdomen
Personality	Active, energetic	Joyful, talkative	Clever, handsome	Impetuous	Intuitive	Blackness	Hesitant	Gentle, creative
Season	Autumn	Autumn	Summer	2nd month (rabbit month)	End of spring	11th month (rat month)	End of winter	3rd month of every season
Animal	Horse,	Sheep	Pheasant	Dragon	Chicken	Pig, fish	Tiger, dog	Cow
Article/object	Gold, circular article	Gold, music instrument	Book, weapon	Vegetable, flower	Cord, stick, feather	Article with core	Stone, fruit	Square article, paper, cloth
Direction	North-west	West	South	East	South-east	North	North-east	South-west
Colour	Dark-red	White	Red	Green	Green	Black	Yellow	Yellow

Analysing Examples Of The Classical Method

Case 1. 19 years' dream comes true

Prince Chong Er, the Prince of the Jin Kingdom in the Spring and Autumn and Warring State Period (403–221 BC) had been in exile for 19 years. He was keen to return to his motherland to reclaim his throne. He set off on his journey back home. One day when he was approaching the border of his motherland, he suddenly felt worried whether he would achieve success in this plan. He asked his minister. The minister drew the hexagram T'ai (no. 11), Peace.

The minister thought this plan would be successful. Part of the text of the I Ching about the hexagram is that: '*Small departs, the great approaches. Good fortune and success.*' Based on looking at the image of the hexagram and reading the relevant interpretation of the I Ching, the minister explained to Prince Chong Er that the small represented the enemy who occupied the kingdom of the Prince and the great indicated the Prince. So the outcome of the Prince's plan was definitely positive. His dream of 19 years came true eventually.

Case 2. Father's Health

In the North-South Dynasty (420–589), a young man of a poor family lived in the North Qi kingdom with his father. The young man's mother had died when he was very young. His father had brought him up. Although life was hard, he loved his father very much and still enjoyed the simple life with his father, regardless of the poor conditions. One day his father suddenly became sick. He was very worried about his father's health. They had no money to pay a doctor. Several days later he remembered the great I Ching. Although he knew very little about the book, he conducted a coin-casting divination. He got the T'ai hexagram (no. 11) without any line changing, as follows:

As soon as he drew the hexagram, he immediately checked the judgement text in the I Ching. He found that the meaning of the hexagram T'ai is Peace. The text on the hexagram is:

> '*The Receptive, which moves downward, stands above; the Creative, which moves upward, is below. Hence their influences meet and are in harmony, so that all living things bloom and prosper'. The judgement about the hexagram is: 'Small departs, the great approaches. Good fortune and success.*'

So he was very happy with this result. He thought it was a very good indication, just as the words told him: all living things bloom and prosper, good fortune. He thought his dearest father would recover very quickly. However, days later, his father did not become better and seemed worse. He was very worried again. He knew where a famous I Ching master lived, Master Zhao Puhe. He went to visit the Master and asked for help. Master Zhao was very moved by the boy's story and was willing to help him. However, as soon as he heard the boy had got the hexagram T'ai, he was terribly shocked. After a long silence, Master Zhao told the boy it was the worst symbol for his father. 'Because,' the Master said, 'the image of the hexagram definitely shows us that the upper trigram is Kun, which represents earth, and the lower trigram is Chien, which generally represents heaven, but also represents an old man, king or father, when you are concerned with people's affairs instead of other events. So the image of the hexagram gives us a tragic picture: an old man lies under soil. It means your father may die soon due to the disease and will be buried.' Although the boy didn't want to believe the indication, and tried his best to save his father's life, unfortunately, his poor father died just two weeks later.

In this case, we can understand that carefully looking at the image of the hexagram and thinking about its symbolism is critically important for prediction. Sometimes this is more important than reading the interpretation text from the I Ching. Master Zhao got the judgement based on observing the image of the hexagram and not from referring to the words from the I Ching. The Classical method is quite flexible; as you see that the same hexagram T'ai Peace gave us completely different results. In the previous case the hexagram T'ai meant auspicious indications for the Prince, but in the second case the same hexagram meant misfortune for the poor boy. The most important thing is to try your best to use your own intuition and not to limit yourself only to rational thinking and logical deduction.

Case 3. The Death of A Martial God

The very famous General Guan Gong of the Sui Kingdom in the Three Kingdom Dynasty Period (221–265 AD) had been regarded as a great martial god in China and other oriental countries for 2000 years. When he lost a battle, the King of the Wu Kingdom wanted to know the fortune of General Guan Gong. The great scholar on the I Ching, Master Yu Fan, conducted a divination to answer the question for King Wu. The hexagram was Chieh (no. 60): Limitation, with the fifth line changed.

Original hexagram   **Final hexagram**

* Denotes changing line

Having looked at the hexagram carefully, Master Yu thought that General Guan Gong would be killed two days later. He explained that the sixth line of the Original hexagram is the symbol of a man's head and the fifth line is the symbol of a man's neck. As the fifth line of the hexagram, which represented the neck of General Guan Gong, was changed from an unbroken line to a broken line, the image suggests something was being cut into two parts by somebody. It meant that the head of General Guan Gong might be cut off by his enemy. Just two days later news of General Guan Gong's death was confirmed: he was captured by his enemy and then beheaded. Since his death the Chinese people have respected him as a great martial god.

In this case, Master Yu made a judgement only by looking at the image of the changing Line of the Original hexagram and inspecting its place in the final hexagram.

Case 4. An Emperor's Fate

Emperor Sui Yang, the well-known despot of the Sui Dynasty (589–618 AD), worried about his power. His minister did a divination for him. The hexagram was Li (no. 30: Fire) with the fourth line changing.

The text on the changing line is terribly inauspicious: it says that '*A large fire with its bright light high comes unexpectedly, then a lot of people are found burnt, then dead, then abandoned.*' In this hexagram, the upper trigram is fire, and the lower trigram is also fire; the image is of a large fire burning all over the world, symbolising a great rebellion or revolution. Very soon a large insurgence happened throughout the country, and the Emperor Sui Yang was captured by the people and killed.

Case 5. Career and Fortune

One day, an old friend of mine visited me to consult me about his career path in government reform. He had worked as a director in a government department for eight years with great success. The head of the department was to be reappointed and there were two possibilities: one was that my friend would hold onto his position as he was very well qualified, and the other possibility was that another candidate, even though they might not be as eligible, might take the position and replace my friend. So my friend was wondering if he would keep his job. I asked him to conduct a divination by coin casting. He drew the hexagram Chia Jen, no. 37: The Family/The Clan with the third line changing.

Original Hexagram   **Final Hexagram**

I looked at the image of the hexagram. The upper trigram is Sun, representing the oldest daughter, the lower trigram is Li, representing the second daughter; both are female and there is no male symbol. So it meant that this job would not be my friend's any more, because he is not female. The text on the hexagram told me that this hexagram is favourable only for the female. I checked the text on the changing line. It said: '*It shows its subject treating the members of the household with stern severity. There will be occasion for repentance, there will be peril, but there will also be good fortune. If the wife and children were to be smirking and chatting, in the end there would be occasion for regret. It says in the Small Symbolism: "when the members of the household are treated with stern severity, there has been no great failure in the regulation of the family. When the wife and children are smirking and chattering, the proper economy of the family has been lost."* ' I have known my friend for years. He is a very kind man. Although he is a highly qualified director in his department, he never treats his colleagues in his department too strictly; they are really like family members and enjoy laughing and joking when they finish their work. Based on the working style of my friend, I thought he might already have lost control of his department and that a woman from his department might replace him as the new director. So I told him the forecast from the I Ching, and suggested that he should look for another job. He totally agreed with my analysis and started to apply for a new position. One month later, my friend told me that he was indeed replaced by a former employee, a young woman, a close relative of a senior official in the government. Fortunately my friend had had enough time to prepare for this change in advance owing to the help of the I Ching, and he soon found a new job for himself and enjoyed his new position.

Case 6. Looking Forward to the Year Ahead

In the Spring Festival 1995, Professor Liu, a client of mine, visited me and asked me if there was good news for him in the coming new year. Professor Liu is a research fellow in a very famous academy. His major is TCM, and he has a lot of experience and a very strong background in researching and writing in this area. Recently however, he had had some trouble with his supervisor. He is a very academic person and weak in public relationships, and though he tried to improve the relationship with his supervisor, there was little progress, as the supervisor is a very difficult man. He hoped that some change would take place in the coming year. I understood Professor Liu and asked him to consult the I Ching by the coin method. He drew the hexagram Chien (no. 1), the Creative hexagram with the third and fourth lines changed.

Original Hexagram   **Final Hexagram**

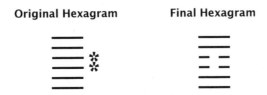

I told him that there would be a big change taking place for him. The text for the Chien hexagram says: '*Heaven, in its motion, gives the ideas of strength. The superior man, in accordance with this, nerves himself to ceaseless activity.*' Meanwhile the fourth line says: '*(We see its subject as the dragon looking) as if he were leaping up, but still in the deep, there will be no mistake.*' So it was possible that Professor Liu would transfer to another department and work under a new supervisor and with new colleagues. This new supervisor would be very kind and easy to communicate with. And also, considering the very strong background of Professor Liu, he might be put in charge of an important research project. In this situation, I suggested that the best attitude for Professor Liu was not just to wait passively but actively to make the necessary preparations. When the time came, he should submit an application to transfer to a new department. Six months later, I received good news from Professor Liu, and his situation had changed just as I predicted. He transferred to another department and a famous professor was his supervisor. This new supervisor had a similar background to Professor Liu, they had a lot of common interests, similar tastes and had set up a good collaborative relationship very quickly. As Professor Liu had taken the opportunity in good time due to accepting the recommendation of the I Ching, now as chief researcher, he is conducting an important international cooperation project and is highly respected in his field worldwide.

Chapter Six

The Mei Hua Method

This method can be used to get a prediction by analysing the relationship between the top and bottom trigrams of the hexagram. One trigram represents self/client while the other trigram represents partner/match or event concerned. This procedure is quite simple and the prediction result can be obtained quickly. It is easy to learn and sometimes the prediction result is so accurate that clients are astonished by it. It is one of the most popular divination methods in many oriental countries. This method is especially suitable for those who have a talent for intuition or insight.

Although it is a wonderful practical method, it has not been introduced into the West so far. Many western people are keen to learn this method. It should be possible for you to understand this method and know how to use it just after reading this book and completing a little practice.

Creating The Hexagram

For the Mei Hua method you do not need coins but you will need to refer to the Chinese calendar (chapter 4) and the Hexagrams (chapter 10).

To help you understand the Mei Hua method I would like to use an example of a case study I conducted when I started to study this method years ago.

President Lincoln was murdered at 10.15 p.m. 14 April 1865. On that evening, President Lincoln went to the theatre with his wife. The other members of the audience were excited to have their President amongst them, and the performance stopped for a few minutes to welcome Lincoln. However, halfway through the performance, at 10.15 p.m., suddenly a

shooting occurred. As soon as Lincoln's bodyguard left his side, a 27–year-
-old murderer entered the President's box, swiftly approached Lincoln and
shot him in the head. The President died instantly.

I imagined that, in order to guarantee the President's safety, two
days earlier we had been invited by the White House to conduct a prediction to confirm the original schedule for President Lincoln. According to
the President's schedule, the calculation is as follows:

Firstly translate the date 10.15 p.m., 14 April 1865 into the Chinese
calendar as follows:

	HOUR	DAY	MONTH	YEAR
HEAVENLY STEM	−*wood	+*wood	+metal	−wood
EARTHLY BRANCH	Pig (−water)	Tiger (+wood)	Dragon (+earth)	Ox (−earth)
TIME NUMBER **	12	19	3	2

Note:

* − = yin, + = yang
** The Earthly Branch of this hour is Pig, Pig's number is 12 (See page 51); The number
of this day is 19, which is obtained directly by checking the Chinese calendar; The
number of this month is 3, which is obtained by checking the Chinese calendar;
The Earthly Branch of this year is Ox, Ox's number is 2.

In order to calculate the number of the day, count the days of the month the
western date appears after new moon. In the Chinese calendar the lunar
month begins on new moon. The new moon for April 1865 was on 27 March
1865, day 1 in the Chinese calendar; count forward and 14 April 1865 would
be day 19.

Then we create a hexagram by a three-step calculation on the number of
the time, including year, month, day and hour. The process is shown as
follows:

Create Upper Trigram

Identify the number of the upper trigram by conducting a calculation based
on the formula:

(no.year + no.month + no.day) / 8 = x … **a** (remainder number)

Please note: the **a** clearly indicates the number of the upper trigram (according to the order of the Early Heaven Sequence of the Eight Trigram Chart, or Ch'ien 1, Tui 2, Li 3, Chen 4, Sun 5, K'an 6, Ken 7, K'un 8. (See figure 6, page 18) When **a** = 0, it is seen as the same as 8). Then it is very easy to find out the trigram based on this specific number **a**. In other words, when **a** = 1, the trigram is Chien, when **a** = 2, the trigram is Tui, etc.

In our example, the result should be:

The year = 2, month = 3, the day = 19

(2 + 3 + 19)/8 = 3 ... 0 (remainder number **a**)

So far, we get the **a** = 0. The 0 is seen as 8, so the number of the upper trigram is 8. According to the order of the Early Heaven Sequence of the Eight Trigram Chart, 8 means trigram Kun, Earth. So the trigram should be Kun:

Create Lower Trigram

Identify the number of the lower trigram by conducting a calculation based on the formula:

(no. year + no. month + no. day + no. hour) / 8 = y ... **b** (remainder number)

Please note: the **b** clearly indicates the number of the lower trigram (according to the order of the Early Heaven Sequence of the Eight Trigram Chart, or Ch'ien 1, Tui 2, Li 3, Chen 4, Sun 5, K'an 6, Ken 7, K'un 8. (See figure 6, page 18) When **b** = 0, it is seen as the same as 8). Then it is very easy to find out the trigram based on this specific number **b**. In other words, when **b** = 1, the trigram is Chien, when **b** = 2, the trigram is Tui and so on.

In our example, the result should be:

The year = 2, month = 3, the day = 19 and the hour = 12

(2 + 3 + 19 + 12)/8 = 4 ... 4 (the remainder number **b**)

In this way, we get the number **b** = 4, so the number of the lower trigram is 4. According to the order of the Early Heaven Sequence of the Eight

Trigram Chart, 4 means trigram Chen, the Thunder. So the lower trigram should be Chen,

☳

So far, we get the Original hexagram by combining the upper trigram and the lower trigram. It is called Fu (no. 24): Return, or the Turning Point as follows:

☷☳

Locate Changing Line

Identify the number of the changing line by conducting a calculation based on the formula:

(no. year + no. month + no. day+ no. hour) / 6 = z ... **c** (remainder number)

c indicates the number/order of the changing line. Please note, when **c** = 0, it is seen as 6.

In our example, the result should be:

The year = 2, month = 3, the day = 19 and the hour = 12
(2 + 3 + 19 + 12)/6 = 6 ... 0 (the remainder number **c**)

As the **c** = 0, it is seen as 6, so the sixth line of the hexagram will change.

So far, we get the Original hexagram Fu (no. 24) and Final hexagram I (no. 27) the Corners of the Mouth, as follows:

Original Hexagram	Final Hexagram
☷☳ *	☶☳

Besides the two hexagrams, we may have a Nuclear hexagram. It is made from the four lines among the Original hexagram as follows:

Original Hexagram	Nuclear Hexagram
– –	– – 5
5 – –	– – 4
4 – –	– – 3
3 – –	– – 4
2 – –	– – 3
——	– – 2

We take the second line of the Original hexagram as the first line of the Nuclear hexagram, and the third of the Original hexagram as the second of the Nuclear hexagram, and so on. Let us put the Nuclear hexagram between the Original hexagram and the Final hexagram. So far we have three hexagrams:

Original Hexagram	Nuclear Hexagram	Final Hexagram

Note: The three upper trigrams are Object trigrams and the three lower trigrams are Subject trigrams.

We can now analyse the process of change, development and the final outcome of the event/matter concerned according to the three hexagrams. Each of them represents one specific phase of the development process respectively: the Original hexagram represents the beginning of the event, the Nuclear hexagram indicates the middle phase of development of this event, and the Final hexagram is the ultimate outcome of the event/matter.

The Five Steps In Mei Hua Analysis

Step 1

Identify Subject trigram and Object trigram.

The Subject trigram represents the self/client who consulted the I Ching to get guidance or answers, while the Object trigram represents the specific partner/match of the client or the event/matter concerning the client.

The principle of identifying Subject trigram and Object trigram in the Original hexagram is very simple. The trigram in which the changing line is located is the Object trigram, and the other trigram without a changing line is the Subject trigram. As soon as the locations of the Subject trigram and the Object trigram are determined in the Original hexagram, these same locations will be followed in the next two hexagrams.

In our example, the Original hexagram, the upper trigram K'un is the Object trigram, because the changing line is located here, and the lower trigram Chen is the Subject trigram. In the Nuclear hexagram, the location of the two trigrams is the same as the Original hexagram, or the upper trigram K'un is also the Object trigam and the lower trigram K'un is the Subject trigram. Then in the Final hexagram, the upper trigram Ken is the Object trigram and the lower trigram Chen is the Subject trigram.

Step 2

Find out the element of the Subject trigram and Object trigram by checking figure 32 on page 63.

In our example, the Object trigram (K'un) is earth, the Subject trigram (Chen) is wood.

Step 3

Look at the relationship of the Subject trigram and the Object trigram, based on the dynamics involved in the Five Elements. E.g. metal births water, water destroys fire and fire melts metal. Refer to figure 3 on page 11.

For our example, when you look at the Original hexagram, the relationship of the two trigrams is that the Subject trigram (wood) destroys the Object trigram (earth).

Step 4

Compare the force of Subject and Object trigrams from two perspectives:

1) By Quantity

Calculate the total number of trigrams in all the hexagrams, including the Original hexagram, Nuclear hexagram and Final hexagram.

In our example, the side of the Subject trigram (wood) has two trigrams (lower trigram of the Original hexagram and the lower trigram of Final hexagram). On the side of the Object (earth) trigram there are four trigrams (upper trigram of Original hexagram, upper trigram of Nuclear hexagram, lower trigram of Nuclear hexagram and upper trigram of Final hexagram). So the Object trigram seems to be prevailing over the Subject trigram in terms of quantity.

2) By Quality

We need to examine the impact on the Subject trigram and Object trigram of the time of year, month, day and hour respectively. Using our knowledge of which of the Five Elements is attached to each of the 12 Earthly Branches, it is possible to speculate on their interaction. We know that the Five Elements' relationships with one another are based on support, drain, control or destruction. For example, when the trigram element is metal and the element of Earthly Branch of the year is fire, the trigram will be destroyed by the year; when the trigram element is metal and the element of Earthly Branch of the month is earth, the trigram will be supported by the month; when the trigram element is metal and the element of Earthly Branch of the day is water, the trigram will be consumed by the day.

In our example, the Object trigram is earth, and the Subject trigram is wood. The Earthly Branches of the time year, month, day and hour are:

earth Ox, earth Dragon, wood Tiger and water Pig respectively.

The Object trigram earth is supported by the earth year and earth month, since they are the same earth. But the Subject trigram wood is supported by the wood day, as they are the same element. It is also supported by the water hour, as water births wood. Comparing the two sides, the Object trigram is obviously stronger than the Subject trigram, because generally the year and month are much more powerful than the hour. The year is respected as god or king in power. The month relates to the season, which in turn determines the status of Five Elements in different seasons. (See figure 4 page 12) So they have greater impact on the trigram than the hour.

Step 5

Get a brief judgement on the outcome by formula.

The first thing that most people are concerned with is whether the final outcome of the event is auspicious or inauspicious, good luck or misfortune. We may get a general answer quickly by analysing the relationship of the Subject trigram and the Object trigram according to a general principle as in the following formula.

(Ot = Object trigram, St = Subject trigram,
o = auspicious, x = inauspicious)

There are 5 possibilities as follows:

Figure 33

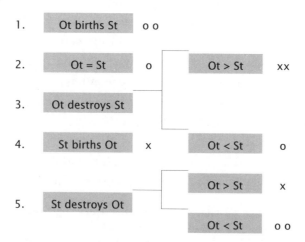

This method gives you a simple and quick response and tells you only if the outcome is positive or negative. It is also easier to see the relationship between the two trigrams. For example, in the third stage above, or when the Object trigram destroys the Subject trigram, you cannot get a correct judgement immediately. You must enter the next box to compare the force of the two sides, then identify which side is stronger. There are two possibilities. This is where: St > Ot, the result is positive, or when Ot > St, the result is negative. But when you compare the force of the two sides, you must carefully look at two aspects – compare them by quality and quantity. It is relatively easy to compare them by quantity. However, when you compare the two sides by quality, the issue becomes more complex again. Consider the impact of time, such as year, month, day and hour, on the trigram, and also think about the influence of space (direction and location, which is also considered in feng shui) or the geography factor on the trigram. With regard to the impact of time on the trigram, we have already discussed this above. However, the influence of space, or the geographical factor, has not yet been discussed. I will explain it by giving you an example later (see case 2 Workshop in London. Page 81).

On the other hand, you may not be satisfied with such a simple answer as positive or negative. You may be very keen to know more details related to the development process of the event/matter, such as the questions of when, where, who, how and what, and ranges including quantitative and qualitative amounts. For example you may want to know a distance, the number or character of people, the quality of a house, or an amount of money. The question may be associated with a very broad area. It may depend on a particular demand from the questioner. Anyway, very often, further in-depth analysis of the development of the event is necessary.

When you conduct further analysis don't forget to refer to the I Ching hexagrams and read the relevant text on the Original hexagram, Final hexagram, changing line and sometimes the Nuclear hexagram and their images. This principle is the same as the Classical method discussed previously.

Case 1. President Lincoln's Murder

Let's continue the prediction for President Lincoln and review the date and hexagram (see page 72):

Translate the date 10.15 p.m., 14 April 1865 into the Chinese calendar as follows:

	HOUR	DAY	MONTH	YEAR
HEAVENLY STEM	–wood	+wood	+metal	–wood
EARTHLY BRANCH	Pig (–water)	Tiger (+wood)	Dragon (+earth)	Ox (–earth)
TIME NUMBER	12	19	3	2

The Original hexagram, Nuclear hexagram and Final hexagram are as follows:

Main Hexagram	Nuclear Hexagram	Changing Hexagram

As you know, the Original hexagram represents the beginning of the event, or in this case the murder itself. The Nuclear hexagram represents the middle phase of the development of the event. The Final hexagram indicates the outcome of the event, or the outcome of the murder case. The Subject trigram represents the client; here it is Lincoln. The Object trigram represents the match; here it is the murderer.

We can see from the diagram above that in the Original hexagram the Subject trigram Chen (wood) destroys the Object trigram Kun (earth). In the Final hexagram, the Subject trigram Chen (wood) destroys the Object trigram Ken (earth) too. It means that from the beginning of the murder until the end of the murder, the relationship of Lincoln and the murderer is always one of conflict. It is a powerful fight between Lincoln and the murderer. But who will be the winner in the end? It depends on the comparison of the force between the two sides. As we analysed before, the Object trigram (the murderer) is much stronger than the Subject trigram (President Lincoln). There are four trigrams with the earth element, or more trigrams that are the same as the Object trigram, and the Object trigram is supported by the year and month. But there are only two trigrams which are the same as the Subject trigram, and this trigram is only supported by the day and hour. According to Chinese philosophy, the year is as powerful as the god, or the king since it controls the world overall during this time. The month represents the season. It is an important link between the year, day and hour. Both the year and the month are powerful and very strong, but the hour is less important. The Object trigram (the murderer) is not only stronger than the Subject trigram (Lincoln) in quantity, but also very much stronger than the Subject trigram in quality. It is obvious that the Object trigram will achieve great success in the fight and the Subject trigram will lose. In other words, President Lincoln will be killed ultimately by the murderer.

Case 2. A Workshop in London

On 28 July 2000, at about 1.30 p.m., my good friend, Jon Sandifer, kindly invited me to give a lecture on the I Ching to his colleagues and friends in the UK. I was very happy to receive this invitation, however I wondered if the time would be good for my audience and whether western people would like to join me, a Chinese man, to discuss this very ancient and maybe diffi-cult topic. I was keen to know the outcome of this plan in advance. I made a prediction about the lecture's outcome and the number of participants.

Firstly I translated the time data — 28 July 2000, 1.30 p.m. from the western calendar into the Chinese calendar:

	HOUR	DAY	MONTH	YEAR
HEAVENLY STEM	–fire	–fire	–water	+metal
EARTHLY BRANCH	Sheep (earth)	Pig (water)	Sheep (earth)	Dragon (earth)
TIME NUMBER	8	27	6	5

Secondly I created the Original hexagram based on the formula (see page 59). I got the number of the upper trigram of the Original hexagram from the formula: $(5 + 6 + 27)/8 = 4 \ldots 6$ (a)

Thus the upper trigram is Kan: water (based on the Early Heaven Sequence of the Eight Trigram Chart. 6 = Kan).

Then I got the lower trigram from the formula: (5 + 6 + 27 + 8)/8 =
5 ... 6 (b)

Thus the lower trigram is Kan: water (based on the Early Heaven
Sequence of the Eight Trigram Chart. 6 = Kan). So we get the Original hexagram by putting the upper trigram and lower trigram together.

**Main
Hexagram**

Then we get the number of the changing line from the formula: (5 + 6 + 27
+ 8)/6 = 7 ... 4 (b)

Because the changing line is fourth, we get the Final hexagram by
changing the fourth line of the Original hexagram.

Based on the principle of drawing the Nuclear hexagram (see page 75),
we get the Nuclear hexagram from the Original hexagram. We put the three
hexagrams together as follows:

Main Hexagram	Nuclear Hexagram	Changing Hexagram

Note: The three upper trigrams are Object trigrams and the
three lower trigrams are Subject Trigrams.

According to the judgement principle as described previously, we can forecast the implementation of this plan as follows.

Let's look at the Original hexagram first, as this hexagram represents the
very beginning of the project. The upper trigram Kan is the Object trigram
(because the changing line is located here) with the element water. The
lower trigram Kan is the Subject trigram with the element water also. Therefore the Subject trigram and the Object trigram are the same element and the
two trigrams support each other. It is definitely a positive sign. The Subject
trigram represents myself, the lecturer of the workshop, and the Object

trigram represents my partner, the organiser and coordinator of the plan, Jon Sandifer. The support relationship between the two trigrams indicates clearly that the two men who initiated the workshop are very good friends and support each other for a successful plan.

Then let's look at the Nuclear hexagram as it represents the middle phase of the project. The Subject trigram of the Nuclear hexagram is the lower trigram Chen wood. (Please remember the Subject trigram is now located in the lower part of the Nuclear hexagram the same as the location of the Subject trigram in the Original hexagram.) Also the location of the Subject/Object trigram in the Final hexagram is the same as the Original hexagram. It means that as soon as the location of the Subject and Object trigram is determined in the Original hexagram, the same location will be followed in the next two hexagrams. The Object trigram is the upper trigram Ken earth, the Subject trigram wood destroys the Object trigram earth. Does it mean the two good friends will start fighting each other? No, the Subject trigram represents the side of holding the workshop, or Jon and me, and the Object trigram represents the side of the audience. The relationship of destruction is by no means considered conflict here. It just means that as hosts, Jon and I warmly and actively invite our friends to attend the workshop.

According to Chinese philosophy, the meaning of destruction is not one of control or conflict, but actually clash. Many times in nature and even in human affairs, when we are looking to achieve a major breakthrough, we need to rely on our full resources. This clash could be the use of explosives or heavy tools to mine gold or diamonds. The yelling and screaming of a leader in battle encouraging the troops can be considered a clash. In essence, a clash is regarded as the agent for encouraging change, creating wealth and is often the polarised force for attraction. This cycle of destruction, drawn from the Five Elements can also mean control and in any relationship control is seen as looking out for or looking after someone, as a parent would a child.

Finally, look at the Final hexagram which represents the outcome of the project. The Object trigram which is located in the upper part of the hexagram (representing participants) is Tui metal and the Subject trigram located in the lower part of the hexagram (representing our workshop) is

K'an water. This means the Object trigram metal births and supports the Subject trigram water. It is the most perfect relationship among trigrams. It is obvious that all participants will actively support the project and enjoy the lecture very much.

After analysing the relationship between the Subject trigram and the Object trigram we need to look at the impact of chi from the cosmos on the project which is represented by the Earthly Branches of date. These are represented by the Subject trigram and the Object trigram. In the Original hexagram, both the Subject trigram (water) and the Object trigram (water) are supported by the day (the Pig day is water). Although they are destroyed by the year (the Dragon year is earth), the month (the Sheep month is earth) and the hour (the Sheep hour is earth), it is not something to worry about. It just means that in the preparation stage of our project there may be difficulties to be overcome. It also gives us an important indication that we must pay more attention to selecting the best date to hold the workshop. By analysing this hexagram we can also understand the reason why timing is always a priority for any plan.

After reviewing the impact of the universe on the Original hexagram, we must examine the Final hexagram which indicates the final outcome of the project. Every event and matter in the world always changes and develops over time. All of us have experienced that something may be difficult at the beginning, however the situation may change and improve later and develop very well. It is possible that we may overcome all difficulties and achieve great success. If only the Final hexagram is a good omen, it means the outcome is hopeful. When we look at the Final hexagram, the Object trigram located in the upper part of the hexagram (element metal) is supported by the three Earthly Branches of the year (Dragon year is earth), month (Sheep month is earth) and hour (Sheep hour is earth). Having so many powerful supporters, the Object trigram is comfortable and becomes very strong. It also means that all the participants are qualified people. Some of them may be well-qualified professionals experienced in my field, some may be experts and scholars with strong backgrounds in studying traditional Chinese culture. All of them are happy to join us. Because there are many supporters from the year, month and hour to the Object trigram, the number of participants should equally be quite big. Furthermore, as the

Object trigram becomes strong the first beneficiary is unquestionably the Subject trigram since the Subject trigram water is birthed by the Object trigram metal. If the expectant mother's health is excellent, who will doubt about her future baby?

We decided to hold the workshop in September. It is a Rooster (metal) month. According to the principle of Combining-Conflict relationship between Earthly Branches (see chapter 4), the Rooster month will closely combine with the Dragon year. When the two elements combine, they create a new element, in this case metal (see chapter 4). It is a very powerful type of metal. It will not only support the Subject trigram of water and the Object trigram of water in the Original hexagram, but will also support the Subject trigram water and the Object trigram metal in the Final hexagram. Therefore both the Subject trigram and the Object trigram in the Original hexagram and in the Final hexagram will become strong in September. It means the workshop will be most successful at this time. Thus the audience, speaker, organiser and coordinator will be satisfied with the workshop and benefit a lot from it.

Regarding the number of participants this is also an important issue for us. We need to do some logistic preparations based on the number of participants in advance, such as finding a classroom, the preparation of tea and lunch, and the preparation of handouts for my lecture. How can we know the precise number two months before the workshop opens? It seems quite a difficult question. But provided we get our hexagram, it will tell us everything. We can get the precise figure by calculating the number of the trigrams of the hexagrams.

If we want to know the number of participants, the solution is very simple. The only thing we need to do is add the number of the upper trigram and the lower trigram of the hexagram. (Please remember the number of the trigram is based on the Early Heaven Sequence of the Eight Trigram Chart, or Chien 1, Tui 2, Li 3, Chen 4 ... See figure 6 — on page 18). First, add the number of the upper and lower trigrams of the Original hexagram. As we know, it represents the first phase of the plan, or the number of our first list of students at the workshop. As the number of the upper trigram Kun is 6, and the lower trigram Kun is 6 too, the total is 6 + 6 = 12. As the number of the changing line should also be counted we add the number of the changing line 4, so the total number of people registering should be 12 + 4 = 16. The Nuclear hexagram and the Final hexagram represent the last two phases of the plan. In order to determine how many participants will join eventually, it is necessary to calculate the total number of all three hexagrams. The number of the trigram of the Nuclear hexagram is 7 (upper trigram Ken) + 4 (lower trigram Chen) = 11, and the number of the trigram of the Final hexagram is 2 (upper trigram Tui) + 6 (lower trigram Kan) = 8. The total is 12 (number of Original hexagram) + 4 (number of changing line) + 11 (number of Nuclear hexagram) + 8 (number of Final hexagram), giving a final total of 35. By now, it is safe to prepare 35 handouts and book a classroom for 35 people for our workshop.

With regard to the projection of numbers by this method, I would like to emphasise the flexibility of this method. Sometimes we get the number by adding the number of trigrams in all three hexagrams, including the Original hexagram, the Nuclear hexagram and the Final hexagram. I did this in the example above. However, sometimes we get a number by adding the number of the trigram from the Original hexagram only and ignoring the other two hexagrams entirely. You may ask me: 'When do you need to add the trigrams from all three hexagrams, and when do you not need to do so?'

Although the Mei Hua method is flexible, I will still offer you a general principle to be followed. The key point to pay most attention to is that we cannot consider the number separately. As I have emphasised previously, we do need to comprehensively review and analyse the Object trigram and the Subject trigram from two aspects. On one hand, we need to check the quantity of the trigram, while at the same time checking its quality which is determined by the impact of chi from the cosmos. Then we can integrate the analysis from the two aspects and make our overall judgement.

Here is the principle: when the quality of the trigram is poor, or the trigram is weak, its quantity/number needs to be reduced. When the quality of the trigram is good, or the trigram is strong, its quantity/number should be increased.

In order to show you how to put this principle into practice, let's come back to our example. Because the Object trigram metal of the final hexagram (as we know, it represents the final number of students) is supported by the earth year, earth month and earth hour, it is very strong, and of high quality. Based on the principle above, we should increase its quantity/number. We therefore need to calculate the number of trigrams from all the three hexagrams and add the number of the changing lines together. Thus finally we get the number of participants as 35. If the situation of the hexagram was totally different or if the Object trigram of the Final hexagram had not been supported by the year, month and hour, or if it had been destroyed by the year and month (if the year and month were fire element, they would destroy the Object trigram metal), then it would be very weak, and we should reduce its quantity/number. In this case we should add the number of trigrams only from the Original hexagram and ignore the other two hexagrams. In that situation, the number should be reduced to 12 (add the number of the trigram in the Original hexagram only) or 16 (based on the 12, adding the number of the changing lines – 4). It means that the number of participants might be 12, or at best 16.

So what was the actual outcome of our workshop? Owing to the excellent organisation by Jon, exactly 35 participants attended our workshop. Most of them were qualified experts in traditional oriental culture. Some of them were well-known scholars in the western world, some of them were reputed practitioners and very experienced in applying eastern wisdom to improve the quality of daily life for themselves and helping their friends and clients. The workshop was a great success. Both participants and organisers were satisfied with the outcome. Although I only had time to provide them with a brief introduction to the I Ching prediction methods, all the participants were excited and gave my lecture their best evaluation and warmest praise. I was impressed and deeply moved by western people's great enthusiasm for traditional Chinese culture. I very much appreciated the support from my good friend Jon and his kind wife Renata, who prepared a wonderful tea and lunch for all the participants. It was the excellent arrangements by Jon and great support from all the members of his family (including his kind mother-in-law and his sweet children) which made the workshop so successful.

Accuracy In Quantity Predictions

I must emphasise that estimating a specific number as accurately as possible is very important work for forecasting when we want to identify certain amounts of quantitative matter such as time, distance, money, or a number of people. The number itself is a critical element for the Mei Hua I Ching prediction method. This is a concept of two ways. Firstly, we may draw a hexagram as our Original hexagram (that is our basic tool with which to conduct predictions,) from a specific number (as we mentioned previously, when we want to create a hexagram, we may translate a specific number into a relative trigram. e.g. 1 = Chien, 2 = Tiu, etc.). Secondly, when we want to analyse a particular hexagram we can get a figure from the trigram of the hexagram (e.g. Chien = 1, Kun = 8…) and we will use this concept very often when we do hexagram analysis later in this book.

I would also like to introduce another principle on how to evaluate the great and complex impact of the universe on a trigram. When we analyse the trigram we should not only consider the influence of time, but also that of space, or the geographical factor and also the weather. The impact of space and weather on the trigram is as significant as that of time, because they are the real chi of the cosmos. In the previous example, although the Original hexagram, the Subject and Object trigram water is not supported by time, it is fortunately supported by the geographical factor and the weather, which represents powerful chi from the universe with great impact on the trigrams. When Jon and I discussed the plan we were sitting in Jon's home. The room was very comfortable and it was a very beautiful day. It was sunny in the early morning, then it started to rain when we began talking about the plan. Here the trigrams are supported by the wet weather. The water from heaven is a dear gift to our plan from our great father God! Furthermore, I noted when I visited Jon, his house is located in a beautiful area close to the river Thames. We sat on the bank to discuss our plan and enjoyed the beautiful landscape. The prosperous water from the river supported our trigrams too. It is a dear gift from our great mother Earth! Thus, we got great support from both heaven and earth. This is huge chi from the universe. So we are very confident that we will achieve final success for our plan! (On the day when we held the workshop, it was also sunny in the early morning. Then close to noon, it began raining slightly again, but it was September, it was a comfortable day, neither hot, nor cold. Also, London is a very wet city and close to the sea. This land is permeated with so much water!

Case 3. A Diagram of A Life Journey

With this method we can not only successfully predict a specific event or particular matter happening in a specific time frame, maybe in months, days, hours, or even in a few minutes, but also comprehensively forecast people's destiny. It may show us a general picture of the whole journey of life for an individual, from their birth, becoming older, to very old age, and finally to their death.

I will give you an example by analysing one person's life journey. It is a real story about a close friend of mine. Seaborn Wang, a Chinese man, was born at 3.30 a.m., 25 May 1948 in south-west China. Let's forecast his life journey by the following steps:

Firstly create a hexagram according to his birthday — 3.30 a.m., 25 May 1948. Translate the date into the Chinese calendar as follows:

	HOUR	DAY	MONTH	YEAR
HEAVENLY STEM	+earth	+metal	–fire	+earth
EARTHLY BRANCH	Tiger (wood)	Dog (earth)	Snake (fire)	Rat (water)
TIME NUMBER	3	17	4	5*

Note: * The number '5' is Heavenly Stem number (yang earth) instead of Earthly Branch number 1 (Rat). This reformed method was initiated by Master Shao.

Then create a hexagram by the 3 steps for calculating the number of time, including year, month, day and hour in this table. (The formula is shown on page 72.)

We get the number of the upper trigram of the Original hexagram from the formula:

$$(5 + 4 + 17)/8 = 3 \ldots 2 \text{ (a)}$$

Thus the upper trigram is the trigram Tui metal (based on the Early Heaven Sequence of the Eight Trigram Chart. 2 = Tui).

Then we get the lower trigram from the formula:

$(5 + 4 + 17 + 3)/8 = 3 \dots 5$ (b)

Thus the lower trigram is the trigram Sun wood (based on the Early Heaven Sequence of the Eight Trigram Chart. 5 = Sun).

So we get the Original hexagram by putting the upper trigram and lower trigram together:

Then we get the number of the changing line from the formula:

$(5 + 4 + 17 + 3)/6 = 4 \dots 5$ (c)

Because the changing line is the fifth, we get the Final hexagram by changing the fifth line of the Original hexagram. Based on the principle of drawing the Nuclear hexagram (see page 75), we get the Nuclear hexagram from the Original hexagram. We put the three hexagrams together as follows:

Original Hexagram	Nuclear Hexagram	Final Hexagram

Note: The three upper trigrams are Object trigrams and the three lower trigrams are Subject trigrams.

When you look at these three hexagrams you may be quite surprised by this idea: can such a simple figure really represent someone's entire life journey? It is such a long journey, often lasting 80 to 90 years! It seems mysterious indeed. However it is true and we will start to understand his fate by carefully analysing these three hexagrams step by step.

As we know, the three hexagrams represent different phases of the development of an event respectively. So the Original hexagram symbolises

The Mei Hua Method | 91

his childhood, the Nuclear hexagram symbolises the middle of his life and the Final hexagram symbolises his old age.

The beginning of the man's life journey is quite difficult. In the Original hexagram, as the changing line is located in the upper trigram, the lower trigram is the Subject trigram and the upper trigram is the Object trigram. The Subject trigram Sun (wood) is destroyed by the Object trigram Tui (metal). It means there were a lot of unhappy experiences in this man's childhood. The Subject trigram represents the boy himself and the Object trigram represents a range of events and people surrounding him. Because the Object trigram metal directly destroys the Subject trigram wood, it means the boy was born into a very poor situation, he was weak and he found it very difficult to find good opportunities to develop himself and no kind people willing to help him at that stage.

The situation dramatically changed when the boy became a teenager. We can understand it by looking at the Nuclear hexagram. In this both the Subject trigram and the Object trigram are Chien trigram (metal). The two trigrams support each other. It means the boy's environment improved a great deal and he received a lot of support from many friends and relatives helping him to achieve great success in his career when he became adult.

The final outcome is his fate in old age. It is shown from the Final hexagram. In this hexagram, the Subject trigram (lower trigram) is Sun (wood), and the Object trigram (upper trigram) is Chen (wood). The two trigrams are the same element so they support each other. It is a very auspicious sign. It means that the man was supported by his friends and relatives continually which made his achievement sustainable.

After analysing the relationship between the two trigrams, we need to compare the quantities of the Subject trigram and the Object trigram. Thus we look at all three hexagrams and calculate the total number of trigrams with the element wood (as the Subject trigram is wood) and those with the element metal (as the Object trigram is metal). It is obvious that there are three trigrams with the element wood, and three trigrams with metal among the three hexagrams (see the hexagram diagram). So in terms of quantity, the two sides are equal. We also need to compare the quality of the two sides, so we will need to look at the impact of the cosmos on the two sides. In the Four Pillars, the year, month, day and hour represent the energy of the cosmos at the moment when the boy was born. It shows that in the Original hexagram, the Subject trigram wood is supported by the water year (Rat is water) and the wood hour (Tiger is wood). Please remember that wood is still prosperous in the early summer. Because the month is May, it is the very early summer with flowers blooming and prosperous vegetation. Furthermore, the man is born in China, a far-eastern country. If you recall, based on the Later Heaven Eight Hexagram Chart the East is the direction of wood. So the Subject trigram wood is very strong in this region. On the other hand, the Object trigram (metal) in the main hexagram is not really strong because the season is summer when metal is weak and China is located in the east where wood is strong but metal is weak. (If the man was born in a western country, the situation would be totally different, as metal becomes very strong in the West.). The Object trigram (metal) is only supported by the earth day (Dog is earth) and consumed by the water year (Rat is water). So comparing quality, the Subject trigram wood is stronger than the Object trigram metal. Integrating the analysis of quality and quantity for the two sides above, the overall judgement is that the Subject trigram wood prevails over the Object trigram metal.

If we look at the text on the hexagram from the I Ching it is also very interesting: the Original hexagram (symbol of the early phase of his life journey) is Ta Kuo, hexagram no. 28: Preponderance of the Great. It says: '*the ridgepole sags to breaking point, one has further to go to get success*'. It is obvious that although it is a difficult time, the Original hexagram encourages the man to struggle to overcome difficulties and seek success. Then the Nuclear hexagram (symbol of the middle age of the man) is Chien, hexagram no. 1: Creative. This hexagram is the first of all 64 hexagrams and means that the man followed the law of change and development, or the Tao, making himself strong and always trying his best to achieve great success. The Final hexagram (symbol of the man's old age) is Hêng – hexagram no. 32: Duration. It means 'forever sustainable' indicating that the man will have good luck until he is very old.

If we review this man's real life journey now, you will be astonished by the result. It was exactly in accordance with the prediction above based on the three hexagrams.

When the man was very young, he was weak and suffered from several diseases. His parents were mistreated during the Cultural Revolution, so he lost a lot of good opportunities for education and finding a job. Also, during a terrible fight with the Red Guard of Chairman Mao, he was shot at with a machine gun at very close range. Thank God, the young man fortunately escaped from death, but many of his friends were killed in that disaster.

When the man became an adult, the situation changed dramatically. He got the opportunity to take part in a national university entrance examination and became a student in the best medical university in China as he got top marks in the entrance examination. As soon as he graduated he was promoted to an important post very quickly and he has been successful in his career in researching, teaching and writing ever since. He achieved a good reputation in China and he has also been recruited as chair of health expert teams by several international bodies such as the World Bank.

In the future, we strongly believe he will remain fortunate, because he has also studied the I Ching for a long time and he knows how to follow the I Ching to do what he should do.

Case 4. Different Ways to Create a Hexagram

There was a very interesting game played by Professor Lin, Dr Tai and myself one day in September 1993. We three colleagues were travelling home by train after attending an international conference on the I Ching. In order to liven up the boring journey we were playing a game of guessing something with the I Ching. Just then, a young girl, a university student who was sitting next to us on the train, asked to join our interesting game. Although she was a stranger, we welcomed her to join us. The first question the girl asked us was for us to try to guess the precise age of her second eldest brother, who was not travelling with her. Professor Lin, Dr Tai and I guessed the young man's age by three different methods separately and strictly kept our methods and results to ourselves until we finished. The three methods we used were as follows:

a) Professor Lin created a hexagram and calculated the age based on the colour of the articles the girl held in her hand. She was holding a red pen and white paper, so Professor Lin thought that the upper trigram should be the Li fire (as the red colour of the pen means Li according to the Eight Basic Trigrams), and the lower trigram should be the Tui lake (as the white colour means Tui lake according to the Eight Basic Trigrams):

So her brother's age should be calculated from the formula: 20 (the lower trigram Tui is number 2 according to the Eight Basic Trigrams) + 3 (the upper trigram Li is number 3 according to the Eight Basic Trigrams) = 23.

b) I created a hexagram and calculated the age based on the character of the particular person. Since the girl was sitting to the west of us I decided that the upper trigram should be the Li (trigram Li means young girl) and the lower trigram should be Tui (the trigram Tui means west relative to the girl's direction) as in the figure above. So the age of her brother is 20 (the lower trigram Tui is number 2 according to the Eight Basic Trigrams) + 3 (the upper trigram Li is number 3 according to the Eight Basic Trigrams) = 23.

c) Dr Tai created a hexagram and calculated the age based on the number of strokes of the Chinese character 'Second Brother' or Er Ge. Er is a Chinese character with two strokes, Ge is a Chinese character with 10 strokes. So he thought the upper hexagram should be Tui (number two means trigram Tui according to the Eight Basic Trigrams) and the lower trigram should also be Tui (the 10 is divided by 8 and the remainder is 2) as follows:

Then, because the time when we were playing the game was 11.30 a.m. or the seventh hour in Chinese time, the first line changed, so the age is 20 (the lower trigram Tui) + 2 (the upper trigram Tui) + 1 (the changing line is 1) = 23.

When the three of us finished our individual calculations, we showed our results to the girl at the same time. She was amazed that, although we had guessed the age of her brother by different ways, our results were identical and absolutely accurate. Her second eldest brother was 23 years old!

Case 5. University Entrance Examination

Chinese higher education has developed rapidly in recent years. Demand is very high and it is difficult to meet people's needs, so competition for the university entrance examination is terribly fierce. This competition not only affects young people but also greatly affects the parents. Many parents are willing to pay any price for their only child's higher education (the modern Chinese couple can only have one child). In many poor families, the parents make every effort to guarantee their child's tuition, even using money that should be for their basic food and clothing. There are many moving stories about it. I had a lot of experience of consulting for these poor parents on their children's education issues. On 13 July 2001, about 10.00 a.m., Ms Yang, a client of mine, came to me and asked the result of the university entrance examination for her son. According to the date when Ms Yang asked me the question, I conducted a prediction for her by the Mei Hua method, as follows.

Firstly translate the date 13 July 2001, 10.00 a.m. from the western Calendar into the Chinese calendar based on checking the thousand-year calendar:

	HOUR	DAY	MONTH	YEAR
HEAVENLY STEM	–wood	–fire	–wood	–metal
EARTHLY BRANCH	Snake (fire)	Ox (earth)	Sheep (earth)	Snake (fire)
TIME NUMBER	6	23	5	6

Create the Original hexagram based on the formula (see previous chapter).

We get the number of the upper trigram of the Original hexagram from the formula:

$$(6 + 5 + 23)/8 = 4 \ldots 2 \text{ (a)}$$

Thus the upper trigram is the trigram Tui metal (based on the Early Heaven Sequence of the Eight Trigram Chart. 2 = Tui).

Then we get the lower trigram from the formula:

$$(6 + 5 + 23 + 6)/8 = 5 \ldots 0 \text{ (b)}$$

Thus the lower trigram is the trigram Kun earth (the 0 should be seen as 8, based on the Early Heaven Sequence of the Eight Trigram Chart. 8 = Kun).

So we get the Original hexagram by putting the upper and lower trigrams together.

Then we get the number of the changing line from the formula:

$$(6 + 5 + 23 + 6)/6 = 6 \ldots 4 \text{ (b)}$$

Because the changing line is fourth, we get the Final hexagram by changing the fourth line of the Original hexagram.

Based on the principle of drawing the Nuclear hexagram (see previous chapter), we get the Nuclear hexagram from the Original hexagram.

Thus we put the three hexagrams together as follows:

Main Hexagram	Nuclear Hexagram	Changing Hexagram

Note: The three upper trigrams are Object trigrams and the three lower trigrams are Subject trigrams.

According to the judgement principle, as I described previously, I forecast the result of the young man's examination as follows.

I looked at the Original hexagram (No. 45: Ts'ui – Gathering Together) firstly, as the Original Hexagram represents the very beginning of the event. The upper trigram Tui is the Object trigram (because the changing line is located here) with the element metal, and the lower trigram Kun is the Subject trigram with the element earth. So the Subject trigram births the Object trigram. It implies that the young man should pay a price for this examination. It is reasonable. In fact, he has already put in a lot of energy and time to prepare for the vital examination. As the Subject trigram represents the young man and the Object trigram represents the examination or the university, the birth relationship between the two trigrams indicated clearly that the young man who wants to study at university has to pay the necessary attention (as well as energy, time and money) to improve himself.

Then I looked at the Nuclear hexagram as it represents the middle phase of the event. Because the Subject trigram of the Nuclear hexagram is the lower trigram Ken earth. (The Subject trigram is now located in the lower part of the Nuclear hexagram the same as the location of the Subject trigram in the Original hexagram. And also the location of the Subject/Object trigram in the Final hexagram is the same as the Original hexagram. In other words, as soon as the location of Subject and Object trigram is determined in the Original hexagram, this same location will be followed in the next two hexagrams). The Object trigram is the upper trigram Sun wood. The Subject trigram earth was destroyed by the Object trigram wood. It means that the young man will face a big challenge not only in this examination but also during the coming years when he studies at university, some difficulties may be economic, some may involve hard study. The young man has a long way to go.

The Final hexagram represents the final outcome of the examination. The Object trigram located at the upper part of the hexagram (representing the examination or the university) is Kan water, and the Subject trigram located at the lower of the hexagram (representing the young man) is Kun earth. So the Object trigram water is destroyed/controlled by the Subject trigram earth. It implies that the young man is able to overcome all difficulties, take the situation under control and finally achieve his objective.

After analysing the relationship between the Subject trigram and the Object trigram, we need to look at the impact of chi/energy from the cosmos, which is represented by the Earthly Branches of date, on the young man and his examination, which are represented by the Subject trigram and Object trigram respectively. In the Original hexagram, both the Subject trigram earth and Object trigram metal are supported by the day as the Ox day is earth, and the month as the Sheep month is earth. Also the Subject trigram is supported, but the Object trigram is destroyed by the year (the Snake year is fire) and the hour (the Snake hour is fire too). It is a very good symbol for the young man. It means that in the preparation stage of his examination and study there are difficulties that need to be overcome. The young man is supported by his parents, his teachers and classmates (they are represented by the year, month and day), and due to his good personality and the hard effort he has made, he will become very strong gradually. So he will achieve final success.

In regard to the average score of the examination of the young man, it is also an important issue for the parents and the young man himself. It seems a quite difficult question, but I must answer it. Because I have the hexagram, it will tell me the answer accurately. I get the precise figure by calculating the number of the trigrams of the hexagrams, or just looking at the number of the upper trigram and the lower trigram of the hexagram. (The number of the trigram is based on the Early Heaven Sequence of the Eight Basic Trigram Chart, or Chien 1, Tui 2, Li 3, Chen 4 … and so on: see the previous chapter). Firstly I found the number of the lower trigram of the Original hexagram is 8 (hexagram Kun is 8). It represented 80. The number of the upper trigram of the Original hexagram is 2 (hexagram Tui is 2). So the average score is at least 80 + 2 = 82. Because the Subject trigram is very strong, the number of the changing line should also be added, I added the number of the changing line 4, so the final score is 82 + 4 = 86.

By now my prediction is basically complete. But then Ms Yang added another question about where her son's university might be located. I told her that it should be located in the north of China. I got the direction from the Object trigram of the Final hexagram. (The Subject trigram and Object trigram represented the young man and his favoured university respectively.) The Object trigram of the Final hexagram is Kan, or water. Based on the direction of Eight Basic Trigrams (see previous chapter), the hexagram Kan is located in the north. So the university is in Beijing, the capital of China, located in the north, where there are a lot of good universities.

One month later, I received a very excited telephone call from Ms Yang. All of my predictions about her son came true. The average score of her son's examination was precisely 85.8, (my prediction was 86). The young man had just received an admission letter from a famous university in Beijing.

Case 6. A Health Issue

On 17 November 2000 about 8.10 p.m., I received a long-distance call from Professor Hu, a client of mine. Her question was about her husband's health. Her husband was also a famous professor; he was just 46 years old but had had hepatitis B for eight years. Professor Hu was wondering if there would be any new problems emerging for her husband. Because Professor Hu lived far away, it was difficult to ask her to do a coin casting, so I decided to make a divination by the Mei Hua method for her. According to the date when Professor Hu called me and asked the question, I conducted a quick prediction as follows.

Firstly I translated the date – 17 November 2000, 8.10 p.m. from the western calendar into the Chinese calendar based on checking the thousand-year Calendar:

	HOUR	DAY	MONTH	YEAR
HEAVENLY STEM	+wood	–earth	–fire	+metal
EARTHLY BRANCH	Dog (earth)	Rabbit (wood)	Pig (water)	Dragon (earth)
TIME NUMBER	11	22	10	5

Secondly, based on the formula I created the Original hexagram as follows: (Please see the previous chapter and the previous case. I have omitted the detailed process of the calculating here, so if you like, you may try to do this very simple calculation to prove the result).

**Original
Hexagram**

Because the sixth line changed (I omitted the calculation process again,) I got the Nuclear hexagram and the Final hexagram as follows:

Original Hexagram	Nuclear Hexagram	Final Hexagram

Note: The three upper trigrams are Object trigrams and the three lower trigrams are Subject trigrams.

According to the judgement principle as described previously, I forecast the possible outcome for Professor Hu's husband as follows:

Looking at the Original hexagram (no. 20 Kuan: Contemplation/View) firstly, as the Original hexagram represents the early stage of the event. The upper trigram Sun is the Object trigram (because the changing line is located here) with the element wood, and the lower trigram Kun is the Subject trigram with the element earth. So the Subject trigram earth is directly destroyed by the Object trigram wood. It definitely indicates that Professor Hu's husband is suffering from a critical disease. The Subject trigram represents the man, and the Object trigram represents the disease or hepatitis B (interestingly the liver is the element wood in TCM). The destructive relationship between the two trigrams indicates clearly that there is a severe fight between the man and the disease.

Then I looked at the Nuclear hexagram as it represents the middle phase of the event. Because the Subject trigram of the Nuclear hexagram is the lower trigram Kun earth and the Object trigram is the upper trigram Ken earth, the Subject trigram earth is the same element as the Object trigram earth. It means that the man's health may be kept stable for a period with medical treatment, or the disease may be under control for a relatively long period. That is also true, as he had received active treatment for eight years.

What is the development of the disease in the coming years? I need to check the Final hexagram very carefully, which represents the final outcome of the development of the disease. The Object trigram located at the top of the hexagram (representing the disease) is Kan water, and the Subject trigram located at the bottom of the hexagram (representing Professor Hu's husband) is Kun earth. So the Object trigram water is destroyed by the Subject trigram earth. It obviously implies that the man is struggling to overcome grave difficulties in order to beat the disease and recover.

So who will be the winner of the vital fight between the man and the disease? It is necessary to compare the forces of the Subject trigram and Object trigram. We also need to look at the impact of chi/energy from the cosmos. In the Original hexagram, the Subject trigram earth is supported by the year (the Dragon year is earth). However it is directly destroyed by the day (Rabbit day is wood) and consumed/exhausted by the month (the Pig month is water). On the other hand, the Object trigram wood is supported by both the month (water) and the day (wood). Furthermore, as the month and day will combine together when they meet each other (the Rabbit and Pig are two key elements among a Great Combination of Three Elements: see previous chapter), they may produce a very strong wood (so long as the Sheep element comes one day). It is a very powerful force to support the Object trigram and destroy the Subject trigram directly. So the Object trigram is very much stronger than the Subject trigram. Although in the Final hexagram, the Subject trigram earth tries its best to destroy the Object trigram water, unfortunately, it is too weak to win the fight. It is a very inauspicious symbol for the poor man. It means that there is great difficulty in overcoming the disease.

What is my recommendation for Professor Hu based on the prediction above? How can Professor Hu face this unfortunate situation? Although it is very difficult, I must tell her the possibility in order to enable her to make the necessary effort and preparations for her husband.

I gave the suggestion to Professor Hu by telephone as follows:

The disease may develop very quickly, especially in the coming months. Because during the current water months, (Professor Hu called me in the Pig month – a water month, and the next month was Rat month – a water month too) the Object trigram wood of the Original hexagram may become stronger and stronger due to great support from the month. Furthermore, as you see, in the Final hexagram, which represents the final outcome, although the Subject trigram earth actively fights with the Object trigram water, as the water month gave very powerful support to the Object trigram, the poor Subject trigram has little chance of winning the fight. So during these two months, great attention should be paid to looking after her husband's health. If possible, it would be better for him to live in a dry room with a beautiful sunny aspect to protect him from wet weather in the winter season (the sunshine is fire, which births the Subject trigram earth). No sooner had I made this point than Professor Hu cried suddenly in a very high voice on the telephone. She told me that, for several years her husband had lived in a very wet room, like a cellar underground without sunlight, in all seasons. She told me that even though her husband was a famous professor, their accommodation was still very poor. Although their house was bigger, the location of the house was worse. Although it has improved in recent years, the feng shui issue has not been highlighted by people so far.

Professor Hu was unfortunate indeed during these cold water months. Her husband's health became worse and worse. Only several days after that call, when Professor Hu asked me to give her advice, her husband died in hospital. Despite making every effort, the doctors were unable to save him. He died in the Pig month – a water month and, as the hexagram indicated, the Subject trigram earth of the Final hexagram was beaten down by the strong Object trigram water.

Case 7. Another Health Issue

1 January 1995: although it is New Year's Day, many Chinese people are still at work, as they pay more attention to the Chinese New Year than the western New Year. About 10.00 a.m., a young lady accompanied by her husband visited me and asked a question about her husband. Her husband, Mr Zhou, is a successful businessman aged 41 and apparently in good health. However he had felt weak recently, so his wife was worried about his health. Based on the time when the lady asked me the question, I got the data about the Heavenly Stems and Earthly Branches and the hexagram from the formula of the Mei Hua method. I listed them as follows (the detailed process was omitted here).

	HOUR	DAY	MONTH	YEAR
HEAVENLY STEM	−wood	+water	+fire	+wood
EARTHLY BRANCH	Snake (fire)	Dragon (wood)	rat (water)	Dog (earth)
TIME NUMBER	6	1	12	11

Original Hexagram	Nuclear Hexagram	Final Hexagram

Note: The three upper trigrams are Object trigrams and the three lower trigrams are Subject trigrams.

I looked at the Original hexagram (no. 7 Shih: the Army) firstly, as the Original hexagram represents the early stage of the event. The upper trigram Kun is the Object trigram (because the changing line is located here) with the element earth, and the lower trigram Kan is the Subject trigram water. So the Subject trigram is directly destroyed by the Object trigram. It definitely indicates that Mr Zhou is in a dangerous situation. He might get a fatal disease, as the Subject trigram represents the man, and the Object trigram represents the possible disease. Then I looked at the Final hexagram, which represents the outcome of the man's health. It is difficult too, as the Subject hexagram water is destroyed by the Object hexagram earth again. It means the man's health may become worse very soon.

What is the final outcome? It is necessary to check and compare the forces of the two sides, or the Subject trigram and Object trigram. Because the Subject trigram is destroyed by the Object trigram from the beginning to the end, it is a very inauspicious symbol. The only hope is that the Subject trigram becomes much stronger than the Object trigram. What are the facts? As the Subject trigram is water, only supported by the month, and destroyed by the year, day and exhausted by the hour, it is much weaker than the Object trigram, which is supported by the year, day and hour. The only advantage for the Subject trigram is that the season is winter, so water is still prosperous. However, because time is going forward, when the earth month and fire months come, the Subject trigram water will become weaker, meanwhile the Object trigram earth will become stronger. Based on my analysis, I suggested that Mr Zhou should see a doctor immediately and have a comprehensive physical examination and actively seek effective medical treatment. The best direction should be the west, as the west is metal's direction. The metal can birth water, or the element of the Subject trigram. He has to give up smoking (I noted he was a smoker, and he confirmed he had a long history of smoking), as cigarettes produce the fire element, which will birth the Object trigram earth, and directly injure his lungs, which are metal element, according to TCM. He needs to protect himself from going to the south, which is fire's direction and strongly supports the Object trigram. The risk season when he needs to be looked after carefully is summer of the following year.

Six months later, Mr Zhou's wife visited me again but she was alone. She told me what had happened to her husband. After visiting me on New Year's Day, she sent him to see a doctor and tests confirmed that he had a problem with his lung. He received treatment from the doctor and moved to a relative's house, which had good feng shui and was located to the west of their original house. Mr Zhou gave up smoking and his health seemed to be recovering smoothly in the first three months, so he was very happy and totally forgot my suggestions and the doctor's advice of leaving work and resting for at least six months. Just then there was some very important business for his company in the south of China. Regardless of his health condition, he went to the south to do his work in April. He was very busy with his work and he started smoking again, but one day he started haemorrhaging seriously. When he was sent to hospital, the doctor's diagnosis was lung cancer in its later stage. Only one month later Mr Zhou died in that hospital, which was located in the south of China. The date of his death was 30 June 1995, 11.00 p.m., or Dragon's day – the earth day, in Horse month – the fire month.

Case 8. Improve a Relationship by Changing your Telephone Number

One day in 1995, Mr Wu, an old client, visited me. He had had a serious fight with his wife and now she wanted a divorce. However, Mr Wu still wanted to save his marriage, which had been very happy for both of them for about 17 years. After asking him some brief questions, I noted that they had changed their telephone number two months before. I guessed this might be what had caused the trouble in his family. So I conducted a divination by using the suspect telephone number 8810903.

I created the hexagram by calculating the telephone number based on the following process:

1. Firstly I divided the digits of the telephone number into two digit groups. The principle is that if the number of digits of the telephone number is even, such as 6, 8, 10, the digits of the number should be divided into two groups equally of 3 (6/2), 4 (8/2), 5 (10/2) respectively. If the number of digits of the telephone number is odd, such as 5, 7, 9, the digits of the number of the first group should be one digit less than those of the second group (because the first group and second group represent the upper trigram and lower trigram respectively, the Chinese think that the upper trigram should be lighter than the lower trigram just as heaven is lighter than the earth), or 2, 3, 4 in the first group and 3 (5-2), 4 (7-3), 5 (9-4), in the second group respectively. In this case, the number of digits of 8810903 is 7, an odd number. It should be divided into 2 groups as follows:

1st group (3 digits)	2nd group (4 digits)
881	0903

2. Then I created the Original hexagram from the two groups based on the formula (very similar to the method of creating hexagrams by calculating time data).

    The number of the upper trigram of the Original hexagram is from the first group based on the formula:

$(8 + 8 + 1)/8 = 2 \ldots 1$ (a)

Thus the upper trigram is the trigram Chien metal (based on the Early Heaven Sequence of the Eight Trigram Chart. 1 = Chien)

    The number of the lower trigram of the Original hexagram is from the second group based on the formula:

$(0 + 9 + 0 + 3)/8 = 1 \ldots 4$ (b)

Thus the lower trigram is the trigram Chen wood (based on the Early Heaven Sequence of the Eight Trigram Chart. 4 = Chen)

The number of the changing line is from the hour when Mr Wu asked the question (he asked me at 10.00 a.m., or the sixth hour in the Chinese calendar) based on the formula:

$$6/6 = 1 \ldots 0 \text{ (c)}$$

Or dividing the number of the hour by 6, then taking the remainder as the changing line's number. If the remainder is 0, it is seen as 6.

By now we get the hexagrams as follows:

Main Hexagram	Nuclear Hexagram	Changing Hexagram
—— *	——	– –
——	– –	——
——	– –	– –
——	——	——
– –	– –	– –
– –	– –	– –

Note: The three upper trigrams are Object trigrams and the three lower trigrams are Subject trigrams.

So the Original hexagram is no. 25 Wu Wang: Innocence/Unexpected, a Six Clash hexagram (see next chapter), which means that total conflict or a terrible fight will happen unexpectedly between wife and husband. If you check the relationship between the Subject trigram and the Object trigram, the Object trigram destroys the Subject trigram, which is also an inauspicious symbol for the family. I advised Mr Wu to submit an application to his telephone company to replace this inauspicious number with the number 8801907, which I specially selected for him. Amazingly enough, only two weeks later, the couple came back to harmony automatically. Why did this telephone number have such a large impact on improving their relationship? Because it is a Six Combine/Harmony hexagram, or T'ai hexagram (no. 11), Peace, which means total harmony and happiness. I omitted the process of creating the hexagram and you may prove it yourself by calculating the telephone number 8801907 to create the hexagram T'ai based on the same formula as I have shown you above.

So far I have introduced you to a new method of creating hexagrams from telephone numbers. Do you trust the great impact of telephone numbers on people's daily lives or not after reading this case? I will give you more examples later – see cases 16 and 17 (page 121).

Case 9. Forecasting the Sex of a Baby

A strict and powerful policy on family planning has been implemented in China. Each couple is only allowed to have one child. Some young couples, and particularly their grandparents, are very concerned about their future baby's sex (generally speaking a boy is more favourable than a girl for most parents based on traditional Chinese culture, however this idea is beginning to change). As an experienced I Ching consultant, I am often asked to predict a baby's sex. There is a range of modern equipment and technology to do this job, however modern equipment can still make mistakes. Also, doctors are strictly prohibited from providing this service based on the national family planning policy. This is one of the reasons why modern people still prefer to consult the ancient I Ching to find out their baby's sex rather than relying on advanced technology.

On 20 November 2000, about 8.00 p.m., a young couple (Mr Yu and Miss He) visited me and Miss He asked me what sex her baby was. I made a prediction by the Mei Hua method for them.

The data on the date and the hexagram are as follows: (the detailed process was omitted here)

	HOUR	DAY	MONTH	YEAR
HEAVENLY STEM	+metal	+water	–fire	+metal
EARTHLY BRANCH	Dog (earth)	Horse (fire)	Pig (water)	Dragon (earth)
TIME NUMBER	11	25	10	5

Main Hexagram	Nuclear Hexagram	Changing Hexagram

Note: The three lower trigrams are Object trigrams and the three upper trigrams are Subject trigrams.

In the Original hexagram, generally speaking the Subject trigram represents the client, and the Object trigram represents the event/matter in question. So in this hexagram (no. 36 Ming I: Darkening of the Light), the upper trigram Kun, or the Subject trigram is the symbol of my client, the mother. (Based on the general meaning of the Eight Basic Trigrams, the trigram Kun is the very symbol of mother). Then the lower trigram Li, the Object trigram, is the symbol of the baby, which is the matter concerning its mother. So the answer is very clear and very simple: based on the general meaning of the Eight Basic Trigrams, you can find the trigram Li representing the second daughter. I swiftly told the couple that their baby is definitely a beautiful girl! However, the young future father challenged me with: 'As everybody knows, there is only one child for each couple, so why does the hexagram indicate a second daughter? We have not had any children before!' 'Wait a minute, it is not necessary to be surprised by it,' I answered, 'I imagine you had an abortion at least once before.' I said to the future mother, 'So the girl is not really your first child, as she should have an older sister or brother who was killed before being born.' The couple nodded. They confirmed that the young woman had had an abortion years before.

Two weeks later, the young woman gave birth to a daughter. She is a very sweet girl. The next case also deals with this subject.

Case 10

17 December 1994 4.30 p.m.: Mr Wang, a young man, visited me and asked me to predict the sex of his baby (his wife was six months pregnant at the time).

The data on the date and the hexagram are as follows:

	HOUR	DAY	MONTH	YEAR
HEAVENLY STEM	+earth	–fire	+fire	+wood
EARTHLY BRANCH	Monkey (metal)	Ox (earth)	Rat (water)	Dog (earth)
TIME NUMBER	9	15	11	11

| Main Hexagram | Nuclear Hexagram | Changing Hexagram |

Note: The three upper trigrams are Object trigrams and the three lower trigrams are Subject trigrams.

My analysis process is very similar to the previous case. In the Original hexagram (no. 59 Huan: Dispersion/Dissolution), the Subject trigram Kan represents the client, and the Object trigram Sun represents the event/ matter concerning the client. So in this hexagram the upper trigram Sun, or the Object trigram, is the symbol of the baby, the matter concerning my client. By checking the general meaning of the Eight Basic Trigrams, I found very soon the trigram Sun represents oldest daughter. So Mr Wang's first child should be a girl.

When the question of the sex of the baby is answered, you may argue with me: 'In the previous case, the Subject trigram Kun, or the earth, represented the mother correctly. So the relationship between the upper trigram and the lower trigram is the relationship of daughter and mother. It is a very convincing explanation indeed. But how do you explain the meaning of the Subject trigram in this case? It is the lower trigram Kan, or the water, instead of earth. Can you say it is the symbol of the mother? What is the relationship between the trigram Sun and trigram Kan?' My answer is very simple: my client has changed in this case. In the previous case, my client was the mother, who asked about her baby's sex. So her symbol is the earth trigram. In this case, my client is Mr Wang, the father. So in this case, the relationship between the Subject trigram and the Object trigram is the relationship of daughter and father. Although the father's general symbol is the trigram Chien, Heaven, however the Subject trigram Kan in our case, the water, represents Mr Wang too. You can check the general meaning of the Eight Basic Trigrams: the trigram Kan is the symbol of the second son, so Mr Wang should have an older brother or older sister. He admitted that he is the second son with one older brother in his family.

When their baby was born, my prediction was proved correct.

Case 11. How to Prevent a Fatal Accident and Guarantee Travel Safety

At a party, my friend Professor Lan told me a true story. One day his colleague Professor Zhou asked him about his travel to Beijing. Based on the time when the question was asked by Professor Zhou, Professor Lan made a prediction as follows:

Time data and hexagram are as follows:

24 December 1987, 9.50 a.m.

	HOUR	DAY	MONTH	YEAR
HEAVENLY STEM	–wood	–fire	+water	–fire
EARTHLY BRANCH	Snake (fire)	Sheep (earth)	Rat (water)	Rabbit (wood)
TIME NUMBER	6	4	11	4

Main Hexagram	Nuclear Hexagram	Changing Hexagram

Note: The three lower trigrams are Object trigrams and the three upper trigrams are Subject trigrams.

The Original hexagram is no. 14 Ta Yu: Possession in Great Measure, meaning great achievement and prosperity. It is a symbol of good fortune and is auspicious based on the general concept and common viewpoint. However, Professor Lan thought it was a warning on air travel, because he thought that according to the image of the Ta Yu hexagram, with the trigram fire above and the trigram heaven below, it is a symbol of fire burning in the sky. It is a very dangerous picture for air travel, as it indicates the aeroplane may explode in the sky.

As soon as Professor Lan told me the hexagram and his judgement as above, I agreed with his swift judgement made by looking at the image of the hexagram with his high intuition. I immediately added more evidence using the Mei Hua method as follows: although the Subject trigram fire is birthed by the Object trigram wood in the Final hexagram, which represented the final outcome, if we check the force of the Subject trigram, which represents Professor Zhou, the Subject trigram fire is very weak in the water month of the winter season. Although it is birthed by the Object trigram wood, it is not enough. Furthermore, north is a risk direction, which symbolises water, the deadly enemy of the fire element. Beijing is located in northern China and our city is located in the south of China.

Based on his brief analysis, Professor Lan recommended that his colleague go to Beijing by train instead of by air. Unfortunately Professor Zhou knew the I Ching only superficially. He insisted on the viewpoint that the hexagram of Ta Yu was an absolutely good symbol, and went to Beijing by air after all. When he arrived in Beijing safely, he telephoned Professor Lan, and said that his previous prediction had been wrong, as the aeroplane was safe. However, Professor Lan insisted on his previous prediction and continued to try and persuade his friend to come back to Chongqing by train instead of by air.

A few days after that telephone call, on 18 January 1988, at 10.17 p.m., the most serious air crash in the history of China's civil aviation happened in Chongqing. The aeroplane crashed into a hill, 5.7 km from Chongqing airport. It was the flight from Beijing to Chongqing. Professor Zhou was just one of the 108 victims of this accident. Besides 98 Chinese passengers, one English passenger and three Japanese passengers were also killed.

I asked Professor Lan if he knew what time his friend's aeroplane left Beijing airport. Professor Lan said his friend had not told him the time before the accident happened. Days later, after the accident, he read in a newspaper that the aeroplane had departed Beijing airport at 7.05 p.m. So based on the data of the aeroplane departure, I conducted the following divination by the Mei Hua method to prove the reason why this accident happened.

The time data and hexagram are as follows:

18 January 1988, 7.05 p.m.

	HOUR	DAY	MONTH	YEAR
HEAVENLY STEM	+metal	+water	–water	–fire
EARTHLY BRANCH	Dog (earth)	Monkey (metal)	Ox (earth)	Rabbit (wood)
TIME NUMBER	11	29	11	4

Original Hexagram	Nuclear Hexagram	Final Hexagram

Note: The three lower trigrams are Object trigrams and the three upper trigrams are Subject trigrams.

The Original hexagram (no. 62 Hsiao Kuo: Preponderance of the Small) shows that the Subject trigram wood destroys the Object trigram earth and the Final hexagram shows that the Subject trigram wood births the Object trigram fire. The relationship between the two sides is already definitely inauspicious. Furthermore, when we check the force of the Subject trigram, it is a very weak wood, as it is directly destroyed by the day metal. And as the month is Ox (earth month), which contains a huge amount of metal within its core (see previous chapter), it is also a very strong force to destroy the weak wood. So the Subject wood is in a vitally dangerous situation indeed.

If you check the image of the hexagrams, (in the first divination by Professor Lan, he made a judgement mainly by looking at the image of the hexagram and in spite of analysing the relationship between the Subject and Object trigrams), you may make a significant discovery. Comparing the hexagrams here with those in the first divination conducted by Professor Lan, the trigram Li, or the fire element is always a very important symbol from the very beginning to the end in all the hexagrams of the two divinations. In the first divination conducted by Professor Lan, the hexagram Li symbolised fire burning in the sky (see the Original Hexagram Ta Yu). In the second divination conducted by me firstly, the hexagram shows that thunder is rumbling up on the mountain (see the Original hexagram Hsiao Kuo, in this hexagram, the trigram Chen, thunder is above the trigram Ken mountain.) Finally a large fire burns following the thunder (see the Final hexagram Feng, in this hexagram, the trigram Li fire is under the trigram Chen thunder). It is a terrible picture of an aeroplane crash. Unfortunately it accurately described the real process of this accident: first the aeroplane crashed into a hill, then it exploded into flames and there were no survivors.

If you don't like the image of the symbol of the hexagram and think it is a metaphor, as this method needs higher intuition and is relatively difficult for a beginner, you can use a simpler and more direct method. What you need to do is reflect on the text on the hexagram and its changing line (see chapter 10). This procedure may take only a few minutes. If you can refer to the original I Ching, you will find the answer very quickly, there are only four Chinese characters in this line: '*a bird flying is evil*'. And also you may find that the text on the sixth line of the hexagram mentions: '*A bird flying far aloft, there will be evil. The case is what is called one of calamity*'. So the large bird – Professor Zhou's aeroplane – is not far from its death. It is an 'evil bird', which killed 108 innocent people!

If only Professor Zhou had paid a little more attention to Professor Lan's warning based on the first divination, and if only he had made a second divination by briefly consulting the I Ching, even by reading the words 'a bird flying is evil' a few minutes before boarding, he might have had a last chance to get an urgent warning from the second divination. If so, maybe he would have changed his mind due to such a strong symbol indicating the fatal risk repeatedly.

Case 12. Changing Jobs

In China today, people have more freedom to change their job than in previous decades. However, it is difficult for many young people to make a wise choice, so they often consult the I Ching to get suggestions. On 29 December 2000, about 12.00 a.m., a young man asked me whether he should remain in his company or resign and seek another job elsewhere.

The data on the date and hexagram are as follows:

	HOUR	DAY	MONTH	YEAR
HEAVENLY STEM	+wood	–metal	+earth	+metal
EARTHLY BRANCH	Horse (fire)	Rooster (metal)	Rat (water)	Dragon (earth)
TIME NUMBER	11	25	10	5

Main Hexagram	Nuclear Hexagram	Changing Hexagram
☰ ☷ *	☶ ☷	☰ ☷

Note: The three upper trigrams are Object trigrams and the three lower trigrams are Subject trigrams.

The relationship between the Subject trigram and Object trigram is supportive of each other firstly based on the Original hexagram (no. 42 I: Increase). But the Subject trigram is destroyed by the Object trigram finally based on the Final hexagram. It means that the company had been doing well previously and the young man had been satisfied with his job in the past. However, the situation changed, not only the condition of the company became worse but also the relationship between the young man and his boss became terrible. Because the Subject trigram and Object trigram represented the young man and his boss or the company respectively, the destructive relationship shows a clash or fight happened between the young man and his boss. So who is the winner of the fight? Can this clash be improved? My analysis of force comparison of the two sides indicated that it is difficult to improve the situation in the future, because the Object trigram metal, which is supported by the year and day, is obviously stronger than the Subject trigram wood, which is supported only by the month but destroyed by the day and exhausted by the year. Furthermore, if you check the text on the changing line from the I Ching, it indicates definitely that: '*He can with advantage be relied on in such a movement as that of removing the capital.*' So the best strategy for the young man is to leave as soon as possible and look for a new job elsewhere. (When making this judgement, I also utilised the concept of the Six Clash Hexagram. As mentioned previously, the Six Clash Hexagram does not mean remaining/immobility but rather means movement/mobility. Since the Final hexagram Wu Wang is a Six Clash Hexagram, I was sure that the young man should change his job.) The favourable direction is east as the Subject trigram is wood, which is prosperous in the east. The young man took my advice and very soon he found a satisfactory job in Shanghai, an eastern city.

Case 13. Promotion

My old friend Professor Wang was an outstanding associate professor in traditional Chinese culture and was loved by his students. He telephoned and asked me if he had an opportunity of being promoted in the current reform of higher education. Based on the time he asked me — 5 July 2001, 2.30 p.m. - I made a divination for him as follows:

Time data:

	HOUR	DAY	MONTH	YEAR
HEAVENLY STEM	-metal	-earth	+wood	-metal
EARTHLY BRANCH	Sheep (earth)	Snake (fire)	Horse (fire)	Snake (fire)
TIME NUMBER	8	15	5	6

Original Hexagram	Nuclear Hexagram	Final Hexagram

Note: The three upper trigrams are Object trigrams and the three lower trigrams are Subject trigrams.

Both the Subject trigram and Object trigram in the Original hexagram (no. 58 Tui: The Joyous/Lake) are metal and they support each other. The Subject trigram fire is birthed by the Object trigram wood in the Nuclear hexagram. They are auspicious symbols. The relationship of the Subject trigram and Object trigram in the Final hexagram is birthing each other. As the Subject trigram metal births the Object trigram water, this kind of relationship is generally referred to as a cost or a drain. Water 'drains' metal in the Five Elements, so it does not influence the good outcome for Professor Wang very much. It merely implies that as a qualified professor working in a university, he is willing to devote himself to a career in education and put all his energy and intelligence into teaching, researching and writing, all of which he finds most enjoyable. I think it also indicates that Professor Wang should pay more attention to preparing well for this promotion evaluation. According to the policy of the higher education system reform, all candidates are required to pass a national test and provide relevant certificates on foreign languages and computer skills before they are promoted. I suggest that Professor Wang should take part in some intensive training courses on foreign languages and computer skills as soon as possible to guarantee passing the test. Of course he will have to pay for doing these training courses in a short period of time, however it is absolutely necessary. The most important evidence in my judgement on his promotion is the Final hexagram no. 60 Chieh: Limitation, which is a Six Combine/Harmony hexagram. This is generally an auspicious symbol and means great success and achieving goals.

Regarding the force analysis, the Subject trigram in the Original hexagram, which represented Professor Wang himself, is not strong at that specific moment. It did not get support from the Earthly Branches of year, month and day at that summer season but rather was destroyed by them. It would be a very inauspicious symbol and hopeless if my friend had been working in the south, where metal is very weak and fire is quite strong. Fortunately, my friend was working in a university located in western China, where metal is very strong and fire is weak (according to the Later Heaven Sequence of Eight Trigram Chart, west is the direction of the Tui trigram, or metal element). In other words, my friend has great support from the direction, which is one of the most important symbols of the universe energy just like the season. It also has an important impact on the development of every event/matter. Furthermore, although it was Horse month at that time (5 July), it is worth noting that it will be Sheep month only two days later. (7 July is the starting point of Sheep month with earth element, which supports the Subject trigram metal.) And it was moving on from summer to autumn very soon. According to the timetable of promotion evaluation, the promotion will be determined in the autumn, when the Subject trigram metal will become very strong because autumn is metal's season. So the fortune of my friend is absolutely positive. Regarding timing, because his Subject trigram is not yet strong enough at that summer season, the final good news about his promotion will arrive two to three months later. During this period he needs to make necessary preparations. He will be promoted in the month of autumn, most probably on an Ox day in Rooster month in this Snake year, when the Great Combination of

Three Elements will be set up. Checking the Chinese calendar, I found that the date should be 11 or 23 September (the two days are Ox days in Rooster month). When the Subject trigram metal gets support from the strong metal produced by the Great Combination of Three Elements from year (Snake), month (Rooster) and day (Ox), he will achieve his target.

On 23 September 2001, or Ox day in Rooster month of Snake year, I received an e-mail from my friend Professor Wang. He was excited to tell me that just that morning he had received his promotion and invited me to attend his celebration party. The time data is Ox day, Rooster month and Snake year. The three animals of day, month and year combine together and build the Great Combination of Three Elements and produce very strong metal to support the Subject trigram in the Original hexagram. Thus my friend achieved his objective.

Case 14. A Gambling Game

Miss Huang, a young businesswoman, visited me and asked if she could win at gambling in Macao. Based on the time she asked me, 8 May 2001 about 12.30 p.m., I made a divination for her as follows:

Time data:

	HOUR	DAY	MONTH	YEAR
HEAVENLY STEM	+wood	−metal	−water	−metal
EARTHLY BRANCH	Horse (fire)	Sheep (earth)	Snake (fire)	Snake (fire)
TIME NUMBER	7	16	4	6

Main Hexagram	Nuclear Hexagram	Changing Hexagram

Note: The three lower trigrams are Object trigrams and the three upper trigrams are Subject trigrams.

You may note that these hexagrams are very interesting: regardless of Subject trigram or Object trigram, all six trigrams in the three hexagrams are metal element. According to the principle of symbolising the trigram, the Subject trigram represented Miss Huang, while the Object trigram symbolised her money, win or loss. Based on general principles of judgement, if the Subject trigram and the Object trigram are the same element and support each other, it means good fortune. Does this mean good fortune for Miss Huang's plan? In this particular case, we need to look carefully at the impact of the date, because there is so much fire element from the Earthly Branches in year, month, day and hour, or all are fire element except the day Sheep. However, you may remember that the Sheep Earthly Branch is also a store of wood, which is fire's mother. So, on one hand the whole chi/energy from the time (including year, month, day and hour) gives strong support to fire; on the other hand, it is a powerful enemy to the metal element, which represents both Miss Huang and her money. By now I believe the outcome is inauspicious for Miss Huang's plan. Furthermore, Macao is located at the very south of Miss Huang's hometown. South is fire's direction, and is the death place for metal! So I made my recommendation to Miss Huang: firstly, she'd better give up this plan to go gambling in Macao; secondly, if she insisted on doing it, the timetable should be arranged for the metal season, or autumn, and she should avoid taking action in the risky summer season, the deadly season for metal.

Miss Huang is the type of person, who superficially consults I Ching sincerely, but does not really trust I Ching. So when she asked me: 'How much will I lose gambling if I go to Macao in the summer?' I answered her immediately: 'About 600,000 yuan, or US $75,000, because,' I explained, 'the total number of the trigrams in the Original hexagram is 2 (upper trigram) + 1 (lower trigram) + 3 (changing line) = 6. Considering the metal is so weak, the loss is not small, so the unit of money should be 100,000 yuan.' Listening to my analysis, Miss Huang smiled and then said goodbye. I was sure that she would ignore my kind warning and would go to Macao very soon because I had already noted that both the Nuclear hexagram and the Final hexagram are Six Clash Hexagrams, which imply serious conflict and quick action, and of course also indicated complete loss.

Just two weeks later, Miss Huang told me on the telephone in a sad voice that she had lost exactly 600,000 yuan when she had gone gambling in Macao in May, the Snake fire month of the summer season.

Case 15. Stock Market Forecast

In the early 1990s, Chinese central government opened a pilot stock exchange in my city. At that time the stock market had a terrible profit margin. As long as you had one original stock ticket, you would win a lot. Some poor people became millionaires overnight just due to buying one kind of original stock ticket. However the stock tickets issued were too few to meet the large demand and it was very difficult for ordinary people to get them. One day my wife asked me to go to a newly opened stock exchange to try buying one. I made a divination according to the time when she asked me, or 26 May 1992, about 9.10 a.m.

Time data:

	HOUR	DAY	MONTH	YEAR
HEAVENLY STEM	+metal	+water	-wood	+water
EARTHLY BRANCH	Snake (fire)	Tiger (wood)	Snake (fire)	Monkey (metal)
TIME NUMBER	6	24	4	9

Main Hexagram	Nuclear Hexagram	Changing Hexagram
✳		

Note: The three lower trigrams are Object trigrams and the three upper trigrams are Subject trigrams.

I checked the hexagram and told my wife about my prediction.

'The symbol is auspicious. Although the Subject trigram wood births the Object trigram fire at first (see Original hexagram, no. 37 Chia Jên: The Family), it destroys the Object trigram earth in the end (see Final hexagram). And the day of wood is a fortunate day for us as it supports the Subject trigram wood, which represents myself. Provided the new stock exchange is located in the east, we will benefit from it because east is wood's direction.' When I was talking about the direction, my wife confirmed to me the new exchange was located directly to the east of my house. 'Because the Object trigram is the symbol of the stock ticket we want to get,' I continued, 'it is strong enough because it is supported by fire month and fire hour, it implies that there are more tickets on sale today. But the destructive relationship between the Subject trigram and the Object trigram means that the process is slow, so we may get the stock ticket in the afternoon instead of in the morning.' But my wife was too keen to buy it to wait any longer, so she asked me to go to the exchange as soon as possible. I followed her to the exchange immediately and conducted the second prediction on the bus to estimate the hour when the ticket would be available for me. I got the hexagram in minutes, according to the hour from 1.00 p.m. to 3.00 p.m. (It is very easy to get a hexagram with the Mei Hua method, once you are familiar with it):

Original Hexagram	Nuclear Hexagram	Final Hexagram
☰ *	☰	☰

'This symbol is obviously much better than the previous one,' I told my wife on the bus, 'The relationship between the Subject trigram wood and the Object trigram wood is supportive of each other in the Original hexagram, no. 57 Sun: The Gentle/Wind. And the Subject trigram wood is birthed by the Object trigram water in the Final hexagram, which implies the final result will be good. So I am sure that during this period of 1.00–3.00 p.m., we will get the stock ticket.' Furthermore, I calculated the number of the Original hexagram: it is 5 (upper trigram) + 5 (lower trigram) + 3 (changing line) = 13, so the accurate time when we get the ticket should be at 1.00 p.m. this afternoon.

What was the actual result? When we arrived at the stock exchange, it was 11.00 a.m. However, there was already a long queue outside the main door of the exchange; over a thousand people were waiting! There was nothing for it but to join the long queue. After patiently waiting for two hours, we got the stock ticket at 1.00 p.m.

Since then my wife has supported my research on I Ching actively, because she believes that it might help her become richer.

Case 16. How to Understand People's Fortunes from their Telephone Numbers

On 19 September 1995, about 10.00 a.m., an old lady visited me and asked about her fortune. It was the first time she had visited me and I hadn't known anything about her before. I got a hexagram for her from her telephone number: 3814836. I calculated the telephone number based on the procedure as in case 12 (page 113) and drew hexagrams according to the result of the calculations. The Original hexagram is no. 32 Hêng: Duration with first line moving.

| Original Hexagram | Nuclear Hexagram | Final Hexagram |

The hexagrams told me: the upper trigram of the Original hexagram is the Subject trigram, which is the Chen trigram. The Chen trigram represents the oldest son, but my client is an old lady. Why does the Subject trigram symbolise a young man? So I guessed that my client, the old lady, was not asking about her own fortune but was actually concerned with the fortune of her oldest son. She acknowledged my first judgement. In fact she was very worried about her oldest son at that time, because he planned to leave home and find a new job. Then when I looked at the Final hexagram, the Chen trigram wood is destroyed by the strong Chien trigram metal. And also the Final hexagram is a Six Clash hexagram, which means quick movement, serious conflict and great difficulty or total loss. Furthermore, because the time data was Pig year, Rooster month, Ox day and Snake hour, the Subject trigram, which is very weak wood, is destroyed by the very strong Object trigram, which is metal supported by the Rooster month (metal) and the Ox day (the store of metal). The Object trigram is also supported by the new strong metal produced by the Great Combination of Three Elements, or metal by the Rooster month (metal), Ox day (earth) and Snake hour (fire). So

I guessed the lady's oldest son was planning to find a job in the west (because the Final hexagram is a Six Clash hexagram, meaning fast movement, and the Subject trigram of the Final hexagram is metal, indicating the west). But west is the most dangerous direction for her son, so I asked her to persuade her son to change his mind. My suggested direction was east, where wood, which represented her son, is prosperous.

Her son did not follow my kind advice, and went to the west after all. The next autumn he was killed in a terrible fight with his colleagues there.

Case 17. Another Telephone Number

At 8.50 a.m. on 17 February 1995 my friend Professor Lin, a famous scientist, asked me about his fortune. The time data is Pig year, Tiger month and Rabbit day. I got hexagrams from his telephone number 2872199 based on the same process as the previous example.

| Original Hexagram | Nuclear Hexagram | Final Hexagram |

The Subject trigram wood is very strong, supported by the year (Pig water), month (Tiger wood) and day (Rabbit wood). The Original hexagram, no. 44 Kou: Coming to meet, with fifth line moving changed to the hexagram no. 50 Ting: The Cauldron. This Cauldron is a very special cooking vessel with two loop handles and three or four legs used only by ancient Chinese nobility. According to the common viewpoint of the ancient Chinese, it is a very special symbol of the highest authority/power of a kingdom/state. The Nuclear hexagram is no. 1 Chien, the symbol of movement of a great man, or president/chairman in power. It means that Professor Li will be appointed as a very senior official with considerable power in the municipal government. If the month moves to Sheep month, when the great wood is built up by a Great Combination of Three Elements, or the year (Pig, water), month (Sheep, store of wood) and day (Rabbit, wood), he may hold the top authority.

Just four months later, in the Sheep month, Professor Li received a formal document from the municipal government. He was nominated as one of the vice-mayors in charge of science, culture and public health in this municipality with a population of 30 million.

Case 18. Forecast Landmark Vote: Olympic Games Bid

Moscow, Russian Federation, 13 July 2001. In a landmark vote of the International Olympic Committee, Beijing was named host city for the 2008 Olympic Games. The Games have never before been held in China, the world's most populous nation. Beijing had emphasised during the 11 months' bid process the overwhelming support of its people for the Games. 96 per cent of Beijing citizens backed the bid. China is also keen to take the opportunity to expand economic openness and raise living standards, spread the values and benefits of the Olympics to China's 400 million youth, and share culture and markets between China and the world in an unprecedented way.

At that exciting time, like most Chinese people, my whole family and I were watching the live TV programme and anxiously waiting for the final decision by the IOC. At 8.00 p.m. Beijing time, (3.00 p.m. Moscow time), Beijing started its final presentation to the International Olympic Committee. As soon as Beijing finished its presentation, at about 8.40 p.m., my wife suddenly smiled at me and said: 'Darling, why don't you forecast the final result of the vote as you are a fortune-teller?' All my family members supported her proposal, so I did a divination immediately, as follows:

Time data (based on Moscow time)

	HOUR	DAY	MONTH	YEAR
HEAVENLY STEM	+earth	−fire	−wood	−metal
EARTHLY BRANCH	Monkey (metal)	Ox (earth)	Sheep (earth)	Snake (fire)
TIME NUMBER	9	23	5	6

Hexagram (based on Moscow time):

| Original Hexagram | Nuclear Hexagram | Final Hexagram |

Firstly, I want to know among the five candidate cities which city may win the vote. Based on the hexagrams chart above, the Original hexagram (no. 49. Ko: Revolution/Moulting) represents the beginning phase of the bid and the Final hexagram no. 31 Hsien: Influence/Wooing (please note the name of the hexagram, which is very meaningful. Every candidate is wooing to be the host city) represents the last decision. The upper trigram is the Subject trigram, representing the IOC. The lower trigram is the Object trigram, symbolising the host city. When I checked the Original hexagram, the lower trigram is Li, fire, it indicated the south (according to the Later Heaven Sequence of the Eight Trigrams.) However, all five candidate cities are located in the northern hemisphere. So I guessed that it implied Sydney, located in the southern hemisphere, which hosted the 2000 Olympic Games. If I want to know the host city chosen for the 2008 Games by this vote, I need to check the Final hexagram, which represents the final result. What does the Final hexagram imply? The Object trigram of the Final hexagram is Ken, Mountain. Its direction is north-east according to the Later Heaven Sequence of the Eight Trigrams (see page 19). I believed I was close to getting the answer, because among the five candidate cities – Beijing, Toronto, Istanbul, Paris and Osaka – only Beijing and Osaka are located in the east. The winner must be one of these two cities, so now the problem is easier to solve. The only thing I have to do is compare the two cities, Beijing and Osaka. I got useful information from the hexagram too. Osaka had emphasised in its final presentation that, as it is an island city surrounded by sea, the Osaka people planned to hold the games on the great Sea, which is a very funny idea indeed. However, there is a disadvantage, as many members of the IOC pointed out that this would cause difficulties with transport.

Let's move back to our hexagrams. If you look at the hexagrams, you will find that, among the three hexagrams, or six trigrams, there is no water element at all! Fire, earth, metal and wood are all there, but no water. So the trigrams tell us they do not support the idea of holding the games on water. What about Beijing? As you know, this is an inland city with great mountains, but little water. The famous Great Wall was built over the mountains of Beijing. So in fact the competition between Beijing and Osaka is a fight between elements, Beijing-earth, Osaka-water. Who will be the winner of the fight? Earth is very strongly supported not only by the trigrams, but also by the fire Snake year, Earth sheep month and earth Ox day. Compared with earth, water is terribly weak. It does not get enough support from the trigrams, or from time factors such as the year, month and day. Furthermore, the water is destroyed by the earth month and earth day, so the stronger earth will absolutely overcome the weaker water. Finally, the clearest indicator is shown from the Object trigram of the Final hexagram, which represents the host city. As you know, it is Ken, and its essential meaning and image is Mountain. It is clear that Beijing, the inland city surrounded by great mountains, will win the battle with Osaka, the island city surrounded by great sea.

Then I needed to answer the question about the result of the votes, which I got from the hexagram drawn based on Beijing time (8.40 p.m.):

Hexagrams (based on Beijing time)

Main Hexagram	Nuclear Hexagram	Changing Hexagram
☷ ☱ *	☰ ☰	☳ ☵

Any number or figure concerning us may be directly obtained by calculating the trigram's number of the Original hexagram (here the Original hexagram is no. 28 Ta Kuo: Preponderance of the Great. Please note the name of the hexagram, which is very meaningful). Because the lower trigram of the Original hexagram is 5 (Sun trigram is 5 according to Early Heaven Sequence of the Eight Trigrams), the vote for Beijing is at least $5 \times 10 = 50$ (as it is very strong, so I see the 5 as ten's digit. It is always necessary for us to do this flexible treatment based on a specific situation), then I add the upper trigram 2 (Tui is 2 according to the Early Heaven Sequence for Eight Basic

Trigrams) and the number of the changing line 3 (the third line is the changing line) So the votes for Beijing should be 50 + 2 + 3 = 55. As 52 votes are needed to win, the votes for Beijing should be over 52, or 55.

By the way, it is worth noting that the Final hexagram is a Six Combine/ Harmony hexagram, which means unity, harmony and completely winning. Furthermore, based on the *Forest of I Ching* by Jiao, the oracle poem on this hexagram is: '*Getting in my car with joyful steps and driving to the family holding great celebration. The kind host of the family gave me a very beautiful coat, then I carried full happiness in the car on my return home.*'

I also tried to forecast Osaka's vote based on the hexagram from Osaka time (about 9.40 p.m.), although I didn't need to.

Hexagrams (based on Osaka time):

Main Hexagram	Nuclear Hexagram	Changing Hexagram

In the same way, I got the vote for Osaka, which is at least 6, as the lower trigram of the Original hexagram (no. 47 K'un: Oppression/Exhaustion. Please note the name of the hexagram, which is also very meaningful, especially compared to the name of the hexagram for Beijing – Preponderance of the Great) is 6 (according to Early Heaven Sequence of the Eight Trigrams. The Kan trigram is 6). The Subject trigram is too weak (it is destroyed by earth day, earth month and exhausted by year fire) to add any more numbers, so I didn't add the number of the upper trigram and the changing line for it. The votes for Osaka will be only 6, or as seen as the unit's digit. By the way, the Final hexagram for Osaka is the very reverse of Beijing: it is a Six Clash hexagram, which means conflict and complete loss.

I gave my forecast to my family members, close friends and relatives by telephone two hours before the vote of the IOC. 'Beijing won the bid for hosting the 2008 Olympic Games at the 112th session of the International Olympic Committee', IOC President Juan Antonio Samaranch announced at 11.10 p.m. (Beijing time), or two hours after my forecast.

The following are the vote totals from the ballot to pick the host city for the 2008 Olympics:

First Round (52 votes needed to win)
Beijing 44, Toronto 20, Istanbul 17, Paris 15, Osaka 6 (eliminated)
Second Round (52 votes needed to win)
Beijing 56, Toronto 22, Paris 18, Istanbul 9.

I extracted a description of this exciting event from a Chinese newspaper as follows and hope to share the great happiness of the Chinese with you:

Tens of thousands of Chinese gathered in a carnival at Beijing's Millennium Monument on Friday night to celebrate the Chinese capital's winning of the right to host the 2008 Olympic Games. Chinese President Jiang Zemin and other government officials joined the carnival.

The square in front of the monument was turned into a sea of joy and smiles at the announcement of Beijing as the winner among the five candidate cities, with tears of excitement flowing on numerous faces, flowers being thrown into the air and firecrackers roaring.

Beijing's plan for the 2008 Games calls for one of the greatest building projects undertaken in China since the construction of the Great Wall. The city will invest more than $20 billion to more than triple the length of its expressway network, expand and upgrade its public transport system and build dozens of competition and training venues by 2008.

Of course, no one can deny that when people from all parts of the world gather in Beijing, interchange between Chinese and Western cultures will be unprecedented in the history of human civilization. When the Olympics embrace Beijing, both are winners.

Case 19. The Largest Dam in the World

The Three-Gorges Dam in China is the largest dam on earth, and China has more large dams than any other country, with 18,820 large dams, or half of all those in the world. So the issue of the impact of the huge Three-Gorges Dam may be influential to the world. The dam is 1983 metres long, 185 metres high and has a 39.3 billion water reservoir capacity. The project is to be completed over 17 years in three phases, from 1993 to 2009. By 1997 the main stream of the Yangtse River had already been dammed. 1.3 million people will be displaced, and 300 million people and farmland along 1500km of the area downstream will also be affected. Despite the importance of the Three-Gorges Dam for the development of China's heartland, neither the World Bank nor the US Export–Import Bank are providing finance.

After about seven years' prolonged and heated argument, a decision had finally to be made by vote of the CNPC (Chinese National People's Congress, China's parliament). As I have worked in the region close to the Three-Gorges Dam area, a friend asked me what the result of the vote would be.

According to the timetable of the ballot, I drew a hexagram and conducted a prediction as follows:

Time data (3 April 1992 at 3.30 p.m.)

	HOUR	DAY	MONTH	YEAR
HEAVENLY STEM	–earth	–earth	–water	+water
EARTHLY BRANCH	Monkey (metal)	Rooster (metal)	Rabbit (wood)	Monkey (metal)
TIME NUMBER	9	1	3	9

Main Hexagram	Nuclear Hexagram	Changing Hexagram

Based on the principle of judgement on the hexagram, I looked at the Subject trigram and Object trigram in the Original hexagram (no. 59 Huan: Dispersion/Dissolution) first. The Subject trigram is Kan water, which symbolised the project, and births the Object trigram Sun wood, which represented the officials who vote on the project. The relationship of the

Subject trigram birthing the Object trigram means cost/exhaust. It is true that if China plans to build the largest dam, the cost will be very big indeed, and will exhaust some essential natural resources. The symbol also implies that initially it is difficult to persuade the officials to support the project due to the big negative impact on the environment and people. However, in the Final hexagram, the Subject trigram is birthed by the Object trigram, implying that the majority will support the project in the end.

When I checked the force of the trigram, at the first stage, or in the Original hexagram, the Object trigram wood is destroyed by the metal year, metal day and metal hour, which implies a large risk. However, in the Final hexagram, both the Subject trigram water and Object trigram metal are supported by the metal year, metal day and metal hour. So the last result of the vote is hopeful.

In regard to the vote totals, as the number of officials of the CNPC was over two thousand, I thought it was easier to estimate the percentage of votes instead of the exact figure. (You may remember that this calculation is relatively flexible. Sometimes I get a number from the hexagram and interpret it as ten's place digit, some times as unit's place digit and so on.) Based on the Original trigram, the number of the Subject trigram is 6 (according to the Early Heaven Sequence of the Eight Basic Trigrams, the Kan is 6). Because the Subject trigram is very strong, supported by the Object trigram and year, day and hour, so the votes are at least 60% (6 × 10 = 60) of the total number of voters, then I need to add the number of the Subject trigram 5 (the Sun trigram is 5) or even more add the changing line 4 (the changing line is the fourth line) on the unit's place. Thus, the final vote is 65%-69% of the voters.

Is the largest dam project going on? As everybody knows, China started this project in 1993. Although at first many officials in the CNPC had disagreed with this project, after acute challenge and heated argument, the final result of the vote was 67.1% (2,633 deputies attended the ballot). So the largest dam project was approved by the CNPC on 3 April, 1992.

Chapter Seven

The Na Jia Method of Prediction

The Na Jia method produces a prediction using precise, logical calculations and by matching each line of the hexagram with the Heavenly Stem and Earthly Branch system – the Four Pillars. For beginners, it might seem complex, but because it involves logical calculations made step by step according to a series of fixed formulae, it is relatively easy to apply and put into practice. It is one of the most popular methods in China, especially in the scientific/academic community. It is also slightly like the Compass School of feng shui. Comparing it with the Mei Hua method, the latter is like the Form School of feng shui. Compass School feng shui emphasises logic, calculation and formulae whereas Form School depends on intuition and insight. Chinese scholars regard the Compass School as a science and Form School as an art.

There are three basic steps:

- Create a hexagram
- Carry out the necessary preparation procedure
- Analyse and make a final judgement

Creating The Hexagram

1) Create a hexagram by the coin method (or create it by making a calculation based on time, as in the Mei Hua method).

For example, when we want to know the outcome of the Lincoln murder, we can get the Original hexagram Fu from the date, as in the Mei Hua method (see the previous chapter):

2) Carry out the necessary preparation procedure
There are five steps:

a) Identify Self line and Response line
b) Match each line with Earthly Branch
c) Match each line with Six Relatives
d) Find out the Favourable/ Unfavourable line
e) Match each line with the Six Gods/Six Animals

This is a relatively complex process, however it is necessary, so we need to discuss it in detail, step by step as follows:

A) Identify Self Line and Response Line.

The Self line and Response line respectively represent the self/client and partner/match or event you are concerned with. We identify them by checking the Eight Palaces.

As in the case of the Lincoln murder, the Original hexagram, Fu, was located in the no. 7 row and no. 1 column of the Eight Palace Chart. The Self line and Response line should be like this:

Note: o = Self line, ▲= Response line

Figure 34 Formula on Location of Self Line and Response Line in the Eight Palace Chart

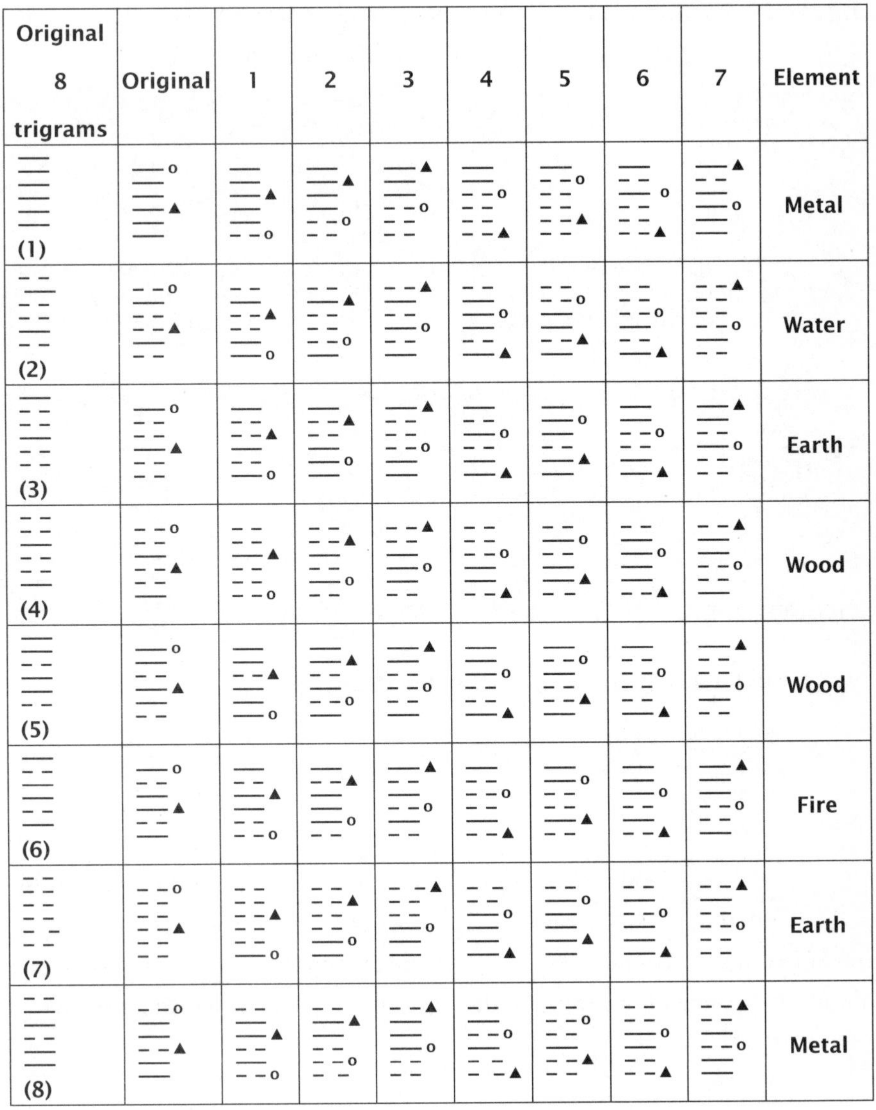

Original 8 trigrams	Original	1	2	3	4	5	6	7	Element
(1)									Metal
(2)									Water
(3)									Earth
(4)									Wood
(5)									Wood
(6)									Fire
(7)									Earth
(8)									Metal

o = Self ▲ = Response

B) Match Each Line with Earthly Branch

Figure 35 Formula for matching each line of the Eight Basic Trigrams with relevant Earthly Branches

Trigram	Ch'ien		K'un		K'an		Ken	
When trigram at top	Dog Monkey Horse	—— —— ——	Rooster Pig Ox	— — — — — —	Rat Dog Monkey	— — —— — —	Tiger Rat Dog	—— — — — —
When trigram at bottom	Dragon Tiger Rat	—— —— ——	Rabbit Snake Goat	— — — — — —	Horse Dragon Tiger	— — —— — —	Monkey Horse Dragon	—— — — — —

Trigram	Tui		Li		Chen		Sun	
When trigram at top	Goat Rooster Pig	— — —— ——	Snake Goat Rooster	—— — — ——	Dog Monkey Horse	— — — — ——	Rabbit Snake Goat	—— —— — —
When trigram at bottom	Ox Rabbit Snake	— — —— ——	Pig Ox Rabbit	—— — — ——	Dragon Tiger Rat	— — — — ——	Rooster Pig Ox	—— —— — —

Match the Fu hexagram with the Earthly Branches

```
= =
= =
= =
= =
———
```

Firstly, let's match the lower trigram Chen with the Earthly Branches using the table in figure 35. We begin by finding out that the trigram Chen is in the seventh column. Because the trigram is located in the lower half of the hexagram, the formula for matching the Earthly Branch is in the second row:

Chen

Dog	— —
Monkey	— —
Horse	———
Dragon	— —
Tiger	— —
Rat	———

Be careful to note that the Earthly Branch is totally different when the trigram Chen is located in the upper position.

Then we match the upper trigram Kun with the Earthly Branch based on the table again. We firstly find out that the trigram Kun is in the second column, then because the trigram is located in the upper half of the hexagram, the formula to match the Earthly Branch is in the first row:

Kun

Rooster	— —
Pig	— —
Ox	— —
Rabbit	— —
Snake	— —
Goat	— —

By now we have finished matching the Earthly Branch for all lines of the hexagram Fu as follows: (The element for each animal is included)

Earthly branch	Element	Hexagram
Rooster	metal	— —
Pig	water	— —
Ox	earth	— —
Dragon	earth	— —
Tiger	wood	— —
Rat	water	——

When you match the line with the Earthly Branch, the same trigram may be matched with totally different Earthly Branches. It depends on where the trigram is located in the hexagram, upper or lower.

C) Match Each Line with Six Relatives

- Firstly, identify which palace the hexagram originates from by checking the Eight Palaces Chart.
- Then find out the element of this palace. It is the Self element.
- Finally, determine the Six Relatives for each line and write it beside the line by checking the table below, noting the birth/destruction relationship of the Five Elements.

The Six Relatives and their general symbols in different areas

Six Relatives	Relation to Self Element	Normally symbolises
Parents	Birth	Parents, document, information, academic,
Officer/devil	Destroy	Husband, supervisor/boss, job/post, devil, robber/thief, disease
Brother	Same	Brother/friend, match, enemy, robber/thief
Wife/money	Destroyed	Wife, money, wealth,
Offspring	Birthed	Children, employee, doctor/medicine, police/bodyguard

Based on the Eight Palaces Chart, the Fu hexagram originates from Kun palace (listed in the first column followed by the Original hexagram Kun). Because the elements of all hexagrams located in this palace are the same as the Original hexagram Kun (Earth), so the Self element of the Fu hexagram is earth also. This step is vitally important. As soon as the key element or the Self element is determined, we can identify the relationship associated with the key element for every line of the Fu hexagram. Since the first line of the Fu hexagram is Rat (the element of Rat is water), it is destroyed by the Self element earth, so its relationship with the Self element should be wife. The second line: Tiger is wood, it destroys the Self element earth, so its relationship with the Self element is officer/devil. The third line: Dragon is earth; it is the same as the Self element, earth, its relationship with the Self element is brother.

Please note that after completing the Earthly Branches and the Six Relatives for the lines of the Original hexagram, you need to do the same for the Final hexagram by matching every line of the Final hexagram with Earthly Branches and Six Relatives.

D) Find out the Favourable/Unfavourable Line

Generally, the Self line and the line supported by the Self line are the Favourable lines. However, you may have more Favourable lines sometimes. It depends on the target of your question, e.g. if you want to be promoted, or if you want to find a boyfriend or get married to a man, the Officer line, which represents the official or husband, is your Favourable line. If you want to make a lot of money from business, or want to find a girlfriend or get married to a woman, then the Wife line, which represents wife/money, is your Favourable line. If you want to publish a paper or enter a higher education institution, or if your question is about your parents' health, the Parent line, which represents parents/academy, is your Favourable line. Remember also that the line which destroys the Self line or destroys your Favourable line is your Unfavourable line.

E) Matching Each Line with the Six Gods/Six Animals

The Six Gods, or Six Animals is another complementary system using symbolism to create an integrated judgement of the hexagram. This process is fascinating and provides you with some complementary indicators to help you make a more detailed judgement. Sometimes people omit this process when making a final judgement.

The names of Six Gods/Animals originate from the names of constellations in ancient Chinese astronomy. They are: Green Dragon, Red Bird, Gouchen (or Polaris), Flying Snake, White Tiger and Black Tortoise. Figure 36 shows how to match them to Relative lines.

Figure 36 Location of Six Gods to Matched Line by Heavenly Stem of Day

heavenly Stem	± wood	± fire	+earth	−earth	± metal	± water
6th line	Black Tortoise	Green Dragon	Red Bird	Gouchen	Flying Snake	White Tiger
5th line	White Tiger	Black Tortoise	Green Dragon	Red Bird	Gouchen	Flying Snake
4th line	Flying Snake	White Tiger	Black Tortoise	Green Dragon	Red Bird	Gouchen
3rd line	Gouchen	Flying Snake	White Tiger	Black Tortoise	Green Dragon	Red Bird
2nd line	Red Bird	Gouchen	Flying Snake	White Tiger	Black Tortoise	Green Dragon
1st line	Green Dragon	Red Bird	Gouchen	Flying Snake	White Tiger	Black Tortoise

Based on the fixed location of the Six Gods, the ordering principle is in accordance with the Heavenly Stem of the particular day on which you draw the hexagram. For example, on the day of 14 April 1865 (see the case on President Lincoln), the Heavenly Stem of the day is +wood, so according to the table in figure 36, the location of the Six Gods in the Original hexagram should be as follows:

Six Gods	Line	Hexagram
Black Tortoise	6th line	— — ✳
White Tiger	5th line	— —
Flying Snake	4th line	— —
Gouchen	3rd line	— —
Red Bird	2nd line	— —
Green Dragon	1st line	———

Then how do you make a judgement on the specific location of the Six Gods? The general symbols of the Six Gods are:

Black Tortoise: bandit/thief, intrigue
White Tiger: extremely dangerous, severe injury
Flying Snake: amazed, plot against
Gouchen: lawsuit/anxious
Red Bird: message, document, affray
Green Dragon: auspicious, happiness, success

When a god is located in the same line as the changing line it is called: 'the god starts action'. Then you may make a judgement based on reading the meaning from the general interpretation about the Six Gods. The Green Dragon symbolises that it is auspicious, and the White Tiger is inauspicious. However these symbols are very flexible, and first you should make judgements mainly based on the previous integrated analysis of the relationship between the Self line and the Response line. When the previous integrated analysis is auspicious, the meaning of the Six Gods should be interpreted as more auspicious and less inauspicious, even for the White Tiger, which is usually a bad sign. On the other hand, when the integrated analysis is inauspicious, the Six Gods should be understood as more inauspicious and less auspicious even for the Green Dragon, which is usually a good sign. The symbolism of the Six Gods is just a complementary indicator; a bad symbol such as the White Tiger will increase the inauspicious aspect when the integrated judgement is negative, whereas a good symbol such as the Green Dragon will increase the auspicious aspect when the integrated judgement is positive.

In our President Lincoln case, as the Black Tortoise is located at the changing line, it means the Black Tortoise starts action. If the previous integrated judgement is totally inauspicious, the Black Tortoise just indicates that the bandit/murderer may complete the murder plan successfully.

Let's summarise the procedure with an example. Let us look at the Original/main hexagram and Final/changing hexagram about the Lincoln murder:

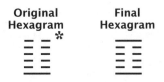

Note: * = Changing/moving line

1. Identify the Self/Response line by checking the Eight Palaces Chart as follows:

Note: o = Self line, ▲= Response line

2. Match each line with the Earthly Branch by checking the table of matching lines with Earthly Branches for the Original hexagram and the Final hexagram.

3. Match each line with the Six Relatives. We find that the Fu hexagram is located in the Kun Palace giving the Self element of this palace as earth. Then we match lines with the Six Relatives, i.e. parents, officer, brother, wife and offspring. These can be represented by fire, wood, earth, water and metal respectively.

4. Identify the Favourable line and Unfavourable line based on our target of concern; in this case, the safety of the President is the priority. We need

to find out which line represents the President and his bodyguard and which line represents the murderer. We can easily find out that the first line is the Self line (water element) and represents Lincoln. The sixth line is the Offspring line (metal element), representing the bodyguard. So the two elements of metal and water are the Favourable elements, which support the Self line water, and the Offspring line is the Favourable line. The fourth line is the Response line (earth element) and represents the murderer. So the Response line is the Unfavourable line, because its earth destroys the Self line's water.

The completed hexagrams are as follows:

Original Hexagram				
Six Relatives	**Earthly Branch**	**Element**	**Hexagram**	**Note**
Offspring	Rooster	Metal	— — ✳	Changing
Wife	Pig	Water	— —	
Brother	Ox	Earth	— — ▲	Response
Brother	Dragon	Earth	— —	
Officer	Tiger	Wood	— —	
Wife	Rat	Water	——— O	Self

Final Hexagram			
Six Relatives	**Earthly Branch**	**Element**	**Hexagram**
Officer	Tiger	Wood	———
Wife	Rat	Water	— —
Brother	Dog	Earth	— —
Brother	Dragon	Earth	— —
Officer	Tiger	Wood	— —
Wife	Rat	Water	———

3) Analyse the Changes and Development of the Event you are Concerned with and Make an Integrated Judgement

The analysis should focus on:

- Comparing relationship and forces between the Self line and the Response line
- Comparing relationship and forces between the Favourable line and the Unfavourable line
- Looking at the force and development of the changing line and its impact on the Self line, Response line and Favourable line

Please note:

a) The principle in judging the relationship between the Self line and the Response line is very similar to the Mei Hua method, i.e. compare the force of two conflicting sides by carefully looking at the impact of time, including year, month, day and hour, on the Self line and the Response line. This can include the Favourable line and the Unfavourable Line respectively and also the influence of space in direction and location.

b) Fundamental to the analysis is also the relationship of the Five Elements and how they act and interact with each other – producing, destroying or consuming.

It is important to use your intuition when you are conducting the analysis. Although the Na Jia method is very much more rational than the Classical method and the Mei Hua method, it is still an I Ching method of prediction so it is still necessary to use your intuition.

Let us look at the same case to analyse the outcome of the Lincoln murder.

A. Compare Relationship and Force for the Self Line and the Response Line

Firstly, let's look at the relationship between the Self line and the Response line. The Self line, water (representing Lincoln) is destroyed by the Response line, earth (representing the murderer). It definitely indicates an inauspicious outcome for President Lincoln.

Secondly, let's compare the force of the two sides. We need to review the time data again:

	HOUR	DAY	MONTH	YEAR
HEAVENLY STEM	−wood	+wood	+metal	−wood
EARTHLY BRANCH	Pig (−water)	Tiger (+wood)	Dragon (+earth)	Ox (−earth)

Based on the date, the Self line (water element) representing Lincoln is very weak, because both the elements of year and month are earth, and destroy water. The element of day is wood, it consumes the weak water, or costs the water energy. Only the hour is the same element of water, but it does not offer enough support to the water. Therefore the Self line is very weak.

On the other hand, the Response line (earth element) is very strong, because it is supported by the powerful earth year and the powerful earth month.

According to the comparison above, the Response line is obviously stronger than the Self line. A strong Response line destroys the weak Self Line, indicating the murderer may kill President Lincoln in the end.

B. Analyse the Favourable Line in Depth

The Offspring line represents the bodyguard. It does not seem very weak and should offer effective protection to Lincoln. However:

1) The Offspring line is a changing line. This is a very special condition and needs to be paid attention to and examined carefully! Changing means moving. Where does it move to? We need to check the Final hexagram, which represents the final outcome. The Offspring line completely disappears in the Final hexagram. It means that when the murderer fired at Lincoln, the bodyguard was absent from the murder area.

2) If we check the relationship between the Offspring line and the month, we find that the Offspring line of Rooster (bodyguard) is combined with the month Dragon. It means that the Offspring line is caught and restricted by the month. So the bodyguard can do nothing to help Lincoln when the murder happens because he is trapped and cannot move any more.

3) If we use the assistant indicator of Six Gods, you find that the Black Tortoise is located at the changing line. This means the Black Tortoise starts action. As the previous integrated judgement is totally inauspicious, the Black Tortoise just indicates that the murderer might achieve the target of his murder plan.

4) If you check the location of the Offspring line, (also an important concept for every feng shui master – location, location and location, the

three priorities of selecting property) we find that the bodyguard line is located far away from the Self line (the two lines are located at the two opposite poles. The Offspring line is at the top of the hexagram, far to the south and the Self line is at the bottom of the hexagram, the very north). It means that the bodyguard moved too far away from the President to conduct his duty.

C. Check the General Picture of the Hexagram

Sometimes we find that there is a special relationship between the upper trigram and the lower trigram in a hexagram. There are two important concepts in the Na Jia method if the relationship of lines of the upper trigram and the lower trigram is like the pattern in the hexagram T'ai (no. 11, Peace). The first line of the lower trigram combines with the first line of the upper trigram (the Rat combined with the Ox – see the relationship between Earthly Branches in figure 28 page 52). The second line of the lower trigram combines with the second line of the upper trigram (the Tiger combined with the Pig) and the third line of the lower trigram combines with the third line of the upper trigram (the Dragon combined with the Rooster). This complete combination relationship between the two trigrams is called a Six Combine/Harmony hexagram. (See the T'ai hexagram in figure 37.)

Figure 37 T'ai Hexagram

When the relationship of the lines of the upper trigram and the lower trigram is like that in the hexagram Chien (no. 1 Creative), here the lines are clashing with each other. The first line of the lower trigram clashes with the first line of the upper trigram (the Rat clashes with the Horse). The second line of the lower trigram clashes with the second line of the upper trigram (the Tiger clashes with the Monkey). The third line of the lower trigram clashes with the third line of the upper trigram (the Dragon clashes with the

Dog). This complete clash relationship between the two trigrams is known as a Six Clash hexagram. (See the Chien hexagram in figure 38.)

Figure 38 Chien Hexagram

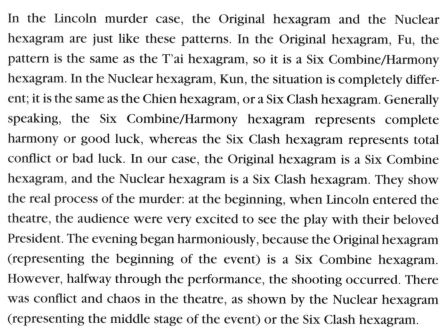

In the Lincoln murder case, the Original hexagram and the Nuclear hexagram are just like these patterns. In the Original hexagram, Fu, the pattern is the same as the T'ai hexagram, so it is a Six Combine/Harmony hexagram. In the Nuclear hexagram, Kun, the situation is completely different; it is the same as the Chien hexagram, or a Six Clash hexagram. Generally speaking, the Six Combine/Harmony hexagram represents complete harmony or good luck, whereas the Six Clash hexagram represents total conflict or bad luck. In our case, the Original hexagram is a Six Combine hexagram, and the Nuclear hexagram is a Six Clash hexagram. They show the real process of the murder: at the beginning, when Lincoln entered the theatre, the audience were very excited to see the play with their beloved President. The evening began harmoniously, because the Original hexagram (representing the beginning of the event) is a Six Combine hexagram. However, halfway through the performance, the shooting occurred. There was conflict and chaos in the theatre, as shown by the Nuclear hexagram (representing the middle stage of the event) or the Six Clash hexagram.

The Six Combine/Harmony hexagram indicates complete harmony or symbolises good luck; the Six Clash hexagram indicates comprehensive conflict, or symbolises bad luck. There is however an important exception to this rule in the Na Jia method. When the question is about somebody who went away or is missing, the Six Combine hexagram means they will not come back, as they are locked/captured by somebody or something and cannot move or return.

Among the 64 hexagrams, only ten are Six Clash hexagrams (all of them are the Basic Trigram except two), and eight hexagrams are Six Combine hexagrams. This means that eight of the hexagrams are the Basic Trigrams shown twice (e.g. the Kan hexagram is the Kan trigram above and below) and the other two hexagrams contain two different trigrams. I list them in the following table to help swift judgement in divination. A summary of the Six Clash Hexagrams and Six Combine Hexagrams is as follows:

The Six Combine Hexagrams

T'ai	Pi	Kun	Chieh	Lu	Pi	Fu	Yu

The Six Clash Hexagrams

Chien	Kun	Chen	Tui	Li	Kan	Ken	Sun	Ta-chuang	Wu-wang

There are several important points in the Na Jia method which can be summarised as:

1. The essential role of the changing line to the Self and Response lines.
2. The invisible changing line and its meaning.
3. Six Clash Hexagram and Six Combine Hexagram: their general meaning and special judgement for health or missing people or objects.
4. The line broken by month, line broken by day and their meaning.
5. The Great Combination of Three Elements and its meaning.
6. Repaid Destruction and Repaid Birth. A special relationship of destruction, and a special relationship of birth, which happens between two lines. The changing line in the Original hexagram is directly destroyed by the new line in the changing hexagram, which is originated/produced from the changing line. The Repaid Destruction is the most inauspicious, because it is just like a son/daughter who wants to kill his/her mother after he/she has been delivered by his/her mother. The Repaid Birth is seen as the most auspicious, because it is just like a son/daughter who feeds his/her mother when she is old.

Case Histories Using The Na Jia Method

Case 1. How to Choose the Right Job to Prevent Misfortune

On 23 February 1995, about 9.45 p.m., Miss Shen, a young lady aged 21, asked me if she could do the job of a taxi driver.

Based on the performance process described in detail, the time data is as follows:

	HOUR	DAY	MONTH	YEAR
HEAVENLY STEM	+fire	–wood	+earth	–wood
EARTHLY BRANCH	Dog (fire)	Rooster (metal)	Tiger (wood)	Pig (water)

Miss Shen cast coins and got the Original hexagram and Final hexagram as follows:

Original Hexagram	Final Hexagram

There are four steps to follow as explained earlier: a) identify Self line and Response line, b) match each line with Earthly Branch, c) match each line with Six Relatives, d) find out the Favourable/ Unfavourable line.

Original Hexagram			
Six Relatives	**Earthly Branch**	**Element**	**Hexagram**
Offspring	Rat	Water	— —
Parent	Dog	Earth	——— *
Brother	Monkey	Metal	— — *o
Brother	Monkey	Metal	———
Officer	Horse	Fire	— — *
Parent	Dragon	Earth	— — ▲
Note: * = Changing line, o = Self Line, ▲ = Response Line			

Final Hexagram			
Six Relatives	Earthly Branch	Element	Hexagram
Parent	Dog	Earth	– –
Brother	Monkey	Metal	– –
Officer	Horse	Fire	———
Brother	Rooster	Metal	———
Offspring	Pig	Water	———
Parent	Ox	Earth	– –

Then, according to the table above, I analysed the change and development of the event according to the question and made an integrated judgement. My analysis focused on: (1) comparing relationship and forces between Self line and Response line, (2) comparing relationship and forces between Favourable line and Unfavourable line, and (3) looking at the force and development of changing line and its impact to Self line, Response line and Favourable line etc. The principle of judgement on the outcome is very similar to the principle of the Mei Hua method, as explained earlier. It involves comparing the forces of the two conflicting sides by carefully looking at the impact of time, including year, month, day and hour on a Self line and the Response line, or the Favourable line and the Unfavourable line respectively. The basis of analysis is always the relationship of the Five Elements and how they interact with each other – birthing, destroying, supporting or consuming/exhausting.

Firstly I looked at the Original hexagram, no. 39 Chien: Obstruction. (The name of the hexagram, Obstruction, is definitely a bad symbol for a driver.) The Self line is Monkey, which is metal and birthed by the Response line. It doesn't seem to be a bad relationship. However it means nothing except that Miss Shen may get a job as a driver one day. If we want to know what the final outcome is – fortune or misfortune – we have to check the force of the Self line and Response line. Both of them are very weak. The Self line Monkey metal is the spring season, death season for metal, and also the Monkey line is directly clashing with the Tiger month, As I mentioned previously, the month is terribly powerful, controlling and managing everything in the whole world. If somebody dares to clash with the month, they will be very unlucky. So when a weak line clashes with a month, it is referred to as the line broken by month and implies great weakness. The Response line

Dragon is earth, which is destroyed by the month wood and consumed by the year and day. Because the Self line and Response line represented Miss Shen and the job of driver respectively, the symbols on the two sides are very weak and it indicates that she is too weak to be competent in this job, even though she may one day work as a driver.

Then I checked the force of the Favourable line and Unfavourable line. Because the Self line is metal, the line with element earth, which births metal, is its Favourable line. You will find the fifth line Dog and first line Dragon are earth element. What is their force? Just as I analysed above, as they are destroyed by month and consumed by year and day both of them are very weak. The Unfavourable line should be the line which destroys the Self line. So the second line Horse fire is the Unfavourable line, because fire destroys metal. What is its force? Fire is at its favourable season spring, and also is firmly birthed by the wood month, so it is very strong. By force comparison of the favourable and unfavourable factors, we understand that Miss Shen will not only face big difficulties (symbolised by the strong Unfavourable line) when she does the driving job, but also she has few friends or relatives (symbolised by the very weak Favourable line) able to support her when necessary, so the general judgement is definitely inauspicious.

Then I need to check the changing lines, which are a meaningful indicator in the Na Jia method. Special attention needs to be paid to them, as they always provide us with very significant information. There are three changing lines in the Original hexagram, or the second line Horse fire, the fourth line Monkey metal, and the fifth line Dog earth. What is their meaning? Firstly, because the fourth line Monkey is Self line symbolising Miss Shen, its moving means that Miss Shen is very actively looking forward to taking the job. The second line Horse fire is an Unfavourable line for Miss Shen, and its moving implies that the difficulty is growing and getting bigger. It also means that the risk is closer to Miss Shen day by day. The fifth line Dog earth, is a Favourable line for Miss Shen; its changing seems to imply that somebody is willing to help her. Unfortunately, the Dog earth is a special element. It is earth element originally. On the one hand, it is also the store of fire, hiding large fire inside, and on the other hand, it may combine together with Horse and Tiger and generate a very powerful new element - fire, which is called a Great Combination of Three Elements. The Horse is the second line and the Tiger is the month. So a great new element fire will be generated by the Great Combination of Three Elements. It is a very vital symbol for Miss Shen. How does such weak metal cope with the terrible fire?

I also added more evidence to try to persuade Miss Shen, who was a very pretty young lady, to give up the very dangerous idea of being a taxi driver. The first evidence is: the Self line of the Original hexagram is fourth line and a changing line, but when the new fourth line in the Final hexagram appeared, it changed itself from original element metal to new element fire. As you know, the fire is the arch enemy of metal, so this kind of destructive relationship – the changing line in the Original hexagram was destroyed directly by the new line at the same location in the Final hexagram – is the worst inauspicious symbol. People call it Repaid Destruction, for example, like a son (the new line in the Final hexagram, which is produced by the changing line in the Original hexagram) killing his mother (the changing line in the Original hexagram). This is a symbol of terrible misfortune especially when it happens on the Self line, which represented Miss Shen herself.

The second piece of evidence relates to the Six Gods/Six Animals. Based on the day when Miss Shen asked her question, the Heavenly Stem is yin wood, so the Six Gods assigned to lines of the Original hexagram are Green Dragon, Red Bird, Gouchen, Flying Snake, White Tiger, Black Tortoise for the first, second, third, fourth, fifth and sixth lines respectively. It implies that the Gods of Tiger, Snake and Bird are starting action (because the fifth line, fourth line and second line are moving lines). The moving of God Tiger means serious injury with serious bleeding, Snake also means unexpected risk, so that symbol indicates very clearly that Miss Shen will have a terrible traffic accident if she becomes a taxi driver in the near future.

What is the possible time of the tragedy? Or when should I warn Miss Shen to look after herself as carefully as possible? I got this information from the changing lines. As I analysed above, the Self line, or the fourth line changed itself from the original Monkey line (metal) to the new line Horse (fire), which is the worst symbol of misfortune. It indicates that the accident may occur in June, the Horse month. Furthermore, the second line Horse fire is the terrible enemy of Self line metal, it is also a changing line, which clearly indicated that the dangerous time is June, the Horse month. Because the very serious crisis warning appeared twice in one hexagram, we should know the most dangerous month is June (Horse month), when fire becomes strongest and metal becomes weakest.

Just exactly as the hexagram indicated, Miss Shen was involved in a horrible traffic accident in June. The poor young girl was almost killed in the crash and her beautiful face was badly injured. A piece of glass from the windscreen went into her left eye and she was left totally blind.

Case 2. A Win-Win Decision

Dr Zhen was warmly invited by a friend of his to be a chief director in charge of a big TCM hospital, run by his friend, but he was not sure if this job was right for him, as he saw himself as an academic person with little experience in business. He called me and I helped him make this divination by the Na Jia method:

The time data is as follows:

	HOUR	DAY	MONTH	YEAR
HEAVENLY STEM	–wood	–water	+metal	–fire
EARTHLY BRANCH	Rabbit (wood)	Ox (earth)	Dog (earth)	Ox (earth)

The hexagrams completed by matching Earthly Branch and Six Relatives:

Original Hexagram			
Six Relatives	**Earthly Branch**	**Element**	**Hexagram**
Wife	Dog	Earth	━ ━ *
Officer	Monkey	Metal	━ ━
Offspring	Horse	Fire	━━━ ▲
Brother	Rabbit	Wood	━ ━
Offspring	Snake	Fire	━ ━
Wife	Sheep	Earth	━ ━ o
Note: * = Changing line, o = Self line, ▲ = Response line			

Final Hexagram			
Six Relatives	Earthly Branch	Element	Hexagram
Offspring	Snake	Fire	———
Wife	Sheep	Earth	— —
Officer	Rooster	Metal	———
Brother	Rabbit	Wood	— —
Offspring	Snake	Fire	— —
Wife	Sheep	Earth	— —

Then I conducted the prediction by comparing the relationship and forces of the Self line and Response line, looking at the force of the Favourable line and checking the force and development of the moving line.

Based on the hexagrams above, in the Original hexagram, no. 16 Yu: Enthusiasm, the Self line Sheep earth represented Dr Zhen, and the Response line Horse fire represented the TCM hospital. As the Response line Horse fire not only births but also combines together with the Self line Sheep earth, it means that Dr Zhen will benefit a lot from this job. In other words, he is competent to be the director. When I looked at the force of the two sides, the Self line is very strong, because it is supported by the earth year, earth month and earth day. It means Dr Zhen is an outstanding person and well qualified to take this position. The support of the Self line also implied that he would be loved and supported by his colleagues, supervisor, partners and clients. The Response line Horse seems less strong than the Self line, but as the Horse fire may combine together with Dog (the moving line earth) and Tiger wood and produce a big fire, which is called a Great Combination of Three Elements, it will become very strong in the next year, the Tiger year. It indicated the business of the TCM hospital would develop very well the next year.

Because economic conditions are also an essential issue for a hospital's development, we should select the Wife line, which represents wealth and economic profit, as our Favourable line. What is the strength of this line? I found there are two Wife lines: one is the Self line and the other is the changing line. The Self line, as I described, is very strong. What about the moving line? You may remember I emphasised previously that the moving line is a very significant indicator, and we must check it carefully. The moving line is Dog earth, supported by year, month and day. Furthermore it changed from earth Dog into a new line fire Snake in the Final hexagram, or no. 35 Chin: Progress. (Please note the meaningful name of the hexagram, Progress, a generally auspicious symbol for a career.) Snake fire is the Dog earth's mother! So this is the most wonderful birth relationship, named Repaid Birth, which is the opposite relationship to Repaid Destruction. It means the Wife line Dog is very strong and it indicates that there is a big market for the TCM hospital.

Finally, as the Original hexagram is a Six Combine Hexagram, it means complete harmony and great success.

Dr Zhen became confident after he heard my analysis, so he accepted the invitation of his friend and went to the TCM hospital. Several years later, his achievements matched my prediction. It was indeed a wise choice for him to go to the TCM hospital. It is a real win-win decision. Both Dr Zhen and his hospital benefited from this choice. He has been supported and loved by his colleagues and employees (this is a big TCM hospital with a large number of employees and clients) and became a well-known figure nationwide. The hospital also profited greatly due to his wonderful management of the hospital's performance and his excellent relationship with his clients and partners.

Case 3. Entering the Best University

On 25 July 2001 at 10.10 a.m, Ms Li's son, a senior middle-school student, asked about the result of his university entrance examination. He had finished the general examination held by the National Education Ministry a week before, so he was anxious to know what the result would be. According to the education system in China, the final result is published at the earliest one month after the general examination.

	HOUR	DAY	MONTH	YEAR
HEAVENLY STEM	–earth	–earth	–wood	–metal
EARTHLY BRANCH	Snake (earth)	Ox (earth)	Sheep (earth)	Snake (fire)
TIME NUMBER	6	5	6	6

Original Hexagram			
Six Relatives	**Earthly Branch**	**Element**	**Hexagram**
Parent	Dog	Earth	———
Brother	Monkey	Metal	——— ▲ *
Official	Horse	Fire	———
Brother	Monkey	Metal	———
Official	Horse	Fire	– – o
Parent	Dragon	Earth	– –

Note: * = Changing/moving line, o = Self line, ▲ = Response line

Final Hexagram			
Six Relatives	**Earthly Branch**	**Element**	**Hexagram**
Official	Snake	Fire	———
Parent	Sheep	Earth	– –
Brother	Rooster	Metal	———
Brother	Monkey	Metal	———
Official	Horse	Fire	– –
Parent	Dragon	Earth	– –

The table shows in the Original hexagram no. 33 Tun: Retreat, the Self line is Horse fire and destroys the Response line Monkey metal. It implies that the student, represented by the Self line, was trying his best to achieve his target, which is represented by the Response line. What is the student's force? The Self line Horse fire is supported by the year Snake fire and the hour Snake. Although the month is Sheep earth, it is still high summer (the average temperature was 28-38°C at the moment when I was doing the prediction), so the Self line fire is very strong on that hot day. It indicated that the student is outstanding and qualified to enter the best university.

The Response line metal represented the university, and is supported by the month earth and day earth. It is also very strong. The best thing is that it is the changing line, and changes into a new line Sheep earth in the Final hexagram. So the Response line metal in the Original hexagram is Repaid Birthed by the very strong Sheep line in the Final hexagram (it is worth noting that Sheep earth is very strong because it is supported by year fire, month earth, day earth and hour fire). It means that the university is keen to welcome the student. If you check the Sheep line more carefully, you will find it is the Parent line, which represents academy according to the general meaning of Six Relatives. Because it is so strong, it implies that the university is the best one with an excellent reputation. Finally, the Final hexagram is a Six Combine hexagram, meaning great success and happiness.

I sent my warm congratulations in advance to the very lucky student, and asked him to relax and await the good news. Twenty days later, the student received an admission letter from Tsinghua University, the best Mainland Chinese university. It is the most famous university in China with the best reputation nationwide, equivalent to Oxford in the UK or Harvard in the US.

Case 4. Disease and Health

On 17 November 2000, about 10.30 p.m., Ms Hu asked about her husband's health. He had suffered from liver disease for eight years, and his health had recently got worse.

Data of time:

	HOUR	DAY	MONTH	YEAR
HEAVENLY STEM	+wood	–earth	–fire	+metal
EARTHLY BRANCH	Dog (earth)	Rabbit (wood)	Pig (water)	Dragon (earth)
TIME NUMBER	11	22	10	5

Original Hexagram			
Six Relatives	**Earthly Branch**	**Element**	**Hexagram**
Brother	Rabbit	Wood	————
Offspring	Snake	Fire	————
Wife	Sheep	Earth	– – ▲
Wife	Dragon	Earth	————
Brother	Tiger	Wood	————
Parent	Rat	Water	———— o ✳

Note: ✳ = Changing/moving line, o = Self line, ▲ = Response line

Final Hexagram			
Six Relatives	Earthly Branch	Element	Hexagram
Brother	Rabbit	Wood	——
Offspring	Snake	Fire	——
Wife	Sheep	Earth	— —
Official	Rooster	Metal	——
Parent	Pig	Water	——
Wife	Ox	Earth	— —

Based on the principle of judgement for the hexagram, I found that there are five negative symbols implying that the patient's life is in danger:

a) In the Original hexagram no. 9 Hsiao Ch'u: The Taming Power of the Small, in terms of relationship between Self line (representing Ms Hu, or client) and Response line (representing Ms Hu's husband, or her target of concern), the Self line water is destroyed by Response line earth. It means her husband's disease is very serious and will bring adversity to Ms Hu.

b) In terms of the changing line, the Self line Rat water is the moving line, but is destroyed by the new line Ox earth in the Final hexagram, or suffers from Repaid Destruction, the worst symbol of misfortune, as I highlighted previously. It means that Ms Hu will be very depressed due to losing her beloved husband.

c) In terms of force of Response line, which symbolises the health of her husband, the Response line earth is directly destroyed by the day wood. Furthermore it is destroyed by the great wood produced by the Great Combination of Three Elements, or the Pig month, the Rabbit day and the Response line Sheep. It implies that her husband's health is beyond cure.

d) In regard to Favourable line, the Offspring line fire, which represents doctor/medicine, is destroyed by month water and is at the death season winter. It implies that there is no effective medicine available to save the patient's life.

e) In regard to other significant indicators, the Final hexagram is a Six Clash hexagram, which is the worst symbol for the patient. There is a general principle for forecasting the patient's health: if the hexagram is a Six Clash hexagram, an old patient will die very soon, but a new patient will recover very soon. On the other hand, if the hexagram is a Six Combine hexagram, an old patient will recover very soon, but a new patient will find it very difficult to recover. Ms. Hu's husband is an old patient having suffered from the disease for eight years, so he will die very soon because he just met the Six Clash hexagram.

The most dangerous date may be the first Ox day, as the changing line shows, or nine days later, so I suggested sending her husband to hospital as soon as possible.

Despite doctors making every effort to save this patient's life, Ms Hu's husband died eventually in hospital on 27 December 2000, an Ox day, nine days after Ms Hu consulted me.

Chapter Eight

The Integrated Method

This process combines the Classical method, the Mei Hua method and the Na Jia method by utilising their strengths, effectively combining them into a new tool. Based on these principles, it is simple, easy to understand, precise and practical. It features the simplest calculation process and the quickest way of getting a conclusion and an accurate forecast. There are three features of this new method:

- The Process of Creating a Hexagram
  Using the Mei Hua method, this is based on only four groups of time number (year, month, day and hour), it does not involve casting coins or other complex processes. It is the simplest and fastest.

- The Analysis Process
  Focus on finding out the key factor which determines the direction and degree of the development of the question concerned. For example, in the President Lincoln murder case, the Favourable line and the Unfavourable line, or the Self line and Response line of the hexagram in the Na Jia method are symbols of the President and the murderer respectively, so they should be the centre of our analysis. Because the Offspring line is the symbol of the bodyguard, it is also a vitally important factor in the outcome of the murder. It needs to be given special attention. If we can identify the key factors, then the outcome is very easy to obtain quickly.

With regard to force analysis, we emphasised analysing the Five Elements of each line and the interaction between key factors. The impact of time or space and sometimes relevant environmental factors such as the weather can play a part. For example, identifying which kind of relationship exists between the Self line and the Response line, birth or destruction? Compare the force of the two sides of Self and Response by checking the impact of year, month, day and hour.

In order to get more information to predict the process in depth with more precision, we use the fundamental parts of the Classical method. These include looking at the image of the hexagram, reading the text on the hexagram and the line and understanding the metaphor. Of course, always pay attention to any significant thoughts from your intuition.

* Make a Conclusion of the Prediction
  We do this by combining all the relevant data in a checklist table. This provides precise deduction and compares the possibilities by using numbers to simplify the final outcome and make it more logical.

Case Histories Using the Integrated Method

Case 1. The three President Murder Cases

Let me show you how to use the integrated method by analysing the three President murder cases.

Every President of the USA, who has become President in a year ending in '0' (e.g. 1860, 1890 and 1960) was certain to die before finishing his term: for example President Lincoln (became President in 1860), President Garfield (1880), President McKinley (1890), and President Kennedy (1960). People have made every effort to try to solve this conundrum; unfortunately they have failed to find any answers so far. However, there is one exception: President Reagan, who took office in 1980, successfully completed his task as 40th President. Although there was an assassination attempt, fortunately he escaped death. Like many people, I have been very interested in studying this great riddle. This is the reason why I probed the three murder cases by the integrated I Ching prediction method.

Lincoln's Murder

I have described this case in detail previously, so I will just review it very briefly here. On the evening of 14 April 1865 President Lincoln went to the theatre with his wife. At 10.15 p.m., as soon as his bodyguard left the President's side, a 27-year-old murderer sneaked into the President's balcony and shot Lincoln in the head. He died instantly.

Firstly translate 10.15 p.m., 14 April 1865 into the Chinese calendar as follows:

	HOUR	DAY	MONTH	YEAR
HEAVENLY STEM	−wood	+wood	+metal	−wood
EARTHLY BRANCH	Pig (−water)	Tiger (+wood)	Dragon (+earth)	Ox (−earth)
TIME NUMBER	12	19	3	2

Then create hexagrams by the Mei Hua method:

Original Hexagram				
Six Relatives	**Earthly Branch**	**Element**	**Hexagram**	**Note**
Offspring	Rooster	Metal	— — ✳	Changing
Wife	Pig	Water	— —	
Brother	Ox	Earth	— — ▲	Response
Brother	Dragon	Earth	— —	
Officer	Tiger	Wood	— —	
Wife	Rat	Water	——— o	Self

Final Hexagram			
Six Relatives	**Earthly Branch**	**Element**	**Hexagram**
Officer	Tiger	Wood	———
Wife	Rat	Water	— —
Brother	Dog	Earth	— —
Brother	Dragon	Earth	— —
Officer	Tiger	Wood	— —
Wife	Rat	Water	———

Kennedy's Murder

On 22 November 1963, in the morning, President Kennedy flew to Texas. He drove through the crowds in an open car and was shot in the back of his head at 11.37 a.m. when he went downtown. The murderer was a 24-year-old man.

The murder took place at 11.37 a.m., 22 November 1963. The time data and hexagrams are as follows:

	HOUR	DAY	MONTH	YEAR
HEAVENLY STEM	+metal	−earth	−water	−water
EARTHLY BRANCH	Horse (+fire)	Snake (−fire)	Pig (−water)	Rabbit (−wood)
TIME NUMBER	7	7	10	4

Original Hexagram			
Six Relatives	Earthly Branch	Element	Hexagram
Brother	Rabbit	Wood	——— ▲
Offspring	Snake	Fire	———
Wife	Sheep	Earth	— — ✳
Wife	Dragon	Earth	— — O
Brother	Tiger	Wood	— —
Parent	Rat	Water	———

Final Hexagram			
Six Relatives	Earthly Branch	Element	Hexagram
Wife	Dog	Earth	———
Official	Monkey	Metal	———
Offspring	Horse	Fire	———
Official	Rooster	Metal	— —
Parent	Pig	Water	— —
Wife	Ox	Earth	———

The Attempted Murder of Reagan

About 2.35 p.m., 30 March 1981, President Reagan left the Hilton Hotel in Washington DC. A murderer aged 25 fired six shots at him. But no sooner had the first shot been fired, than the loyal and devoted bodyguard protected the President with his body regardless of his own safety, pushed the President into his car and sent him to hospital immediately. Although the President's lung was injured in this murder attempt, he was not wounded fatally due to the timely protection of his bodyguard. He recovered quickly and was back at work only twelve days later.

According to the time when the murder attempt took place, 2.35 p.m., 30 March 1981, the time data and hexagrams are as follows:

	HOUR	DAY	MONTH	YEAR
HEAVENLY STEM	–fire	–fire	–metal	–metal
EARTHLY BRANCH	Sheep (–earth)	Sheep (–earth)	Rabbit (–wood)	Rooster (–metal)
TIME NUMBER	8	25	2	10

Original Hexagram			
Six Relatives	Earthly Branch	Element	Hexagram
Brother	Rabbit	Wood	——— o
Offspring	Snake	Fire	———
Wife	Sheep	Earth	— —
Official	Rooster	Metal	——— ▲ *
Parent	Pig	Water	———
Wife	Ox	Earth	— —

Final Hexagram			
Six Relatives	Earthly Branch	Element	Hexagram
Brother	Rabbit	Wood	———
Offspring	Snake	Fire	———
Wife	Sheep	Earth	— —
Offspring	Horse	Fire	— —
Wife	Dragon	Earth	———
Brother	Tiger	Wood	— —

Based on the three hexagrams for the three cases above, I analyse the outcome by comparing the favourable/positive indicator (+) or unfavourable/negative indicator (–) as in the following checklist table:

Analysis of the Three Presidents' Murder Cases

	Lincoln	Kennedy	Reagan
1. (MEI HUA) Relationship of Object/Subject & force	Subject trigram destroys Object trigram, but the Object very much stronger than Subject, so Subject finally lost (–) (–)	Object trigram finally destroys Subject trigram (–)(–)	Object trigram finally births Subject trigram (+)(+)
2. (NA JIA) Relationship of Response line /Self line and force	Response line destroys Self line (–) And the Response stronger than Self line (–)(–)	Response line destroys Self line (–) And the Response line stronger than Self line (–)(–)	Response destroys Self (–), but weaker than Self, because Self supported by month & a big wood bureau by day, month and line. And the Response clashed by month (+)(+)
3. (NA JIA) Overview of hexagram	Six Combine in Original hexagram changed to Six Clashing in Final hexagram (–)(–)	Original hexagram changed to Six Clashing in Nuclear hexagram (–)	Six Clashing in Original hexagram, however improved in Final hexagram
4. (NA JIA) Offspring (symbol of bodyguard)	The Offspring line located far away from Self & behind the murderer, moves away & disappeared finally (–)(–)	The Offspring line clashed and destroyed by month (–)(–)	Located between Self & Response & block murderer, it is also strong & supported by month (+)(+)
5. (CLASSICAL) 5th Line (symbol of President)	The 5th Line is very weak (–)(–)	The 5th Line is very weak & clashed and destroyed by month (–)(–)	The 5th line is strong & supported by month and the Great Combination of Three Elements. (+)(+)
6. (CLASSICAL) The text of I Ching	Disaster (–)(–)	Evil (–)(–)	Regret (–)
7. Final judgement	All are (–) or 13 (–), no (+). So, President died.	All is (–),or 12 (–),no (+). So, President died	3 (–), but 8 (+). So, President injured but escaped from murder finally

Analysis and Judgement

1. According to the time data and relative hexagrams and comparing the checklist table opposite, it is obvious that the two hexagrams of the first two Presidents, Lincoln and Kennedy, were very similar.

   1) In the Mei Hua method, the Subject trigram is destroyed by the Object trigram or the Subject trigram is weaker than the Object trigram, which is a symbol of extreme misfortune for the two Presidents.

   2) In the Na Jia method, the weak Self line is destroyed by the strong Response line, which is also an extremely unfortunate symbol for the two Presidents.

   3) In the Na Jia method, the Offspring line, representing the bodyguard, is weak or absent. So the two Presidents had no way to escape the calamity because there were no favourable factors to protect them (indeed, the vital factor, their bodyguards could not carry out their responsibility), but only those very strong unfavourable factors which directly destroyed them. This is an extremely unfortunate symbol for them.

   4) In the Classical method, in terms of image of line, the fifth line for the two Presidents, which generally represents emperor/president (see the previous chapter on Place of Line) is very weak, because it is destroyed by the earth month and earth year (Lincoln) or it is destroyed by the water month and the winter season (Kennedy) respectively. It is also an inauspicious symbol for the two Presidents.

   5) In the Classical method, the text on the hexagram and line from the I Ching definitely indicates disaster or misfortune with the Presidents.

2. Compared with the previous two cases, the attempted murder of President Reagan should have failed because his hexagram was totally different from those of the first two presidents. Let's compare it with those of the two previous presidents in terms of the four aspects as follows:

   1) In the Mei Hua method, the Subject trigram of the Final Hexagram is birthed by the Object trigram, an auspicious symbol for Reagan,

2) In the Na Jia method, although in Reagan's hexagram the relationship of Self line and Response line is still a destructive relationship, its outcome is completely contrary to those of the first two Presidents. In the case of Reagan, the Self line, which represents Reagan, is supported by month wood directly and supported by the very strong wood of Great Combination of Three Elements built up by the Rabbit month, Sheep day and Pig line. On the other hand, the Response line Rooster representing the murderer clashes with the month Rabbit (called line broken by month), so it is damaged terribly by month. So the outcome of the fight between the Self line and Response line is definitely clear: the very strong Self line will overcome the weak Response line absolutely. So the force competition between the two sides is the key determinant factor for the outcome of the conflict. The main reason why President Lincoln and President Kennedy died is that the Self line of their hexagram is much weaker than the Object line.

3) In the Classical method, when we look at the line image, the fifth line of Reagan's hexagram, which represents the President, it is much stronger than those of the previous two Presidents, because it is supported by the wood month and spring season,

4) In the Classical method, when we look at the line image, the Offspring line representing the bodyguard is strong and located at the central position (the fifth line) between Self line and Response line. So it is like a big block preventing the murderer from getting close to the President; and it effectively protected the President from the murder.

In short, there are a lot of favourable factors surrounding Reagan and they were more numerous and stronger than the unfavourable factors. Among them, there are three very important factors. Firstly, in the Mei Hua method, the Subject trigram representing Reagan is birthed by the Object trigram. Secondly, in the Na Jia method, the key Favourable line, or Offspring line is very strong and in a very good position, so it took the dangerous situation under control very quickly. Thirdly, the Self line, representing the President, is very strong. Thus President Reagan escaped being murdered in the end.

3. When I checked the text of the I Ching, I found that some text on the hexagram and line exactly indicates the outcome and the text on the changing line of Lincoln's hexagram clearly states: '*The Emperor will suffer from calamity ultimately.*' The emperor would refer to President Lincoln in this case. If we check the English translation version of the I Ching by Wilhelm, the original text of this line is: '*the ruler did not travel through the provinces ... misfortune from within and without ... in the end suffer a great defeat, disastrous for the ruler of the country for ten years.*' The text on the Response line of Kennedy's hexagram is: '*We see one to whose increase none will contribute, while many will seek to assail him ... There will be evil.*'

So far, with the integrated I Ching prediction method, I have demonstrated that the murders of the three Presidents could have been forecast, provided that I had known the timetable of the Presidents' activities before the tragedy happened. There are at least three reasons to support this assumption of mine. Firstly, the time, which is the basic and unique data for my calculation for this specific hexagram on the Presidents' activity and relative prediction, is always unchangeable. Secondly the hexagram on the Presidents' activity, which may be made by me at any time, is unchangeable, as the formula of drawing the hexagram is fixed and unique. Thirdly, the judgement on this specific prediction of the Presidents' murders is unchangeable, as the principle of judgement for this method is set up and relatively unchangeable (although it is flexible sometimes, the main general principle is fixed. E.g. in the Mei Hua method, a relationship that a strong Subject trigram is birthed by a strong Object trigram is always an auspicious symbol.). So based on the specific time data on the presidents' murders I may draw an identical hexagram and make the same prediction at any time, no matter when I draw it, either today or any day hundreds of years from now! E.g. the time of the murder of Lincoln is 10.15 p.m., 14 April 1865, or Pig hour of nineteenth day, third month in Ox year in the Chinese calendar. This data is fixed forever, so the Original hexagram Fu with sixth line changing drawn based on this data and calculated according to a fixed formula is also fixed. If I had conducted a prediction for President Lincoln days before the murder happened, I would have drawn an identical hexagram. Because the Mei Hua, Na Jia and Classical methods and the relevant principle of judgement on the hexagram were set up thousands of years ago, the result of judgement on the specific hexagram Fu with sixth line changing, made before the murder happened, would be completely the same as today. This is the reason why I can justify the I Ching method not only by forecasting cases, which may happen in the future, but also by analysing cases which happened many years ago.

Now I'd like to make an assumption: if President Lincoln and President Kennedy had consulted the I Ching, they might have learnt something, changed their timetable and escaped death. Thus the history of the US might have been different. Unfortunately, it is only my assumption. However, President Reagan did consult a famous astrologer in San Francisco before he attended any important event. I knew this from newspapers and it was confirmed by a memoir entitled *Reagan and Me* published in the late 1980s, written by the former Director of the White House Office and Minister of Finance. This was also confirmed by a publication by the First Lady, Nancy Reagan. I guess this is the answer for the great brain-teaser, Why is President Reagan the only President who acceded to his presidency in a year ending in '0', but escaped from murder. Although Reagan did not consult the I Ching, he did get help from another reliable ancient prediction method – western astrology! I believe the prediction of the astrologer was very close to the prediction from the I Ching. Although I don't know about western astrology in depth, I have tried to predict people's fate using both western astrology and eastern astrology, which originated from the I Ching, at the same time. The results are very similar. So, all roads lead to Rome, provided the direction is right. You may agree with me, when you read the story about the two predictions on the satellite launch. Although they were made by a Qigong master and by the I Ching method separately, the results were very similar.

Another question about the fates of President Lincoln and President Kennedy is why was it necessary for them to die before finishing their term as president? I will explore this interesting issue in my next book, and tell you how to understand people's fate with the Four Pillars method; about God's code for everybody, which is allocated to them as soon as they are born, which influences and determines their fate in all life processes.

Case 2. Win Money by Forecasting the Stock Index

On 23 July 2001, at 9.30 a.m., Ms Xiao asked me about the future trend of the stock index of the Shanghai Stock Market.

I did a forecast for her with the integrated method as follows:

Time data:

	HOUR	DAY	MONTH	YEAR
HEAVENLY STEM	+earth	−fire	−wood	−metal
EARTHLY BRANCH	Snake (earth)	Pig (water)	Sheep (earth)	Snake (fire)
TIME NUMBER	6	3	6	6

Original Hexagram			
Six Relatives	**Earthly Branch**	**Element**	**Hexagram**
Brother	Tiger	Wood	——— ▲
Parent	Rat	Water	— —
Wife	Dog	Earth	— —
Official	Rooster	Metal	——— O ✳
Parent	Pig	Water	———
Wife	Ox	Earth	— —

Final Hexagram			
Six Relatives	**Earthly Branch**	**Element**	**Hexagram**
Official	Tiger	Wood	———
Parent	Rat	Water	— —
Brother	Dog	Earth	— —
Brother	Horse	Fire	— —
Official	Dragon	Earth	———
Parent	Tiger	Wood	— —

Analysis and Judgement

1. With the Mei Hua method, the Subject trigram of the Original hexagram earth is destroyed by the Object trigram wood, which is very strong, as it is supported by water day, and the Half Great Combination of Three Elements, or Pig day and Sheep month. It is an inauspicious symbol, and means the stock index will fall a lot and continue to do so for several days.

2. With the Na Jia method, the Self line metal of the Original hexagram is Repaid Destroyed by the changing line Horse fire of the Final hexagram, which indicated that the Horse day (30 July) is the worst day with a big loss on the stock index, also the Wife line Ox directly clashes with the Sheep month (it is called line broken by month) and destroyed by a very strong Response line wood (Unfavourable line), which is very strong as it is supported by wood of Six Combine of Pig day and Response line Tiger and also wood of the Half Great Combination Three Elements, or Sheep month and Pig day,

3. With the Classical method, the name of the Original hexagram no. 18 Ku: Decay definitely indicates a sharp drop on the stock index, and the text of the hexagram also clearly implies saving money and waiting for improvement.

4. Timing, as everybody knows, is critically important in making decisions whether to buy or sell stock and it is also the most difficult problem and the biggest challenge for every market forecaster. So I estimated it using three I Ching methods together.
   - Firstly with the Na Jia method, the valley bottom of the daily line of the stock index, or the lowest point, should be on the Horse day (30 July), which is the best time to buy stock. The changing line shows very clearly (the metal of Self line in the Original hexagram is directly Repaid Destroyed by the new Horse line in the Final hexagram). The turning point should be the first metal day, or Monkey day (1 August) because it can overcome the Unfavourable line wood (it is also Response line), and supports the Self line metal. So the index drop will continue till the seventh day of the market (the space is 7 days from Pig day to Sheep day). Then it stops dropping and starts to go up on the eighth day (the first metal day is Monkey day, or eighth day from the Pig day).
   - Secondly with the Mei Hua method, as the Subject trigram earth is destroyed by the Object trigram wood, as long as the wood is controlled by metal day the situation may be improved. The first metal day is Monkey day; also the Subject trigram is Ken, no. 7, so it indicated the turning point is seven days later.

- Finally with the Classical method, the text on the hexagram states accurately: '*Carrying out what his father wants to work is a good thing, of course, it will benefit him. After his consideration in seven days he begins to know how to do it.*' (quoted from *A New Translation of the I Ching* by Luo Zhiye, Qingdao Publishing House, China 1995). If based on the original I Ching in Chinese, the ancient words indicate: '*Three days before the yang wood day and three days after the yang wood day*'. It also indicated definitely that the Monkey day (1 August) is the turning point of the fall of the stock index line. Because the Heavenly Stem of Horse day (30 July) is yang wood based on the thousand-year calendar, or the Horse day is the yang wood day, then the Monkey day is the third day after the Horse day. (You may prove it by checking the Chinese calendar, or the thousand-year calendar.)

5. Based on my analysis above, I immediately drew a daily line diagram for forecasting the stock index trend in the next eight days as follows.

   What is the actual result? From the day I conducted the forecast, there was a continued fall in the stock index for seven days with a drop of 222 points (from 2178 to 1956, or 10.2%). It was the most serious continual fall of the stock index in such a short period of one week for the previous five years. However, Ms Xiao won a lot from this big change due to having my correct forecast in advance.

   You may check and prove my forecast of the daily line diagram of the stock index by comparing it with the real line of the daily stock index for the eight days shown overleaf.

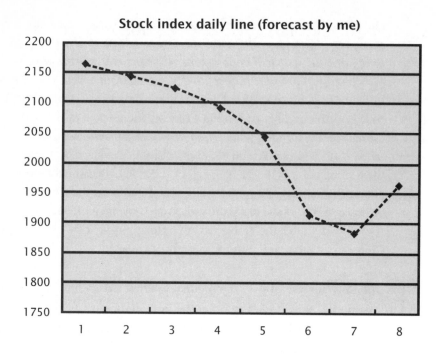

Stock index daily line (forecast by me)

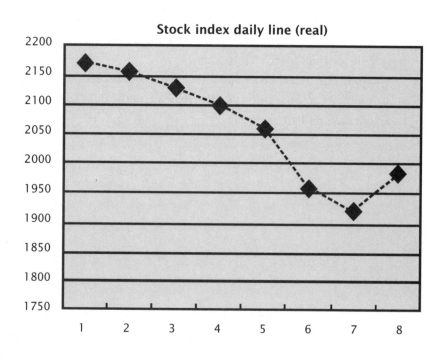

Stock index daily line (real)

Case 3. Comparison of Pearl Harbor and the World Trade Center Attack

In this case, let's compare and analyse two attacks on the USA with world-wide impact that have happened in the last six decades (60 years is a meaningful cycle based on the Chinese calendar as I shall describe later); the terrorist attack on the World Trade Center and the Pentagon in 2001, and the surprise attack on Pearl Harbor in 1941.

Time data:

Pearl Harbor attack: Hawaii, 7.49–9.45 a.m. 7 December 1941.

WTC & Pentagon terrorist attacks: New York and Washington DC, 8.45– 9.40 a.m. 11 September 2001.

Pearl Harbor				
	HOUR	DAY	MONTH	YEAR
HEAVENLY STEM	+earth	−earth	−earth	−metal
EARTHLY BRANCH	Dragon	Ox (earth)	Pig (water)	Snake (fire)
TIME NUMBER	5	19	10	6

WTC and Pentagon				
	HOUR	DAY	MONTH	YEAR
HEAVENLY STEM	+wood	−fire	−metal	−metal
EARTHLY BRANCH	Dragon	Ox (earth)	Rooster (metal)	Snake (fire)
TIME NUMBER	5	24	7	6

Comparing the data in the tables above, it shows that the two cases are very similar as follows:

- The Heavenly Stem and Earthly Branch of the years of both events are identical, the Heavenly Stems are yin metal and the Earthly Branches are Snake, yin fire. (The time between them is sixty years. Based on the Chinese calendar the same year will repeat again after a sixty-year cycle.) So certain similar events might repeat again sixty years later.

- The days of both events are also very similar. Both Earthly Branches are Ox day, yin earth. The months are different, however both of their characters are yin elements in Heavenly Stems and Earthly Branches.
- The year always has a great impact on the development of events and matters in the world. Because in the two years (1941 and 2001), the relationship between Heavenly Stem – yin metal and Earthly Branch yin fire is complete conflict and battle (yin fire always fights with yin metal), it means that a huge battle might happen in this year.
- In the two events, all the three groups of main time data, the year, month and day, are yin element in Heavenly Stems and Earthly Branches. Compared with yang, the general symbols of the yin element imply dark, blackness, sneakiness, negativity and grief. So the energy of the universe on that day was too yin and seriously lacking in yang, the balance and harmony of yin–yang was completely lost. When such an imbalance happens in the universe, there might be huge violent conflicts and bloody tragedies taking place on that particular date.
- As the two events happened at Dragon hour, which is a very powerful flying animal with a fierce and cruel temper, it indicates that a terrible fight in the sky might happen at this time considering the three time factors, year, month and day I mentioned above.

Based on the analysis and comparing the time data for the two events above, we can understand the reason why the two tragedies are so similar. Let's probe the two cases in depth with the I Ching method.

Firstly we draw hexagrams for the two cases with the Mei Hua method, or calculating the number of time. Then we match them with the earthly branches and Six Relatives according to the principle of the Na Jia method as follows.

Pearl Harbor Incident

Original Hexagram			
Six Relatives	**Earthly Branch**	**Element**	**Hexagram**
Official	Snake	Fire	——
Parent	Sheep	Earth	— —
Brother	Rooster	Metal	—— O ✲
Wife	Rabbit	Wood	— —
Official	Snake	Fire	— —
Parent	Sheep	Earth	— — ▲

Final Hexagram			
Six Relatives	**Earthly Branch**	**Element**	**Hexagram**
Wife	Tiger	Wood	——
Offspring	Rat	Water	— —
Parent	Dog	Earth	— —
Wife	Rabbit	Wood	— —
Official	Snake	Fire	— —
Parent	Sheep	Earth	— —

Based on the principle of the Na Jia method, we do the analysis as follows:

1) Official Line – the sixth line, Snake fire. The Official line is a general symbol of authority, so it is the first Favourable line, the symbol of the victim of the event, Pearl Harbor, USA. It is very weak because it is the line broken by month (the Snake fire clashed with and was destroyed by the month Pig water). As it is the sixth line located at the top of the hexagram, it is too high to be safe, just as the text states that 'arrogant dragon causes to repent'. (See text for the sixth line of the Chien hexagram). In terms of its political, economic and military status, the USA was the top of the world.

2) Parent Line – the fifth line Sheep earth. It is a symbol of authority with great power to protect people, so it is the symbol of the navy base at Pearl Harbor. It is also a Favourable line. It is very weak because it is terribly destroyed by strong wood produced by the Great Combination of Three Elements built up by Pig month, Rabbit line and Sheep line, which is an invisible changing line.

3) Brother Line – the fourth line Rooster metal. The general symbol of Brother line is competitor, match or enemy. In this case it is the symbol

of the Japanese armada, the sneaky enemy, so it is the first Unfavourable line. It is very strong because it is supported by the Great Combination of Three Elements of the year Snake, the changing line Rooster and the day Ox. (Although the fourth line is also Self line, we don't see it as the USA but as Japan in this case. The judgement on the Favourable or Unfavourable line is relatively flexible and needs to be considered comprehensively. It is easy to understand that since we see the Official line fire as our first Favourable line for the USA, its opposition element metal, the Brother line should be the Unfavourable line.)

4) Response Line – the first line Sheep. The general symbol of the Response line is the event/matter concerning us, so we see it also as the symbol of the Japanese armada in this case. It is located at the bottom of the hexagram, which implies that the armada of Japan is hidden in the deep, the tricky enemy in the shadows will start up a sneak attack.

5) If we look at the image of the Original hexagram, the upper trigram is Li, fire and the lower trigram is Kun earth. It is the symbol of the navy base of the USA completely destroyed by the Japanese army and a huge fire burning covering Pearl Harbor represented by the earth trigram.

6) If we check the force of the trigram with the Mei Hua method, the Subject trigram (representing the US navy base) earth is very weak. It is destroyed by the great wood produced by the Great Combination of Three Elements built up by Pig month, Rabbit line, Sheep line of the Original hexagram. It indicates that the loss to the USA is extremely heavy due to its navy base being completely destroyed by the Japanese army.

7) If we look at the year – the Snake fire – we see the symbol of the great energy of the universe, which influences all events in the world. It is the symbol of the international community in this case. It supports the Official line Snake fire, which represents the USA, and destroys the Brother line, which represents the Japanese army. So it means that the international community and the UN represented by the year strongly supports the USA and condemns the surprise attack by Japan represented by the Brother line metal. Although this surprise attack was successful, Japan will pay a great price for it in the future.

WTC & Pentagon Incident

Original Hexagram			
Six Relatives	**Earthly Branch**	**Element**	**Hexagram**
Official	Rabbit	Wood	—— *
Parent	Snake	Fire	——
Brother	Sheep	Earth	– – o
Brother	Ox	Earth	– –
Official	Rabbit	Wood	——
Parent	Snake	Fire	—— ▲

Final Hexagram			
Six Relatives	**Earthly Branch**	**Element**	**Hexagram**
Wife	Rat	Water	– –
Brother	Dog	Earth	——
Offspring	Monkey	Metal	– –
Brother	Ox	Earth	– –
Official	Rabbit	Wood	——
Parent	Snake	Fire	——

Based on the principle of the Na Jia method, we do the analysis as follows:

1) Official Line – the sixth line, Rabbit wood. The Official line is a general symbol of authority, so it is the most favourable line, the symbol of the victim of the event, the WTC and the Pentagon in the USA. It is very weak because it is not only the line broken by month (the Rabbit wood clashes with and is destroyed by the month Rooster metal) but is also destroyed by the strong metal of the Great Combination of Three Elements built up by the year Snake, month Rooster and day Ox. As it is the sixth line and located at the top of the hexagram, it is too high to be safe, just like the text said 'arrogant dragon causes to repent'. (See text for the sixth line of the Chien hexagram). The WTC, with its twin towers, was famous as the highest skyscraper at over 400m high.

2) Parent Line – the fifth line Snake fire. It is a symbol of authority with great power to protect people, so it is the symbol of the WTC and the Pentagon, the USA's defence building. So it is also a Favourable line. It is very weak because it is terribly destroyed by strong metal produced by

the Great Combination of Three Elements built up by year Snake, Rooster month and Ox day. (It is worth noting that generally speaking, fire should destroy metal, but if the fire is too weak to control metal, it will be seriously injured by metal. It is just like a very weak policeman who cannot capture a very strong robber and might be killed by the robber.)

3) Offspring Line – the fourth line of the Final hexagram metal. The general symbol of the Offspring line is child, employee and soldier, however because it destroys the Official line, the most favourable line wood representing the USA, we see it as the first Unfavourable line and the symbol of the terrorist hijackers in this case. It is the strongest metal because it is supported by the great metal of Great Combination of Three Elements built up by the year, month and day.

4) Response Line – the first line Snake. The general symbol of the Response line is the matter concerning us, so we see it as the symbol of the terrorist hijackers in this case. It is located at the bottom of the hexagram which implies that they are hidden in the deep; the tricky enemy in the shadows will start up surprise attacks on the WTC and the Pentagon.

5) If we look at the image of the Original hexagram, the upper trigram is Sun. Although its general meaning is wind, it is also the symbol of aircraft because when an aircraft is flying it is like a wind blowing through the sky. The lower trigram is Tui, the lake, however its element is metal (the twin towers of the WTC were steel structures) and is also the symbol of something like a big building broken down based on the essential concept of Eight Basic Trigrams. So it is the picture of the steel sky-scraper collapsing after the crash of the aircraft.

6) If we check the trigram of the hexagram with the Mei Hua method, although the Subject trigram metal is very strong, unfortunately the final outcome is exhaustion because the Subject trigram metal births the Object trigram water in the Final hexagram. It implies that although the USA is the strongest country it will lose a lot from these terrorist attacks.

7) If we look at the year – Snake fire, it is the symbol of the great energy of the universe, which always greatly influences events in the world. It is a symbol of the international community and the UN in this case. It supports the Favourable line – the Parent line Snake fire, which represents the USA and destroys the Unfavourable line – the Offspring

metal representing terrorism. So it indicates that the international community and the UN firmly supports the USA and condemns the surprise attacks by international terrorism represented by the Offspring line metal. So although the terrorist attacks on the WTC and the Pentagon were well organised and successful, international terrorism will pay a relative price for it in the future.

Comparing the two cases above by analysis of the Na Jia method and the Mei Hua method, you may find that there are several similarities. They are as follows:

A) The first Favourable line, the Official line representing the USA is very weak and always at the top location, which is a dangerous position, too high to be safe.
B) The Response line is always located at the bottom of the hexagram, which is too low to be obvious, so it is the symbol of the enemy in the shadows.
C) Comparing the force of the two sides, the first Favourable line is very weak but the first Unfavourable line is very strong, which indicates the sneak attacks will be successful.
D) Inspecting the force of the trigram with the Mei Hua method, the Subject trigram representing the USA is very weak, which implies that the USA will suffer greatly from these attacks.
E) Checking the year, it determinedly supported the Favourable line, which indicates that the USA can obtain support from the international community eventually.

Based on the similar points above, our conclusions about the process and outcome of the two events are very similar: the USA lost a lot of lives and money from the surprise terrorist attacks, which were earthshaking disasters with great worldwide impact. Due to its support by the international community, the USA will recover from these attacks soon and the Japanese army and international terrorism will pay their relative price for their surprise attacks eventually.

Of course there are some differences in the hexagrams for the two cases, because they have their specific situations. They are symbols flexibly representing the Japanese army and terrorism respectively, however the differences do not influence the general judgement of the last outcome for the two cases.

When we check the judgement with the Classical method further, we will find some meaningful indications. The texts on the lines of the hexagrams are as follows:

Pearl Harbor incident: the Original hexagram is no. 35: Chin. The text on this changing line is: '*One advances like a marmot* (burrowing rodent), *however firm and correct it may be, the position is extremely dangerous.*' Everybody knows the navy base of the USA (admiralty port) seems as firm as possible, however it is dangerous indeed when they are unaware, because the enemy can make a successful surprise attack. The Japanese armada (including submarines) approached Pearl Harbor stealthily, like a marmot advances underground.

WTC and Pentagon incident: the Original hexagram is no. 61: Chung Fu. The text on the changing line is: '*A crowing rooster tries to mount to heaven, even with firm correctness, there will be terrible misfortune.*' The twin towers of the WTC were so high that they seemed to be in heaven and firm enough. But when the terrorist hijackers attacked them with aeroplanes, the unbelievable tragedy occurred. The aeroplanes crashed into the WTC and the Pentagon just like crazy roosters and the noisy crowing of the rooster is like the explosion of the planes. The terrorist attacks are just like an urgent alarm call of a rooster crowing at dawn, which has awakened not only the USA, but also the whole world to take united action against terrorism and protect the peace of the world. The hijackers tried to mount the sky and bring huge tragedy, so here is the metaphor of the crowing rooster to symbolise the planes instead of the silent marmot, which appeared in the case of Pearl Harbor and symbolised the Japanese armada. It is worth noting that in Chinese, the aeroplane and rooster are the same sound – 'Ji'. Chinese people are keen on puns and they have always liked to make puns about aeroplanes and roosters since the aeroplane appeared in the world. Sometimes when Chinese people say rooster, in fact, they are actually talking about an aeroplane.

Please note that although the metaphors for the two cases based on the I Ching are different, however the eventual indications are very similar and both are absolutely inauspicious. One indicated extreme danger and the other indicated terrible misfortune. In terms of the different metaphors of the I Ching, they are also perfectly appropriate to the particular situation for the two cases respectively. Because the text was written several thousand years ago, it was impossible for the ancient Chinese to know about the aeroplane, submarine and skyscraper, so they described the activities of animals such as the rodent and rooster as metaphors to symbolise modern events in their oracle.

Satellite and Missile Launch

On 14 August 1992, at 8.00 a.m., after consulting Master Chen, the famous Chinese Qigong Master, and carefully adjusting the original schedule of the satellite launch and choosing the best time, China launched satellite 'Long March No. II' successfully. According to a Chinese newspaper report, Master Chen was awarded a prize of 200,000 yuan (or US $24,000) from the relevant sector in charge of the satellite launch for his great contribution to the timing of the launch.

I checked the time data of the satellite launch, and got a hexagram to confirm that the Master's recommendation was correct. I made a judgement using the Classical method, mainly by checking the text of the hexagram and the line from the I Ching, however I created the hexagram not by coin casting, but by the Mei Hua method (calculating the time data based on a fixed formula). This is very common when we conduct the Classical method. The Original hexagram is the hexagram Sheng (no. 46) or Ascending with the first line changing.

Original Hexagram	Final Hexagram
▬▬ ▬▬ ▬▬ ▬▬ ▬▬▬▬▬ ▬▬▬▬▬ *	▬▬ ▬▬ ▬▬ ▬▬ ▬▬▬▬▬ ▬▬▬▬▬

The name of the hexagram very clearly indicated ascending to the sky. (Please always pay attention to the name of the hexagram you draw, which often gives you a very concise and distinct answer in one word. I will remind you of this again in later cases.) The text on the changing line is *'allowing to ascend, or welcomed in his advance upwards, great good fortune.'* It indicates very clearly that it is the best time to launch the satellite. The Final hexagram is T'ai (no. 11), the Peace hexagram; its name also means that the final outcome will definintely be a great success.

Failed Satellite Launch

According to a short report in a Chinese newspaper, *The Digest Weekly* of 13 February 1995, on 26 January 1995, at about 6.40 a.m. the Satellite Launching Centre of China failed to launch a satellite called 'Asia and Pacific No. II'. Only 49 seconds after departure the satellite exploded in the sky, then it fell and crashed into a local farmer's house, killing all six members of the family instantly. I checked the time when the satellite was launched, and got the hexagram by the Mei Hua method or calculation of time again. The Original hexagram is Kou (no. 44), Coming to Meet, with the fifth line changing.

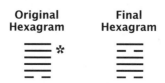

|Original Hexagram|Final Hexagram|

The text on the changing line is: *'A melon covered with willow leaves, hidden lines, then an aerolite descended from the sky (!!)'* Please note the last six words in the sentence. The satellite was a real aerolite fallen from the sky when it failed to enter its orbit! The word 'descending' is extraordinarily interesting as it is the antonym of the word 'ascending' which, in the I Ching, described the first case of the satellite Long March No. II. If you read the I Ching in English translation, it is difficult to find the word 'aerolite' in this line as quoted above. For example, James Legge's translation of the text of this line is: *'a good issue will descend as from heaven.'* So the great English translator translated the 'aerolite' as 'good issue', which descended from the sky. Richard Wilhelm's translation is: *'A melon covered with willow leaves, hidden lines, then it drops down to one from heaven.'* The great German translator translated it as a melon. However, I checked it directly from the original I Ching in ancient Chinese, and the last words of ancient Chinese in this line's text are only four ancient Chinese words: '(an) aerolite descends from sky.' So it is a serious warning for translators who want to help people comprehensively understand the I Ching to be careful when they translate this most complex book. Generally speaking, many words of text in the I Ching on hexagrams and lines are metaphorical, however before we try to interpret the metaphorical meaning, the best way is first to translate the original meaning of the text. Furthermore, in terms of interpreting and understanding the I Ching, the text may be interpreted and understood as different symbols in different situations. You should fully consider the specific situation to get the best interpretation. For example, when our question was whether the satellite would be launched success-fully, the assumption is that everybody hopes it will be *ascending* to the sky instead of *descending* from heaven. So the auspicious symbol and inauspicious symbol are also comparative concepts.

When I did the analysis above, I felt sadness and regret for the person who was in charge of that failed launch and made the last stupid decision. That tragedy, with a large waste of money and loss of six innocent lives, could have been prevented, if only they had consulted the I Ching before making the timetable for the satellite launch. At least they heard the story from their colleagues on the successful launch of Long March No. II due to consulting Master Chen, and should learn something from the wise people who consulted Master Chen to guarantee a successful launch.

Disaster with Large Death Toll

While this book was being written, a terrible disaster shocked the whole of China. On August 2 2001 an article entitled 'Up to 300 may be trapped in tin mine in south China' in *China Daily*, the English language newspaper, reported that:

> Over 200 miners and technicians have been trapped in the Nandan mine in Gangxi Province of China. The accident was caused by water stored in a nearby mine rushing into the mine where the victims were working.

The local TV reported on Monday in a news flash that over 300 people were trapped in a mine of Nandan county. The mine should have been shut since local sources within Nandan county said management of the mines was poor and mishaps have occurred before. But county authorities have not taken action because the tin mines are the major source of local income. Two weeks after the accident, it is confirmed that the disaster happened at 3.30 a.m., 17 July 2001.

I was shocked by this miserable news and also could not help wondering what the hexagram drawn from that time would tell us. I want to study this case in depth to provide more evidence for my readers to justify the method of creating hexagrams according to the time data of when an important event will happen so that we may prevent it in advance. As I mentioned in a previous chapter, because there is a necessary or inevitable correlation between a specific time and an event, it is possible to precisely predict this event according to the specific time using the Mei Hua method, which can uncover the special correlation between time and event. This is the basic theory for our method. I want you to fully understand and trust that there is an inevitable correlation between time and event, and I always want to give you more examples to justify it.

This Original hexagram drawn based on the time data (3.30 a.m., 17 July 2001) is the Hsu hexagram (no. 5): Waiting, with fifth line changing and the Final hexagram is T'ai (no. 11) Peace:

| Original Hexagram | Final Hexagram |

These hexagrams are interesting enough as a special hexagram has appeared again in the Final hexagram T'ai (no. 11), or Peace. You may remember it appeared previously at least twice. The first time, it symbolised an ancient prince's good luck, which is an auspicious symbol because the text on this hexagram is very good. The second time, it symbolised a father's death (see page 64), which is a symbol of misfortune because the image of the hexagram is like an old man buried under the earth. In this case, I think it implies very clearly that there are a number of men (the Chien trigram is the male symbol and all the miners are male) buried under the earth (the Kun trigram means earth and the mine is underground). If you look at the Original hexagram and the Final hexagram, their images indicate the process of the disaster from beginning to end very precisely. At the beginning of the accident, the water flowed into the mine and soon flooded and covered the mine hence all the miners were flooded by the water. The image of the Original hexagram is Kan, the water trigram (representing the flood) above and Chien, heaven trigram (representing the miners) below. In the end, all the miners, who failed to escape from the disaster, were killed. The Final hexagram shows that the miners (represented by the Chien trigram) were buried under the mine (represented by the Kun, earth trigram).

From this analysis, you can understand also how important it is for our judgement to inspect the image of the hexagram.

When analysing this case I did it by looking at the image of the hexagram and inspecting its symbol and change, and not by using other methods such as Mei Hua (except to create the hexagram) and Na Jia. However, I checked another famous ancient book – *The Forest of I Ching*, written by the great scholar, Master Jiao Gan (in the Western Han Dynasty, 206 BCE–23 AD) who was the personal tutor of Master Jin Fang, the great initiator of the Na Jia method. As I mentioned previously, the *Forest of I Ching* by Jiao has been one of the important methods of I Ching prediction in China, so I consult it often. Based on the *Forest of I Ching* by Jiao, the short oracle poem on the hexagram Hsu with fifth line changing says: '*Under the despot king Chu, the people are exhausted from awful exploitation. A disaster happened from stream of Chien due to an evil action by the brother of king. People run and tried to flee from this disaster, however they died in pig's (water) room eventually.*' I was too astounded and amazed to calm myself when I read this poem. It is the actual situation of this disaster. Based on the continuing media reports on this disaster it appeared that before getting the job every miner had to sign an extremely unfair contract with the boss of the mine because they were so poor. According to a reporter who got the contract from Ms Wei, the wife of one of the victims, the contract stated clearly that: 'If the miner dies when he is working in the mine, his family will get nothing from the mine authority except for 20,000 yuan (or US $2,400). There is no economic or legal responsibility on the part of the mine's authority for the miner's death.' When you know the process and the cause of the disaster, it is possible to see the boss of the mine and his management staff as the despot king and his evil brothers as symbolised in the ancient oracle poem.

Let's come back to the real world in Nandan county, where attempts by grass-roots officials to cover up the disaster alarmed the central government of China. The death toll remained unconfirmed for more than two weeks after the accident. But locals feared up to 200 may have died when workers drilled into a shaft filled with water to prevent a collapse, flooding the mine. The Chinese Premier Zhu Rongji has vowed to hold provincial leaders responsible for major accidents at facilities administered by them. So China's central government sent an investigation team to determine the truth behind the accident. The team investigating the 17 July flooding of the Nandan mine said the county's top officials were being held responsible for the disaster. A Chinese paper, *Southern Weekend*, reported that the Longquan Mining Ore Company had tried to cover up the disaster by paying families of the victims 20,000 yuan (US $2,400) each and using strong arm tactics to get the families to sign waivers vowing secrecy. Meanwhile many of the dead miners had been difficult to identify because they carried no official papers and were believed to be migrant workers.

Five top officials of Nandan county in the Guangxi province were either dismissed from their posts or suspended from duties after that tin mine disaster. Seventy alleged gang members and twenty employees of a tin mine company were arrested a day after it was revealed that there was collusion between gangsters and local officials to cover up the mine accident. It is reported that the tin mine industry accounts for 70 per cent of local government revenue and mine owner Li Dongming, who is under arrest, is said to have personal wealth of about one billion yuan (US $120 million).

Chapter Nine

Questions and Answers

1. How do you make a correct judgement if the results of predictions from different methods conflict?

This is a very common question. Everybody has had this experience: before making a very important decision, we like to consult several people to get more useful comments and suggestions. The people you consult are probably from different sectors and have different viewpoints. So the comments and suggestions are likely to conflict with each other. The more people you consult, the more complex the answers from them may be. It is very similar to the situation when you consult the I Ching by different methods. If you asked the same question with the Mei Hua method, Na Jia method and Classical method separately at the same time, you might get a positive answer from Mei Hua, but a negative answer from Na Jia, and a neutral answer from the Classical method. What can you do if you face this kind of situation? There are several alternative ways to be recommended.

- Compare the force of the two sides in quantity and quality. If there are two positive answers from two methods (e.g. Mei Hua and Na Jia methods), but only one negative answer from one method (e.g. Classical method), generally speaking you should agree with the positive judgement. The more important thing is to inspect the degree and intensity for the two sides. Sometimes there is one negative answer, and two positive answers, but you take the negative answer instead of the positive one provided the negative answer is extremely bad such as an indication of a big disaster/tragedy. Based on the same principle, if there is one extremely good answer and two slightly negative answers, you may select the positive one.

- Pay special attention to any significant foreboding which suddenly comes to you just at the specific moment when you are conducting a prediction. For example if you hear somebody suddenly cry in a very sad voice, it is inauspicious; if you hear somebody suddenly laugh with a cheerful voice, it is auspicious. Sometimes a significant foreboding is a more important symbol than any hexagrams. One extremely inauspicious foreboding may counteract three good symbols of a hexagram and one wonderful foreboding is able to offset several bad symbols of a hexagram.

- Just wait patiently, and avoid making a final decision straight away. You need to ask again. When the symbols from the first time you ask are not very clear, perhaps it was interfered with by some factors from the outside or you may have failed to keep calm when conducting that prediction, or maybe the significant foreboding has not appeared, so you may wait for another chance. Generally speaking you may get the chance soon as long as you sincerely respect the I Ching method.

- Seek help from other reliable prediction methods available to confirm your first judgement. The suggested methods are western astrology, face-reading, palm-reading, the Four Pillars method etc. Based on my experience, the Four Pillars method is the best one. In fact, I have often made I Ching predictions combined with the Four Pillars analysis and have achieved great success with this strategy.

2. If asking the same question with the Mei Hua method and the Na Jia method simultaneously, can we create hexagrams in different ways? E.g. can we draw a hexagram by time calculation with the Mei Hua method and draw another hexagram by coin casting with the Na Jia method?

Yes, but you should conduct the coin casting before you do the time calculation in order to make sure that your mind is completely calm and equable when you do the coin casting and avoid interfering because of the result of the time calculation. If you do the time calculation first, you might know the hexagram and relevant judgement from the Mei Hua method before you start the coin casting; whether it is positive or negative, the result of the Mei

Hua method might affect you and then it might be difficult to smoothly conduct the next process of coin casting, which always requires absolute peace of mind. Otherwise you might get a worrying hexagram from the coin casting eventually. And relatively, the time calculation is just an objective formula procedure and is not influenced by the subjective emotion of an individual. So you should do the coin casting first, then conduct the time calculation.

3. What is the meaning of the changing line?

It is always a very valuable indicator in the Na Jia method and needs to be paid special attention. Its general meaning is as follows:

- Providing you with a right answer directly, especially when there is only one line changed, just as in the Mei Hua method. Sometimes you can get a very clear answer from reading the text of the changing line by checking the I Ching directly.
- Directly representing the matter/event concerned and you can find the development/changing trend and process by inspecting and analysing the line carefully.
- Representing the third important force of impact on the line besides the time factors. A weak Self line may become strong due to accepting support from the changing line; or on the other hand a strong Response line may become weak due to being destroyed by the changing line.
- Indicating some specific details associated with the target matter/ event, such as time, direction, particular character/attributes of an article or a person etc.
- Implies that the original changing line will become stronger due to its movement (changing line means movement). If the changing line is weak originally, it will become strong; if it is strong originally, it will become stronger, e.g. you drew a hexagram in Tiger month, and the changing line of the hexagram is metal Rooster. The Rooster line should be very weak if it had not moved, because the metal is weak in the month of spring season. However it becomes strong due to its movement. When a line changes, this means it is actively moving with energy and is able to escape from any control and destruction.

4. What is the invisible moving/changing line and its significance?

As I mentioned, the changing line is a significant indicator for our prediction judgement. There is another kind of line, which is as important as the changing line. It is the invisible moving/changing line. It also means movement of the line. The difference is that it is invisible. We refer to it as the invisible moving line provided the line was originally still but directly clashed with the Earthly Branch of the day, when you drew the hexagram. E.g. If you drew a hexagram on a Rabbit day, the line of Rooster in your hexagram is the invisible moving line because it directly clashed with the Rabbit day. (See the Six Clash Relationship of Earthly Branch in the previous chapter). However I must remind you that there is an important precondition: the Rooster line is not extremely weak originally. If it is too weak (such as a Rooster line in Horse month) and clashes with the Earthly Branch of the day, we don't see it as the invisible moving line, instead it is line broken by day. The line broken by day is an extremely weak line and is always a negative symbol.

5. Which prediction method is best if there is an urgent need to make an immediate decision? If, for example, at the last minute before boarding an aeroplane, you get information to persuade you to give up this flight for a special reason, should you change your mind?

If you are very familiar with the Mei Hua method, you may draw a hexagram in a few minutes (sometimes you can get a hexagram without any calculation with pen and paper and instead can estimate it in your mind. Please see the previous chapter on different swift ways of creating hexagrams on page 93 – on guessing a brother's age). Then you get a swift judgement very quickly. If you are highly intuitive and experienced in assessing foreboding, you may make a judgement according to any foreboding you observe, which might just be a sudden sense or feeling or an idea flashing into your mind. There is another alternative. Some people conduct a very simple coin casting to make a quick judgement. You throw one coin once, then make a decision based on the side of the falling coin. The judgement standard may be set up by you in advance, e.g. it is seen as a positive symbol when it is heads, but a negative symbol when it is tails.

6. How do you calculate the time data to do a prediction with the Mei Hua method when the month is a Leap month?

This is a big problem. If people aren't familiar with the Chinese calendar system, they often make mistakes in this situation. In this case, there are thirteen months in one year, or two duplicated months. There are two fifth months in 2001, or after the fourth month, there are two fifth months following, then the next month is the sixth month. The second fifth month is named Leap fifth month. The principle of the Mei Hua method is that in a Leap month that you should calculate the number based on the number of the Leap month, but you must put the Earthly Branch into the time data table strictly according to the Twelve Seasons' Festival (Every Seasons' Festival is a specific date representing the starting point of the relative month, which is easy to locate in the Chinese calendar). This is a very important concept which is never affected by the appearance of Leap month. For example, on 13 July 2001 you conduct a Mei Hua prediction. Based on the thousand-year calendar this day is in Leap fifth month, and the time data is:

	HOUR	DAY	*MONTH*	YEAR
HEAVENLY STEM	–wood	–fire	*–wood*	–metal
EARTHLY BRANCH	Snake (fire)	Ox (earth)	*Sheep (earth)*	Snake (fire)
TIME NUMBER	6	23	*5*	6

So in this Leap fifth month (which would be sixth month if there had not been the Leap month), you should take 5 as the month number to do the calculation and get a hexagram. But, you must put the sixth month's Earthly Branch (Sheep) instead of that of fifth month's Earthly Branch fire (Horse) into your time data table to consider the impact of the month on the hexagram. Because 13 July is after the Season Festival Xiao Shu, which is 7 July and means the starting point of the Sheep month, so the Leap fifth month should be seen as Sheep month. Please be careful, as the outcomes of predictions are totally different when you put the sixth Sheep month (earth element) into the table and when you put the fifth Horse month (fire element) into the table.

Another very common confusion, which is similar to the one above, concerns the starting point of the year. Based on the Chinese calendar, the starting point of the year is neither in accordance with the first day of January in the western calendar, nor the first day of the first month (Tiger month) in the Chinese calendar. It is the Season Festival Li Chuan and its Chinese meaning is Start of Spring. It is always in accordance with the date of 4 or 5 February in the western calendar (see page 33).

7. How do you use time data to calculate hexagrams and make judgements, when conducting the Mei Hua method in different places in the world, such as the USA or South Africa, and so on?

Generally speaking you should directly translate the data of Local Time in the western calendar into the Chinese calendar and find the Heavenly Stem and Earthly Branch by checking the thousand-year calendar.

E.g. About 2.35 p.m., 30 March 1981 (Washington time), President Reagan left the Hilton Hotel in Washington DC. If you want to predict Reagan's safety issue with the Mei Hua method, you should take the time data from Washington time and translate it into the Chinese calendar and find the Heavenly Stem and Earthly Branch by checking the thousand-year calendar. Then continue with your next prediction procedure. But I don't have personal experience of practising this method in the southern hemisphere. I guess that the system of the Chinese calendar is not relevant to the southern hemisphere. The reason is not only because the seasons in the southern hemisphere are completely opposite those in the northern hemisphere, but also because the Heavenly Stem and Earthly Branch should be matched to every day for this area in a completely different order. It is a very big question indeed. However, special research should be done to solve the question for the application of the I Ching method in the southern hemisphere, no matter how difficult it may be.

8. How can you use the I Ching method as an important guide for feng shui practice?

It is quite complex, however it is also a very good question. In order to answer this question, I'd like to remind you that direction and time are two essential concepts for feng shui assessment and remedy. So my answer will focus on these two points.

Firstly, it is a vital key point to identify the right direction for a particular client. However, the direction is by no means only focused on house location or arrangement of furniture, as many people think, as this is a very superficial understanding of feng shui indeed. The direction should refer to the energy or chi of the universe; it is represented not only by geographic location in a relatively limited area, such as house location and furniture arrangement, but also by the impact of a large area such as a country, or a continent. Furthermore, the most important thing is that it is represented and influenced by the Five Elements, which include matters from a very wide area such as career/ profession, diet, favourable colours, lifestyle, social relationships and so on. In short, it should be represented by everything in the wide physical and mental environment surrounding people, from both without and within. So it is quite difficult to find out what is the most necessary element for a particular person and even more difficult to find the right feng shui remedy for them. Even though, in terms of the concept of direction in a narrow sense, such as the direction of house location and furniture arrangement, some people also make the wrong decision due to not knowing what is the necessary element for a specific person. For example, when the most favourable element for a man who was ill and wanted to move to a better house, is metal, you suggest that he buys a beautiful house with a good landscape in the south. And you advise him to have his front door facing south, (it is a common viewpoint to prefer the south as the front door's direction). It seems that you have given good feng shui advice to the man, but in fact you have made a terrible mistake. You may kill the man if he accepts your recommendation!

Secondly, with regard to time in feng shui, it is important to look at the changeable impact of the universe's energy on a particular person in a specific period. Because the energy/chi of the universe is always changing, so the impact on a person is also very changeable. It is better to represent it and estimate it carefully by Five Element analysis with the Heavenly Stem and Earthly Branch system of the Chinese calendar.

Before you give any advice on feng shui remedies to your client, the top priority is to identify and clarify what is the key favourable element for the specific client. So long as you find it, you may give correct advice to them, otherwise you may mislead your client, so we should take great care to identify the key element to make the correct feng shui remedy. But as I mentioned above, as there are so many factors, from direction aspect and time aspect that influence a person's energy/ element, it is quite a difficult task to answer this complex question. The I Ching method is one of the best tools to help you identify people's key element and clarify the most favourable element accurately and swiftly. (I think the Four Pillars method is another one of the most useful tools to solve this complex problem.)

How do you identify people's key favourable element with I Ching? I believe I have given you a lot of examples in the case studies in this book. Next you might ask me how do you decide on a correct feng shui remedy for a particular client when the favourable element has already been identified? I have mentioned that you should give comprehensive suggestions on how to strengthen the favourable element and how to reduce the unfavourable element. I'd like to highlight it again: not only thinking about house location and furniture arrangement etc. (of course these strategies are necessary, however they are not enough) but also considering the career, lifestyle, diet, social relations and so on. I am afraid I can't discuss it in more detail here.

9. Can I consult the I Ching without drawing a hexagram?

Yes, you may open the Book of Changes randomly and turn to any page, and then look at whichever hexagram it is. Note intuitively any significant foreboding associated with your question.

10. Can I consult the I Ching if I have not got the book to hand?

Yes, in fact many people carry out the Mei Hua and Na Jia methods purely from the image of the hexagram and analysis of the relationship of the Five Elements of the trigram and line and regardless of the explanation text on the hexagram and line from the I Ching. However, the pre-condition is that you are familiar with the Eight Basic Trigrams and 64 Hexagrams and understand the basic principles of the Mei Hua or Na Jia methods.

11. You mentioned that the I Ching can forecast everything in the world; can it help people with things such as stealing or crime?

No, because the I Ching emphasised that Tao (the great Way), or the natural law controlled everything in the world. What the I Ching may help us to do is understand the natural law (Tao) well and tell us how to follow the law in our specific situation. Of course the I Ching teaches you strategies to make a success of your project, however they are strategies to improve your capacity to obey the Tao or natural law instead of teaching you skills to fight the natural law. You can't violate or escape from the Tao, or the natural law ever! According to natural law, anybody who is evil or has committed a crime will be repaid by the great Tao, which is as powerful as the Christian God. And whoever committed the crime has to pay a terrible price for they have done. Furthermore, the I Ching asks people to keep honest and sincere within (Inner Truth) when they consult it, or else the I Ching will not advise them. As everybody knows, if someone wants to carry out a criminal plan, it is impossible to keep honest and sincere within. In short, the I Ching, the Bible of eastern people, teaches us to do right, and never allows us to do any evil actions. If people complain that they have failed to get the right answer from the I Ching, it is often because they are not honest, and the I Ching then won't tell them the truth.

12. How do you pick up the right symbol of a specific indicator such as Self line/Response line, Subject trigram/Object trigram etc. for our target of concern? Why in the book do you sometimes symbolise one thing by two indicators, e.g. in the President murder case, you symbolised the President by both the Self line and the fifth line at the same time?

Yes, the I Ching method is a very flexible method. On one hand, one indicator may have more symbols, e.g. the fifth line may represent the president or emperor (in terms of the judgement of place of line, as I mentioned previously that the fifth line is the place of king), sometimes it may represent the neck of a person (in terms of the judgement of image of hexagram, as I mentioned that the sixth line is a symbol of a person's head and the fifth line is a symbol of a person's neck). On the other hand, one matter/event may be symbolised by two or more indicators at the same time. For example, the President may be symbolised by the Self line (in terms of general principle of the Na Jia method), fifth line (in terms of the place of line), Official line (in terms of the judgement of the meaning of the Six Relatives) and Subject trigram (in terms of the judgement of the Mei Hua method) respectively at the same time and in the same hexagram. So there are no strict fixed criteria for each symbol, there are only some general principles to interpret them. It depends on your particular purpose and method of prediction and your intuition of understanding the I Ching method.

13. With regard to selecting the right time to calculate and create hexagrams, there are several questions:

- **How do you select the right time to calculate and create a hexagram for a prediction about a specific matter/event, which happens in a limited period?**

It is quite flexible. However there is still a general principle. It is important to be aware of noticing any specific moment when something associated with you happens suddenly. E.g. when you get a telephone call or an email, which is associated with the matter concerning you. Or when something which is related to the matter happened, or will happen such as a certain moment of a plane departure or arrival, or a child leaving its family and so on.

- **How can you select the right time if the event lasts for a long period? E.g. 2008 Olympics bid campaign in China.**

You may select the time from any significant moment associated with the event. E.g. the specific time when the Beijing mission for the Olympic Games bid made its final presentation in Moscow. Or you may pick the time at random, e.g. somebody asks you suddenly about the result of the bid. The moment when the person asks you the question is the right time to create the hexagram.

- **How do you pick the right time, if there are two different times associated closely with the question? For example, a friend asks me a question on an international call, he is in Washington DC, US, while I am in Beijing, China. Then which time should I use, the local time in Washington, or the local time in Beijing?**

This is a flexible question indeed. If the question is focused on my friend's side such as his relatives, business in the US and so on, it is better to use the local time in Washington DC. If the question is focused on something that happened in China such as his relatives or business in China, it is better to use the time in Beijing. Sometimes you may draw two hexagrams according to the two local times respectively, then look at one as the main indicator and refer to the other one as an assistant or complementary indicator. E.g. when I predicted the 2008 Olympics bid, I used the local time in Moscow to create the main hexagram, and the local time in Beijing and the local time in Osaka to create complementary hexagrams.

14. Can I ask the I Ching the same question repeatedly if I fail to get a satisfactory answer from the first divination?

Yes, although there was a saying in the text of the Meng hexagram of the I Ching: 'first asking is OK, repeated asking will be rejected.' However, based on my personal experience and several masters' experience, you may ask a question two or more times, provided you pick the time correctly and keep honest within.

15. How can you improve your intuition?

There are many ways to do this. Study I Ching and try to put it into your daily life; practise tai chi, qigong, yoga and so on; it is also important to keep your mental and physical state natural and free from any stress and worry.

16. How do you identify a Great Combination of Three Elements?

The Great Combination of Three Elements is an important concept in the Mei Hua and Na Jia methods. Like the changing line, as long as this great combination is set up, it will greatly influence the hexagram, trigram and line of hexagram. There are several situations which may build the Great Combination of Three Elements, as follows:

- All three elements are from the Earthly Branch of day, month and year (e.g. Snake year, Rooster month and Ox day) or hour, day and month (e.g. Tiger hour, Horse day and Dog month),
- All three elements are from lines in your hexagram and at least two of them are changing lines, e.g. Pig line, Rabbit line and Sheep line are in your hexagram and the Pig line and Rabbit line are changing lines.
- Two among the three elements are from the Earthly Branch of day and month (please note: the hour and year are useless in this situation) and the other one is a line of the hexagram, e.g. you drew a hexagram on Tiger day in Horse month, and there is a Dog line in your hexagram, no matter whether it is a changing line or still line.

- Two among the three elements are from the lines in your hexagram, one of them is a changing line (visible or invisible changing line), and the other one is from the Earthly Branch of day or month, e.g. you drew a hexagram on Rat day, two lines are Monkey and Dragon in your hexagram, and the Monkey or Dragon line is changing.

It is worth pointing out that when there are only two among the three elements which may set up the great combination, you need to be careful in making your final judgement. This situation is called a Half Great Combination of Three Elements. As long as it comes to that day or month, which is the missing one among the three elements, the Great Combination will appear and its impact will be effective, e.g. you drew a hexagram in Dragon month, and the Self line of your hexagram is Rat line, which is not strong at that time because the Rat water is destroyed by Dragon month earth. However, you need not worry too much, as you have already got a Half Combination and you need to wait for the coming Monkey day or Monkey month. When the Monkey day or Monkey month arrives, the Self line Rat water will become very strong due to the support of the Great Combination of the Three Elements. So, the missing element among the three elements (the Monkey in this example) is a very useful and significant indicator, which often gives you the accurate time when you made your prediction.

17. Can I discover the best time for making an important decision by consulting the I Ching? Or pinpoint the best time to start an important action or plan?

Yes, in fact I have already given you some examples on how to time things in advance to guarantee a successful plan in the case dealing with stock market forecasting.

I have often been asked how to select the best date to start an important plan, such as visiting a VIP who may greatly influence people's fate, putting a great deal of money into an investment project, such as selling or buying stock, or booking a plane ticket for a long distance flight. There is a special timing technique. You might hear that there are lots of methods of timing. However, some are too complicated to put into practice and some are unreliable. I'll give you a very simple, swift and reliable one. It is really unique, because I invented it myself years ago and use it often when I want to make an important decision. Until now I have kept it to myself. Although I have used it for my close friends, they only know the result and never know why and how to do it. So it has not been made known to others so far. But now, I'd like to offer it to my dear readers and I hope you benefit from it and enjoy using it in your daily life.

I learnt and reformed this timing technique from my study and research on the I Ching. There are several ways to use timing. The first way is to find a significant indicator from your previous hexagram (such as changing line, Favourable line, Response line and number of Subject trigram etc.), which may obviously indicate or imply the accurate time for carrying out your plan, or the time of your last target achieved. The second way is to make a range of hexagrams according to a range of time data from possible dates for carrying out your plan; then choose the best hexagram by comparing these hexagrams; finally, locate the time which has the best hexagram associated with it. E.g. you plan to hold an important meeting and need to make appointments with relevant people in advance. Based on the schedule, there are three days in the coming week (e.g. Monday, Tuesday and Wednesday) available for all participants. So which is the best day? You must make this decision in advance. The alternative is to draw a range of hexagrams according to the time data of the three days. Maybe there are twelve original hexagrams in total for the three days, or four hexagrams for each day. Then if you find that the best hexagram is the one drawn from the morning of the coming Tuesday from 9.00–11.00 a.m. (Snake hour in the Chinese calendar), you have the answer. The important meeting should be held at that time.

Finally, I'd like to recommend the Four Pillars method again. I believe it is one of the best ways to do timing.

18. Can I do a prediction for another person such as a client or a friend etc?

Yes, although there are some people who disagree with this idea (including the great English scholar on I Ching, Christopher Market), there is a lot of strong and trustworthy evidence on how to do it to help others. In China, besides the senior official Grand Diviner in ancient dynasties who did nothing except make predictions for the emperor, full-time diviner has been a professional career (some people saw them as fortune-tellers) as common as a doctor of TCM. It is very easy to find professional diviners who provide predictions for clients on the streets of Hong Kong, Taiwan, and urban areas of Japan today. And there is a very famous old saying in China: 'The real sage must originate from doctors and diviners.' Some TCM doctors provide both medical treatment and an I Ching prediction together. You might note that lots of the cases in this book were conducted by me in order to help other people, and not just for myself.

Chapter Ten

The Hexagrams and Lines

This chapter provides you with an overview of the imagery of each of the 64 hexagrams based purely on the symbolism invoked in the combination of the two trigrams. These are simply the editor's interpretation and with time and practice it is up to you to take the subject further.

When you are consulting the I Ching from any of the four methods in this book you may need to either (a) consult the meaning of a moving line or (b) see what the final outcome of a hexagram is once the changing line has been adjusted.

What is a brief, almost transliteration of the meaning in each of the changing lines, is wide open to interpretation. I have left them largely as they are in early Chinese texts and it is up to you, the reader, to interpret the metaphors involved.

Personally, I have several translations, or versions, of the I Ching which I refer to. If you find this system as fascinating as I do then I highly recommend that you check out any of the full versions of the I Ching which are mentioned in the bibliography at the back of the book. As Professor Wang Yang repeats throughout this book, intuition plays a large part in your interpretation of any prediction. If you are completely new to the I Ching then the following summaries of the hexagrams will prove useful.

The Hexagrams

Upper Trigram / Lower Trigram	Ch'ien	Chen	K'an	Ken	K'un	Sun	Li	Tui
Ch'ien	1	34	5	26	11	9	14	43
Chen	25	51	3	27	24	42	21	17
K'an	6	40	29	4	7	59	64	47
Ken	33	62	39	52	15	53	56	31
K'un	12	16	8	23	2	20	35	45
Sun	44	32	48	18	46	57	50	28
Li	13	55	63	22	36	37	30	49
Tui	10	54	60	41	19	61	38	58

Key to the Hexagrams

To find the hexagram that the oracle has given you as an answer to your questions, locate the lower trigram on the left and the upper trigram on the top of the chart. Then turn to the hexagram text that the number indicates.

1. Ch'ien/The Creative
Above: **Heaven**
Below: **Heaven**

The two trigrams here, Heaven, represent all the yang qualities. This can involve masculinity, firmness, leadership, activity, creativity and action. In essence, this hexagram calls for firm action.

Line (6)   Know your limitations. Do not bite off more than you can chew.

Line (5)   The dragon is in the sky, it would advance you to see the wise man.

Line (4)   The dragon is coiled and ready to spring. There is no danger.

Line (3)   The wise man keeps his wits about him at all times.

Line (2)   Seek counsel from a wise man.

Line (1)   Avoid taking rash or spontaneous action.

2. K'un/The Receptive
Above: **Earth**
Below: **Earth**

Here the double trigrams of Earth embody the full spirit of yin which represents femininity, patience, peace and reliability. Rather than be the initiator of action, simply go with the flow or the tide.

Line (6)   Success comes from maintaining your self-belief.

Line (5)   Wearing yellow clothes at the beginning brings good luck.

Line (4)   Your potential is locked up.

Line (3)   Maintain a high moral principle.

Line (2)   Keep still and everything will be to your advantage.

Line (1)   Be wary of premonitions.

3. Chun/Sprouting
Above: **Water**
Below: **Thunder**

The lower trigram here, Thunder, represents the dawn and spring. Above it lies Water. The symbolism here is that of initiation of any project, but caution is required as any new life-form or action is fragile at the beginning. Remaining still is good advice.

Line (6)   Hesitation and regret.

Line (5)   Saving in moderation is beneficial, hoarding could be disastrous.

Line (4)   Be patient and everything will turn to your advantage.

Line (3)   When hunting, always be accompanied by an expert tracker.

Line (2)   Life appears like a merry-go-round, but you make little progress.

Line (1)   Going around in circles.

4. Meng/Youthful Folly
Above: **Mountain**
Below: **Water**

In this trigram, Water lies under the Mountain. Water, in this instance, can represent the curiosity of youth which can be restless and have no roots, whereas the Mountain represents knowledge or a teacher. This trigram can symbolise what Zen teachers describe as 'having a beginner's mind'. To be willing and open to learn.

Line (6)   Youth needs strong moral guidance.

Line (5)   Immaturity and youthful trust can bring good fortune.

Line (4)   Without education you will meet difficulty.

Line (3)   Avoid being seduced by wealth.

Line (2)   Embrace the naivety of youth.

Line (1)   Show the youth the results of indiscipline as a warning.

5. Hsu/Waiting
   Above: **Water**
   Below: **Heaven**

Water above Heaven means that the skies are heavy and full with rain. It is obviously always wise to wait until the heavy rain passes. Waiting can provide an education of its own – patience, perseverance and having the confidence to overcome difficulties, as well as understanding the importance of timing your move.

Line (6)   Unannounced visitors that you welcome with honour will bring later good fortune.

Line (5)   Fast and you will receive good blessings.

Line (4)   Hide out of sight away from your home.

Line (3)   If you are unprotected in the open you will be robbed.

Line (2)   In the beginning blame and gossip is rife, but the outcome is beneficial.

Line (1)   Hedge your bets and remain on the fringe of activity.

6. Sung/Conflict
Above: **Heaven**
Below: **Water**

Heaven represents father, authority, morality and clarity, whereas Water represents the middle son who is the expert arbitrator within the family of the trigrams. All disputes can be settled with the assistance of the wisdom of an elder (Heaven) combined with the skilful diplomatic nature of the middle son (Water). In this situation, seek advice to resolve the dispute.

Line (6)   In a legal dispute, you are initially supported and it is undermined three times.

Line (5)   Success in legal matters initially.

Line (4)   Let go of the conflict and trust your own judgement.

Line (3)   Make sure your vision and dream are in tune with your leader or misfortune occurs.

Line (2)   Little success in legal affairs. Leave home as soon as possible.

Line (1)   Let go of the conflict and despite the gossip good fortune prevails.

7. Shih/The Army
Above: **Earth**
Below: **Water**

Using the Five Element theory, earth controls water. In this situation the sometimes ambiguous and dangerous nature of Water is controlled by the gentle passive supporting earth. The symbolism here is of honour, loyalty and working on your own inner strength, integrity and honesty.

Line (6)   Gain support from the leaders and not the masses.

Line (5)   Make use of local resources.

Line (4)   Taking shelter on the left is safe.

Line (3)   Defeat will occur if you procrastinate.

Line (2)   The command of the army is sound and secure.

Line (1)   Whether moving forwards or backwards, maintain your rhythm.

8. Pi/Holding Together

Above: **Water**
Below: **Earth**

The advice in this hexagram suggests that working cooperatively together in the face of difficulty or disaster will bring
greater success. It is wiser to group together now, rather than
seek help by joining a group when it is too late.

Line (6)   Those that support you have no leader and can bring
          you harm.

Line (5)   Declare who your supporters are to the world at large.

Line (4)   Find support from beyond your closest friends.

Line (3)   Those that believe in you at present are not necessarily
          those who will support you.

Line (2)   Those that you can trust are closest to you.

Line (1)   Surround yourself with co-workers who trust you.

9. Hsiao Ch'u/The Taming Power of the Small

Above: **Wind**

Below: **Heaven**

The trigram Wind is always associated with the feng in feng shui. It is a gentle, intuitive, almost psychic quality. Heaven always represents judgement and wisdom. In essence, this hexagram suggests that you should use your intuition in the widest possible sense to come up with a clear and focused judgement.

Line (6) The storm has passed, you may now proceed with caution.

Line (5) Extend love, honesty and gratitude.

Line (4) Dissolve your anxieties and fears and believe in yourself.

Line (3) The wheel is off the vehicle. The driver and passenger blame each other.

Line (2) There is no harm in being supported.

Line (1) There is no harm in returning home safely yet empty-handed.

10. Lu/Treading
Above: **Heaven**
Below: **Lake**

The trigram Tui (the Lake) is the youngest and most yin of the trigrams, yet above her sits the ultimate yang trigram (Heaven) or authority. This hexagram suggests that you need courage and agility to take on or confront power, authority or events that are far greater than you.

Line (6)   Good luck will prevail if you return.

Line (5)   Advance without hesitation but be wary of future danger.

Line (4)   If you tread on the tiger's tail with trepidation ultimately you will be rewarded.

Line (3)   If you tread on the tiger's tail you will be bitten.

Line (2)   The road is flat and this is a good sign for the prisoner.

Line (1)   Be modest and wear simple shoes.

11. T'ai/Peace
Above: **Earth**
Below: **Heaven**

This is the perfect combination of heaven and earth, male and female, yin and yang. This is a meeting of heaven and earth, bringing sincerity, honesty and integrity and confidence to what you do. Heaven is now on earth.

Line (6)   Your supporters are distracted and this suggests problems.

Line (5)   Good fortune at the beginning.

Line (4)   Speak the truth and avoid paying lip service to others simply to appease them.

Line (3)   Despite the turbulence of life, maintain your self-belief and enjoy good nourishment.

Line (2)   Long journeys can be rewarding if you keep to the straight and narrow.

Line (1)   The leader or the boss will enjoy good fortune.

12. P'i/Standstill
Above: **Heaven**
Below: **Earth**

Although heaven and earth are represented in this hexagram in their correct position, the oppressive yang energy of the downward force of heaven prevents the creativity and spirit of yin from flourishing. The symbolism here is of stagnation and small possibilities.

Line (6) Whatever was in the way has gone now and peace follows.

Line (5) By removing the stumbling blocks, the wise man is successful.

Line (4) Go with the judgement of the leader or the government and work together with your neighbours.

Line (3) When you are acknowledged, accept it from the bottom of your heart.

Line (2) An unscrupulous person is successful by falsely appeasing others.

Line (1) Great luck, fortune and success.

13. T'ung Jen/Fellowship with Men
Above: **Heaven**
Below: **Fire**

This hexagram can be seen as a group of friends in the woods gathered around a fire at night under the heavens. The warmth, the companionship, the inspiration and the friendship that are generated can lead to new levels of possibility.

Line (6)   To develop friends and friendships beyond your home or workplace is beneficial.

Line (5)   Bring everyone together to fight a good cause and remember to relax afterwards.

Line (4)   Go close to the edge, but do not fight your adversary into the corner.

Line (3)   Having made all your preparations and observations, you discover it is wise to wait.

Line (2)   Fellowship should be extended to all men - not just your own family.

Line (1)   Going out of your way to bring people together will bring good fortune.

14. Ta Yu/Possession in Great Measure
Above: **Fire**
Below: **Heaven**

Fire above in this hexagram can be seen as the sun at the peak of its development at noon or mid-summer. When you are at your peak of success be generous and rewarding to others around you. Giving is a blessing to others.

Line (6)   If the heavens smile on you, everything brings you good fortune.

Line (5)   Good fortune comes from deep and trusted friendship.

Line (4)   It does no harm if you do not show off.

Line (3)   The lieutenant can acknowledge the general, but the masses do not have this opportunity.

Line (2)   There is no harm undertaking transportation with large vehicles.

Line (1)   Get rid of the cause and the damage is not serious.

15. Ch'ien/Modesty
Above: **Earth**
Below: **Mountain**

The Mountain trigram is always associated with knowledge, deep security and stillness. Above it in this hexagram lies Earth protecting and strengthening the Mountain's quality. This hexagram represents the strong, silent individual who does not need to show off or brag.

Line (6)   If you have a reputation for modesty you can gain success in punitive action.

Line (5)   There is success in being tough with those who do not share their success with their friends.

Line (4)   Be modest in every aspect of your life and success will follow.

Line (3)   A happy and successful old age becomes those who are modest.

Line (2)   Good fortune to someone who despite their fame can remain modest.

Line (1)   A modest and careful person can gain great fortune by travelling widely.

16. Yu/Enthusiasm
Above: **Thunder**
Below: **Earth**

The lower trigram of Earth can be seen as heavy, still or stagnant. To motivate its chi, fiery active weather above it can change its nature. Out of this stagnation can come inspiration, passion and activity.

Line (6)   If you are self-indulgent late into the evening it will bring no harm.

Line (5)   Seek guidance about your illness.

Line (4)   Let your friends share your success and pleasures.

Line (3)   Procrastination or flattery brings regret.

Line (2)   Like a rock, maintain your principles and this will bring you good fortune.

Line (1)   You have a reputation for seeking sensory pleasure and this brings bad luck.

17. Sui/Following

Above: **Lake**

Below: **Thunder**

The Lake can represent reflection, intuition, vision or dream. Thunder can be expressed as power and initiative. Here the symbolism suggests that you would be wise to pursue your dreams.

Line (6)   Freedom follows incarceration.

Line (5)   Remain true to all that is just and fair and innocent.

Line (4)   If you are true to yourself no harm will come to you if you seek success.

Line (3)   Never forget that home is where your heart and responsibilities ultimately lie.

Line (2)   Whatever occurs do not let go of your responsibilities.

Line (1)   You will gain a lot by socialising away from home.

18. Ku/Decay
Above: **Mountain**
Below: **Wind**

Wind is a wood element and here it is suppressed by the heavy downward force of the earth element Mountain. Here the imagery suggests that there is a temporary obstacle or an overriding burden of responsibility that is preventing you from moving. In nature this would be similar to a pile of earth temporarily burying a new shoot.

Line (6)   Be free of all corruption and avoid serving a leader.

Line (5)   Resolve your father's mistakes with honour.

Line (4)   It brings sorrow to have to resolve your father's mistakes.

Line (3)   Although it is regrettable there is nothing wrong with sorting out your father's problems.

Line (2)   When resolving the issues of an older relative, let go of the principle that older people are wiser.

Line (1)   Having the unswerving support of a son, a father can avoid a disaster.

19. Lin/Approach
Above: **Earth**
Below: **Lake**

The reflective often visionary nature of the Lake is pushing upwards towards the receptive quality of Earth. Something is about to begin and you need to be decisive, focused and energetic in seeing it through.

Line (6)   Leadership by sincerity brings good fortune.

Line (5)   A good ruler uses wisdom.

Line (4)   A good leader listens and understands their people.

Line (3)   Glossing over the truth or sweetening the pill will bring no reward to the ruler.

Line (2)   Nothing can go wrong if as a ruler you treat people with humanity.

Line (1)   A great leader is successful if they have humanity.

20. Kuan/Contemplation
Above: **Wind**
Below: **Earth**

The grounded open and receptive qualities of Earth below are supporting the more intuitive nature of Wind above. An ideal opportunity to slow down, take stock and reflect. Before initiating something new, it would be wise to pause for a moment.

Line (6)   By observing and interfacing with other cultures the wise person learns.

Line (5)   All will be well with a leader who really understands his people.

Line (4)   When in Rome do as the Romans do.

Line (3)   Manage your staff by listening and watching.

Line (2)   Prying and gossiping undermine your sincerity.

Line (1)   Childish behaviour in a leader holds them back.

21. Shih Ho/Biting Through

Above: **Fire**
Below: **Thunder**

The Fire trigram is associated with illumination and inspiration. It is one thing to feel inspired about something and another to have the motivation and energy to pursue your dream. Here the combination is perfect, bringing determination and stamina.

Line (6)   You are carrying too many responsibilities and this can be inauspicious.

Line (5)   There is danger, but no disaster.

Line (4)   Finding an arrowhead or bullet in the meat, the omen is that you remain faithful to the cause in times of difficulty.

Line (3)   Sickness after eating preserved meat, but there is no long-lasting effect.

Line (2)   There is no harm if you bite off more than you can chew.

Line (1)   Naked feet are threatened but there is no harm.

22. Pi/Grace
Above: **Mountain**
Below: **Fire**

The Mountain is always symbolic of stability, the family or the establishment. While Fire is a powerful form of chi, it lies below this trigram (Mountain) and is attempting to break into the stronghold. This is possible with grace, humility and modesty.

Line (6)   Dress or decorate with white for success.

Line (5)   Decorate your home modestly. All will be well.

Line (4)   It is auspicious to wear white.

Line (3)   If you are well-dressed and faithful good luck will occur.

Line (2)   It is beneficial to decorate your hair, your beard or your moustache.

Line (1)   You would benefit by walking instead of taking a vehicle.

23. Po/Splitting Apart
Above: **Mountain**
Below: **Earth**

The first five lines of this hexagram are yin and the only stability lies at the top. There is little stability in this hexagram and it suggests that everything will fall apart very soon, paving the way for new possibilities. You have little support.

Line (6) After the harvest the largest fruit is not consumed.

Line (5) All is auspicious when the favourite concubines enter the bedroom together.

Line (4) If you cut or graze yourself when the bed breaks it brings bad luck.

Line (3) There is damage, but no irretrievable loss.

Line (2) It is dangerous if the frame of the bed breaks or collapses.

Line (1) Bad luck occurs if the leg of the bed breaks.

24. Fu/Return

Above: **Earth**
Below: **Thunder**

This hexagram suggests new beginnings. The first line of the hexagram is yang and all the others are open and receptive. Life lies ahead of you – this is a process of rebirth.

Line (6)   If you lose your way, physically or emotionally, on your journey it is bad luck, but not a disaster.

Line (5)   Always return when it is urgent.

Line (4)   Come home alone taking the safest route.

Line (3)   Constantly returning from your journey shows trouble but not disaster.

Line (2)   Take care of things or make repairs before returning to your journey.

Line (1)   After setting out on a journey you return soon.

25. Wu Wang/Innocence
Above: **Heaven**
Below: **Thunder**

The Heaven trigram in the upper position can reflect your vision and dream, whereas the lower trigram Thunder symbolises initiation and action. A wise interpretation of this hexagram is to be yourself, be receptive to new possibilities and allow events to unfold with trust.

Line (6)   It can be disastrous to take action without being clear about your purpose.

Line (5)   An unexpected illness can be prevented without taking medicine.

Line (4)   The unexpected can be anticipated by divination.

Line (3)   Be wary of an unexpected disaster.

Line (2)   Always travel with a clear sense of purpose.

Line (1)   Travelling with no thoughts of reward or results will bring good luck.

26. Ta Ch'u/The Taming Power of the Great
Above: **Mountain**
Below: **Heaven**

This hexagram depicts a very powerful combination of stability and control. Grounded by Heaven, which can represent father, authority or control, the trigram above, the Mountain, symbolises stability and wisdom. Believe in yourself and remain focused.

Line (6)   A wide open sky and a level road and horizon ahead of you will bring a favourable result.

Line (5)   Restraint will bring great success.

Line (4)   Learn to harness and discipline your stamina as this will bring good luck.

Line (3)   There is advantage in travelling.

Line (2)   The wheel has come off the vehicle.

Line (1)   When under threat, retreat.

27. I/Providing Nourishment
Above: Mountain
Below: Thunder

There is a strong self-reflective quality represented in the upper trigram of Mountain and the action from below – Thunder – suggests that you need to chew very well. Chewing in this sense is not literal, but more in a contemplative way.

Line (6) An adventure or journey at present, however dangerous, could manifest as luck.

Line (5) Avoid undertaking dangerous journeys at present.

Line (4) Develop your courage, sincerity and honesty.

Line (3) Avoid undertaking anything vitally important at present.

Line (2) This is not a time to take punitive action.

Line (1) Bad luck can occur if you ignore the prediction.

28. Ta Kuo/Preponderance of the Great
Above: Lake
Below: Wind

The wood element that supports the Wind trigram can be represented in this imagery as that of a tree. In this situation the tree is submerged in the lake. The wood can also be represented as the ridgepole of a house with enormous pressure bearing down on it. The symbolism here is of a sense of being completely overwhelmed by pressure.

Line (6)   You find yourself out of your depth, but there is no misfortune.

Line (5)   The woman rediscovers her youthful spirit and finds a young man. No disaster yet no success.

Line (4)   The burden has lifted from your shoulders, but be wary of accidents.

Line (3)   You are burdened by responsibilities that can bring bad luck.

Line (2)   You rediscover your youthful energy.

Line (1)   A good time to self-reflect and be modest.

29. K'an/The Abysmal
Above: **Water**
Below: **Water**

The yin nature of water reflects the dark, the night, the winter and the still. A double measure of this element spells trouble. However, the strength of water lies in courage and flexibility. The solution here is to draw on your inner reserves and flexibility to see through this crisis.

Line (6) Misfortune. Possible dangers or difficulties for three years.

Line (5) Be patient and the danger will pass.

Line (4) Make an offering or prayer to ward off the danger.

Line (3) This is a dangerous line. Dangers occur when leaving or coming back.

Line (2) Only aim for modest success when you are faced with danger.

Line (1) You are surrounded by danger. Be careful.

30. Li/The Clinging
Above: **Fire**
Below: **Fire**

Fire can represent warmth, inspiration, passion and vision. Double this quality up and the result could be exhausting! Fire always needs fuel – oxygen and wood. Make sure that you have support for your vision and expression.

Line (6)   When the leader or the boss takes punitive actions, he goes for the opposing leader and not their supporters.

Line (5)   Despite your tears, your grief and worry, good fortune does emerge.

Line (4)   The irresponsible son who was once sent away now returns and is killed.

Line (3)   Bad luck occurs if you hunt at sunset or sing without being accompanied by musical instruments.

Line (2)   Catching birds or animals with a yellow net will bring luck.

Line (1)   Always observe respect and offer a prayer when you begin a new venture.

31. Hsien/Influence
Above: **Lake**
Below: **Mountain**

There is a subtle symbolism in this hexagram. As hot air rises in nature towards the heavens, the cooler mountainous air forces the moisture to return to the lakes, rivers and streams. Here your reflective inner knowledge (Mountain) can have a powerful yet subtle influence on others.

Line (6)   In expressing yourself, your face and tongue tremble through emotion.

Line (5)   You are overcome by emotion, but there is no difficulty.

Line (4)   You are procrastinating. Whatever you decide your friends will support you.

Line (3)   Stay still and avoid travelling far.

Line (2)   It is safer if all the family remain together at present.

Line (1)   You tingle all over with emotion.

32. Heng/Duration
Above: **Thunder**
Below: **Wind**

This is a very strong combination of two wood elements. The vision, sensitivity and intuition of Wind below influences the more action-orientated Thunder trigram above. This hexagram suggests that with all action remember your purpose and vision.

Line (6)   If the grass appears greener on the other side, no good will come of it.

Line (5)   Always be motivated by your inherent moral principles.

Line (4)   There is no wildlife in the pastures. The larder is bare.

Line (3)   In the end you will be humiliated if you cannot maintain your principles.

Line (2)   Be free of any regrets.

Line (1)   Know your limitations.

33. Tun/Retreat
Above: **Heaven**
Below: **Mountain**

The two lower lines of this hexagram are yin and it is capped by four strong yang lines. Traditionally in China a mountain always had a cave and the imagery was that this was where sages dwelt in order to reflect and meditate. Here the imagery suggests that you retreat, go within yourself, self-reflect and review the big picture.

Line (6)   Having had great success from hard work and struggle you deserve to retreat in comfort.

Line (5)   You will be rewarded for achieving what you said you would do.

Line (4)   Retreating into your own space is not always easy. Be ready to undertake whatever is needed to achieve this.

Line (3)   Retreat to the security of your own space and focus on that which is vital to you at present.

Line (2)   You have great faith in either a leader or a principle. This faith should free you not tie you.

Line (1)   Avoid danger as soon as you notice it. Do not leave yourself open to attack.

34. Ta Chuang/The Power of the Great
Above: **Thunder**
Below: **Heaven**

This is a very powerful hexagram. Below is the full power and authority of yang breaking through and being fed by the energy of spring and Thunder. Avoid being a bull in a china shop and make sure that, with all this power behind you, you are going in the right direction.

Line (6)   Overcome difficulties and good fortune will appear.

Line (5)   If all is chaos around you, maintain your centre.

Line (4)   Be absolutely focused on your inner strength.

Line (3)   The sage treats every occurrence naturally, whereas unnecessary pride or vanity can get in the way of others' progress.

Line (2)   Be consistent in all that you do and good fortune will prevail.

Line (1)   Despite any temporary disabilities, if you remain faithful to your cause you can progress.

35. Chin/Progress
Above: **Fire**
Below: **Earth**

The imagery here is of almost perfect balance. Fire is represented here as the sun shining brightly above the earth. Everything appears sunny, bright and fortunate. You will prosper and be popular.

Line (6)   You are on the leading edge of an advance. There are difficulties but no serious hazards.

Line (5)   Let go of your doubts and move forward to your advantage.

Line (4)   If you are impatient, speedy and greedy in your advance it will be disastrous.

Line (3)   Everyone trusts you and your self-doubt disappears.

Line (2)   Rely on your inner strength. You are truly blessed by your grandmother.

Line (1)   Be flexible in your dealings with others. Success or promotion is possible.

36. Ming I/Darkening of the Light
Above: **Earth**
Below: **Fire**

This is a difficult hexagram. Fire is buried under the Earth. All is dark. Since Fire represents inspiration and passion, it means that these aspects cannot be seen at present. Hold on to your vision and dream.

Line (6) You have bitten off more than you can chew and are being grounded initially by the failure. It is auspicious to take a more prudent road in the future.

Line (5) Although surrounded by misguided people, remain close to your hidden inner faith. No one can take this away from you.

Line (4) You discover hidden plans or gossip that could harm others. You are not affected and escape unscathed.

Line (3) Despite the darkness, you have the stamina to take on what you consider to be wrong.

Line (2) Injury to the leg. You need powerful assistants.

Line (1) Despite taking on a challenge your mentor will blame you.

37. Chia Jen/The Family
Above: **Wind**
Below: **Fire**

In China the centre of the family's home was always the fire, the hearth. This is an auspicious hexagram as it suggests that the flames of the fire are fed by oxygen/Wind. The imagery here suggests that you support your family, be involved with your family and reconnect with domestic life.

Line (6)   Leadership, honesty and faith in one another brings good fortune to the family in the end.

Line (5)   It is a good sign if your boss or an official visits the family, it is no cause for concern.

Line (4)   Wealth will bring great fortune and prosperity to the family.

Line (3)   Discipline within the home and family in the short term is painful, but necessary to avoid hardship.

Line (2)   Go about any domestic duties with humility and you will be rewarded with good fortune.

Line (1)   Guard and protect your home as best you can to ward off inauspicious events.

38. K'uei/Opposition
   Above: **Fire**
   Below: **Lake**

Two kinds of opposition are at play here. Firstly, the Fire and the water of the Lake, and secondly the fire and the metal element which the Lake represents in the trigrams of the I Ching. Both these trigrams have a social aspect to them and this opposition in this hexagram suggests loneliness and alienation.

Line (6)   Being alone makes you unduly anxious about your security. You can relax when you realise that there is no threat to you.

Line (5)   All doubts and regrets disperse. Spend time socialising and eating with your own family.

Line (4)   When riddled with self-doubt you may meet someone who befriends and inspires you. There are dangers but nothing serious.

Line (3)   Another person's misfortune or experience needs to be a learning curve for you. Do not allow your concerns to hold you back unduly.

Line (2)   No harm comes from meeting an official or your boss in the street.

Line (1)   Avoid wasting time on small matters. Issues will resolve themselves without effort.

39. Chien/Obstruction
Above: **Water**
Below: **Mountain**

Both of these elements in nature are very powerful and difficult to traverse. Climbing a mountain in any weather is a challenge, and any body of water has its dangers. For success in this situation you need to fall back on your own inner strength and shed yourself of any unwanted baggage.

Line (6)   Despite leaving and travelling in difficult circumstances the journey will be easy and bring you good fortune.

Line (5)   Your friends are always faithful if you run into serious difficulty.

Line (4)   There are always difficulties when you are coming and going.

Line (3)   It would be wise to return home if you run into danger or trouble.

Line (2)   Officials and assistants carry the burden of problems for their leaders.

Line (1)   You have many obstacles, difficulties and challenges on your travels, but you are praised on your return.

40. Hsieh/Deliverance
   Above: **Thunder**
   Below: **Water**

Water represents depth, strength and also the unknown. Imagine being in a boat during a thunderstorm. The wisest course of action is to return home and find shelter. With this hexagram it is best to use common sense, listen to your intuition and go with the tide.

Line (6)   Keep your aim and your sights high to overcome difficulties.

Line (5)   Others around you will trust your intuition, leadership and wisdom at this time.

Line (4)   Your friends encourage you to get out of a situation that could do you harm.

Line (3)   Be wary of being robbed or attacked.

Line (2)   This line shows good fortune.

Line (1)   There are no dangers in this line.

41. Sun/Decrease
Above: **Mountain**
Below: **Lake**

The lower trigram of the Lake, which is the youngest and most reflective of all the trigrams, is being held back by the pressure of the Mountain above. The situation here suggests that it would be wise to simplify your life, get rid of your clutter and work on the basics. The best way forward to express yourself is to keep it simple.

Line (6)   Travelling is auspicious. Investment rather than securing your stock is also wise. Others can help you.

Line (5)   If you are given a very fine gift do not turn it away. This will bring you good luck.

Line (4)   You need to take care of any sickness immediately.

Line (3)   You may find that a business partnership dissolves. However, on your first attempt to initiate something new, you may find a new partner.

Line (2)   Remain firmly on course and it would not be wise to take legal or threatening action.

Line (1)   You would be wise to deal with any health issues immediately. Be aware of potentially high costs involved.

42. I/Increase
   Above: **Wind**
   Below: **Thunder**

Both these trigrams are drawn from the wood element which invokes the spirit of growth, spring and youth. Together in this hexagram they are very auspicious. The yang trigram of Thunder is pushing up toward Wind suggesting growth, expansion and increase. An excellent time to initiate action.

Line (6) Through procrastination you are criticised by others and gain nothing.

Line (5) Without any doubt you are successful in what you pursue provided you are honest and help others.

Line (4) It is wise to warn your superior of any imminent problem.

Line (3) If you make a mistake, report it to your superior. No harm will come.

Line (2) Stay purposeful with your vision and dream.

Line (1) It is favourable to initiate and undertake a new project. Everything goes smoothly.

43. Kuai/Breakthrough
Above: **Lake**
Below: **Heaven**

This is a very powerful hexagram as the full force of Heaven, strength, authority or father drives the trigram upwards towards the Lake. Have the courage and the strength to pursue your dreams.

Line (6)   Prepare yourself against unexpected events or problems.

Line (5)   Avoid being stubborn. Take the easiest route possible.

Line (4)   You act out of hardship because you have been criticised. Few people listen to you.

Line (3)   It is possible that you lose face, but if you are wise you will leave without regret or hesitation.

Line (2)   You may warn others too late about imminent danger, but it is not a problem.

Line (1)   If you travel unprepared or are not fit enough to undertake the journey there will be problems.

44. Kou/Coming to Meet
Above: **Heaven**
Below: **Wind**

All the upper five lines of this hexagram are yang, but the lower one, being yin, provides some instability. The lower trigram of Wind is always gentle, changeable and easily influenced by emotions or even the weather. Be wary of sudden changes or the unexpected.

Line (6)   It's time to take on someone who is blocking your progress. After the confrontation remain resolute with your purpose.

Line (5)   Work together with others and you will reap unexpected rewards.

Line (4)   You are down on your luck. Rather than isolate yourself surround yourself at this time with support and share your problem.

Line (3)   You are not in a powerful position. Avoid taking on any further burdens.

Line (2)   Protect all that is yours and avoid sharing anything unnecessarily at this time.

Line (1)   Slow down and remain still. This is not an auspicious time to travel.

45. Ts'ui/Gathering Together
Above: **Lake**
Below: **Earth**

In this hexagram the Lake enjoys the stable, receptive influence of the Earth below. This is the natural space for water to gather and meet. Water in Chinese philosophy and medicine can also be symbolic of the process of healing and tranquillity. The suggestion here is that you pull together your whole being: body, mind and spirit.

Line (6)   It is possible to lose money or security. It is not a disaster.

Line (5)   Stick to your vision, dream and purpose and everyone will believe and follow you. A few may not.

Line (4)   You receive and deserve excellent good fortune and no criticism.

Line (3)   Spending time socialising and complaining about your life will not further you at present.

Line (2)   Make small yet sincere offerings to your colleagues to help you through present difficult times.

Line (1)   It is absolutely vital to maintain your vision, dream and purpose. If you doubt yourself, disaster can strike.

46. Sheng/Ascending
Above: **Earth**
Below: **Wind**

The wood energy represented in the lower trigram Wind represents the full force of energy in the late spring. This hexagram suggests that you are on the way up, your ideas and initiatives will be listened to: an excellent time to seek promotion. Let your ideas be heard by someone in authority or influence.

Line (6)   Maintain your course and purpose but you are heading into new territory. Be alert.

Line (5)   Driven by your inner belief make solid yet steady progress toward success.

Line (4)   Be patient in your progress and you will be rewarded.

Line (3)   Before closing the deal make sure it is really worth it.

Line (2)   This is an auspicious time, success and promotion lie ahead – celebrate with your closest friends and allies.

Line (1)   You are lined up for promotion and very good fortune.

47. K'un/Oppression

Above: **Lake**
Below: **Water**

Here, the body of the Lake – water – has been drained out and sits below it. This hexagram can suggest depletion and exhaustion. In this situation you need to draw on the courage that water can give so that you can rely on the courage of your convictions to see you through at this time.

Line (6)   You are in the way of your own progress. Reflect on what needs to change and you will begin to succeed step by step.

Line (5)   If you feel you are under too much pressure at work, relieve the tension by encouraging a cooperative effort.

Line (4)   Despite being caught in a logjam and feeling exhausted you will slowly lift yourself above this state of affairs.

Line (3)   Little comfort at home and difficulties and pressures surround you elsewhere.

Line (2)   A sensory lifestyle will tire you and ultimately be unrewarding. You will succeed once you overcome this phase.

Line (1)   You feel trapped and embroiled by events that have gone out of control.

48. Ching/A Well
Above: **Water**
Below: **Wind**

A well or a spring is central to all rural communities. The wood trigram of Wind was always associated in this hexagram with a bucket and the Water above as the well. The implication from this hexagram is that you need to share your resources cooperatively with your friends, family and associates.

Line (6)   Do not allow others to take advantage of your skills, wisdom and talent. They can drain you.

Line (5)   You are a source of talent and inspiration to others. Do not hide yourself away.

Line (4)   Water in this instance reflects communication. Review what is blocked and maintain contact with others.

Line (3)   Few people currently recognise your skills and talents. However, tune in to what others have to offer.

Line (2)   Avoid wasting your time doing things too hastily which can ultimately damage the outcome.

Line (1)   The spring is full of mud and undrinkable. You have struck rock bottom.

49. Ko/Revolution
Above: **Lake**
Below: **Fire**

Here the strong powerful element of Fire rises up and melts the metal element of the Lake above. This hexagram suggests transformation and revolution. To take advantage of this 'melting point', timing, support and a vision are vital.

Line (6)   While bringing about change, stay purposeful, stay still (physically) and change will occur as fast as lightning.

Line (5)   Draw on your inner strength and courage before undertaking major changes.

Line (4)   It is a good time to make changes that are deep and profound. Remain purposeful.

Line (3)   Before taking new fresh action, carefully evaluate all the risks and costs.

Line (2)   Choose an auspicious date to make changes. A yin earth day is the most auspicious.

Line (1)   Before making any sudden or radical changes make sure that you have adequate security.

50. Ting/The Cauldron
Above: **Fire**
Below: **Wind**

All early civilisations owe their development to the harnessing of fire. Initially it was used for cooking and later for transforming rocks and minerals into weapons and tools. In this hexagram the wood energy of Wind supports the Fire and it is vital to remember that fire needs control or order. Bring structure into your life.

Line (6)   The best fortune can occur if you can keep a cool head while others around you panic.

Line (5)   You have the situation under firm control. Listen and act out of inner wisdom.

Line (4)   Difficulties arise if you are impetuous, hasty or rash. The system can break down.

Line (3)   The situation is too hot to handle at present. Be patient and the outcome will be successful.

Line (2)   Abundance prevails and you have a deep sense of inner security.

Line (1)   All plans and progress seem to have been upset. Make use of this situation by making a clean break.

51. Chen/The Arousing
    Above: **Thunder**
    Below: **Thunder**

This is a very powerful hexagram with two trigrams that represent not only the full growth of spring, but the action and high charge of thunder itself. In this hexagram passions can run high, excitement borders on terror and the impetus behind any new action you undertake could possibly burn you out. Keep yourself grounded.

Line (6)   The shock waves are affecting those around you. The storm will soon pass and you will be unaffected. Do not take an aggressive stance.

Line (5)   Lightning strikes all around you, yet despite some minor problems there is no real danger.

Line (4)   Difficulties and turbulence all around you, but they come to nothing.

Line (3)   A very turbulent time. However, it does not affect you adversely if you had a sense of what was coming.

Line (2)   Plenty of unexpected surprises. This is a good time to take cover temporarily.

Line (1)   A shock out of the blue leaves you temporarily confused. However, you learn something valuable from the experience.

52. Ken/Keeping Still
Above: **Mountain**
Below: **Mountain**

This is a time of immense stability and stoicism. A range of mountains evokes an image of power, tranquillity and stillness compared to a solitary one. A time of self-reflection, of study and stillness is implied. Do not be in a hurry.

Line (6)   Know your limits. Time for you to deliver some home truths to others.

Line (5)   Remain calm and still and be very careful of what you say.

Line (4)   A time to relax and not worry about turbulent events surrounding you.

Line (3)   If you allow the tension of remaining still to affect you, you will become unduly stressed. Take a break from what you are doing at present.

Line (2)   It is frustrating at present to feel stuck and isolated. Be patient.

Line (1)   Your wisest course of action is to remain still and avoid doing anything impetuous.

53. Chien/Development
Above: **Wind**
Below: **Mountain**

The development of plants, trees, cereals, rocks and river beds in nature is gradual and slow. There is progress, but it takes time. With this hexagram the wood element is growing out of the Mountain. Trees on a mountainside take longer to grow than those enjoying the warmth and security of the valleys below. Remain purposeful, but remember that progress is slow.

Line (6)   You have achieved far more than you dreamt of. Others may be envious of you.

Line (5)   Ultimately you succeed. You can make it to higher places.

Line (4)   Events seem to be running smoothly at present. However, this is only for a short time.

Line (3)   Be careful that others do not undermine your success. You are possibly out of your depth at present.

Line (2)   You can enjoy a temporary respite. Socialise and share your success with your friends.

Line (1)   It is easy for you to be blamed at present for making a mistake associated with the learning process. Admit your mistake and no one will blame you.

54. Kuei Mei/The Marrying Maiden
Above: **Thunder**
Below: **Lake**

The Lake trigram symbolises the reflective, the fun and the joyful side of life. It is also our self-expression. In this hexagram self-expression is driven by the impetus of Thunder above which can make our actions reckless and impulsive. Avoid making hasty or rash decisions.

Line (6) The offer sounds good, but in reality there is little on the table. Nothing favourable.

Line (5) Avoid being ostentatious. A good day for a deal is the 16th day of the month.

Line (4) There are going to be delays. It is not a problem.

Line (3) Flattery you receive goes nowhere to advance your position.

Line (2) Despite not being able to see the whole picture, you can still make progress. Take one step at a time.

Line (1) It is possible, even without full support, to make progress. You may also need legal help.

55. Feng/Abundance
Above: **Thunder**
Below: **Fire**

This is a very active and fulfilling hexagram. The Fire below heats the wood energy of Thunder above. This is truly one of the most spectacular hexagrams. Action, success, gain and glory are all associated with this hexagram. Take this opportunity and make the most of it!

Line (6)   You give the impression that you are successful and abundant. This outward expression could be hiding the possibility that all is not well.

Line (5)   Your inner fire brings inspiration and warmth to others. Celebrate with them in your success.

Line (4)   You feel obstructed, confused and lost. A good time to seek counsel from a superior.

Line (3)   You cannot see the wood for the trees. You may be blown off course, but you will recover your position quickly.

Line (2)   Avoid oversleeping in the morning or working late into the night at present. Avoid overindulging.

Line (1)   You will meet someone in authority who can help you in the next ten days. Make good use of their offer and you will be rewarded.

56. Lu/The Wanderer
Above: **Fire**
Below: **Mountain**

In China travelling sages were associated with wisdom and solitude – like the Mountain itself. They are looking for inspiration (fire). By being unattached and unburdened by responsibility, you can expect little in the material world, but plenty of inspiration. This hexagram suggests movement, transition and restlessness, and remember that when you travel, you are more vulnerable.

Line (6)　Be careful not to gamble what you have gained. Avoid making fun of other people's mistakes.

Line (5)　You miss out on an important deal, however in the future you will gain respect and fame.

Line (4)　Despite your travels, endeavours and success, you are not fully satisfied or content.

Line (3)　Be careful of sudden or rash action that leads to loss while travelling or in a business deal abroad. You can lose a close ally.

Line (2)　While travelling you find temporary support that benefits you greatly.

Line (1)　On your travels be generous and supportive of others, otherwise it can spell disaster.

57. Sun/The Gentle
Above: **Wind**
Below: **Wind**

The Wind trigram is associated with intuition and flexibility. When reading this hexagram the message is to proceed gently and intuitively while at the same time acknowledging your vulnerability as you have few roots. Take advantage of your intuition and flexibility at this time.

Line (6)   If you gamble at this time, you could lose everything.

Line (5)   Do not let go of your vision or dream at present. The auspicious day is yin water day.

Line (4)   This is a good time to reap your rewards. Look forward not backwards.

Line (3)   You will cause yourself needless trouble if you waste too much valuable time looking for answers outside of yourself.

Line (2)   This is a good time to consult the I Ching or discuss your plans with a confidant or mentor.

Line (1)   Take care of the small or mechanical details within your project. Maintain your belief and review what support you have.

58. Tui/The Joyous
Above: **Lake**
Below: **Lake**

In the Later Heaven Sequence of trigrams, the Lake is associated with the West. This is symbolic of sunset, harvest and self-reflection. It is also the most pleasurable time of day when families and friends relax and share their insights. This hexagram suggests that you need to relax, socialise and share what is on your mind.

Line (6)   This is a good time to get noticed. Do not shy away from showing the world your skills and talent.

Line (5)   A time to question who you really can trust at present.

Line (4)   See through to completion what you have started. Keep to your word.

Line (3)   Your judgement will be impaired if you believe what others think you want to hear.

Line (2)   Speak your truth from the bottom of your heart. Do not waste your time by flattering others.

Line (1)   Smile and the whole world smiles with you. Relax and enjoy yourself.

59. Huan/Dispersion
Above: **Wind**
Below: **Water**

This hexagram suggests an unsettled period of time. If you are travelling by boat in windy conditions it is easy to be blown off course. The secret of success with this hexagram, or indeed when sailing in rough conditions, is to know where you are going.

Line (6)   You have come through the difficult recent events unscathed. You will succeed.

Line (5)   Despite the recent overwhelming events, someone in authority makes you an excellent offer.

Line (4)   The current overwhelming events can actually be turned to your advantage. It is the time to start a bright new adventure.

Line (3)   This is not a dangerous time even though you currently feel overwhelmed.

Line (2)   Despite the overpowering tide of current events, you will persevere and succeed.

Line (1)   You need strong support of friends, family or colleagues to get out of a tough situation.

60. Chieh/Limitation
   Above: **Water**
   Below: **Lake**

In the natural world, water likes to find the easiest route and the lowest ground. As an element it represents the freedom to travel unrestrained. However, this freedom needs to be tempered by discipline. For example, water needs a glass or bowl or bottle to contain it, a river needs a bank. The imagery here suggests that although you enjoy your freedom, you need to have discipline and structure in your life.

Line (6) This is a time for reinvention. Use a whole new fresh approach to your work and creativity.

Line (5) It is quite safe to let go. You can spend freely without harm.

Line (4) By temporarily holding back on your outgoings and restraining your impetuosity you will have great success.

Line (3) This is a time to show a little restraint in terms of your financial outlay. The outcome, however, is not inauspicious.

Line (2) This is not a time to hold back. Nothing ventured, nothing gained. Travel or change is auspicious.

Line (1) A good time to keep your head down and avoid undertaking risky journeys or projects.

61. Chung Fu/Inner Truth
Above: **Wind**
Below: **Lake**

Both trigrams in this hexagram mutually support each other. In times of excessive heat the Wind – tree – can shade the Lake. Support and nourishment from the Lake in turn feeds the roots of the tree. The two central lines of this hexagram are yin, surrounded and protected by yang above and below. Protect whatever you believe or possess with attention and love.

Line (6)   Beware of being like Icarus and flying too close to the sun! Remain steadfast and humble.

Line (5)   Using your highest ideals maintain your purpose and dream.

Line (4)   Be wary on the 16th day in the Chinese calendar. You may lack important support that day.

Line (3)   A time for celebration and success. However, remember those less fortunate than yourself.

Line (2)   Share your warmth and love with your family and those close to you.

Line (1)   This is a good time to meditate and centre yourself. Be ready for the unexpected.

62. Hsiao Kuo/Preponderance of the Small
Above: **Thunder**
Below: **Mountain**

In this hexagram, the grounded Mountain trigram at the base provides stability, perseverance and inner knowledge. Above lies Thunder which is action and instability. The combination of these two trigrams suggests that you would be wise to be cautious, remain focused, keep your head down and not try to make major initiatives or moves.

Line (6) Be careful not to bite off more than you can chew. Do not make promises that you cannot keep. Otherwise, this will bring you certain misfortune.

Line (5) Be grateful for small mercies. You will have success but it will not be as great as you dreamt.

Line (4) A time to be alert. There's no danger in making progress while at the same time there is no danger if you are alert to it.

Line (3) Do not bite off more than you can chew. Overindulgence could be harmful at this time.

Line (2) If you cannot meet with your superior, be content with meeting their assistant. This can be auspicious.

Line (1) Avoid running before you can walk. Take care of the small details.

63. Chi Chi/After Completion
Above: **Water**
Below: **Fire**

There is a very beautiful and poetic symbolism of balance in this hexagram. The rising heat of fire below heats the water, which in turn sends droplets below to cool the fire. When fire and water are balanced, transformation can be perfect. This perfect balance cannot last. Take advantage of the situation, every element is in balance, and you are in luck.

Line (6)   You could easily get into something well over your head. A dangerous, but not calamitous time.

Line (5)   This is not a time to be ostentatious. Walk your talk and this will speak volumes.

Line (4)   You waste a lot of valuable time on minor problems. Be prepared for every eventuality.

Line (3)   It will take all your inner strength, stamina and perseverance to succeed. There is no one better than yourself to undertake it. Do not delegate.

Line (2)   You will lose something of material value. There is no need to waste time searching for it. Within a week all is recovered.

Line (1)   In any new venture there will be minor mishaps at the beginning. None of these will hold you back indefinitely.

64. Wei Chi/Before Completion
Above: **Fire**
Below: **Water**

The Water trigram at the base of this hexagram is sending its energy downwards, whereas the Fire trigram above is dispersing its energy above. The two forces are pulling away from each other. It will take time and effort to pull these two forces back into harmony. The symbolism here suggests that you need to keep a firm grip on your vision and destination as you are not quite there yet. If you are a good 100 metre sprinter, do not aim at the 100 metre line, but at an imaginary line 10 metres beyond.

Line (6) Do not allow your success to go to your head. Celebrate in full but avoid getting a hangover.

Line (5) Share your success with others. Socialise, relax, unwind and have fun with your companions.

Line (4) A project that you have taken years to develop is about to bear fruit. What you achieved was groundbreaking.

Line (3) Be prepared to take on new ventures or travel. This is not a good time for you to undertake litigation.

Line (2) Take a hold of the situation and slow down. No prudence in rushing at present.

Line (1) Those around you are already aware of your initial mistakes. Everyone is watching to see if you will repeat them.

Select Bibliography

Anthony, Carol K, *A Guide to the I Ching,* Anthony Publishing Company, Stow, MA, USA, 1980

Chu, W K, & Sherrill, W E, *The Astrology of the I Ching*, Routledge & Kegan Paul, London, 1976
        An Anthology of I Ching, Routledge & Kegan Paul, London, 1977

Sandifer, Jon, *Feng Shui Journey,* Piatkus, London, 1999
        Feng Shui Astrology, Piatkus, London, 1997

Walters, Derek, *Chinese Astrology*, Watkins, London, 2002
        The Chinese Astrology Workbook, Aquarian Press, London, 1988

Wilhelm, Richard, *The I Ching*, Routledge & Kegan Paul, London, 1951

Contact Details

The Author

Professor Wang Yang
Department of Preventive Medicine
Chongqing University of Medical Science
No 1 Yixueyuan Road
Chongqing 400016
P.R. China

Email: wangyang@public.cta.cq.cn or yangw_89@yahoo.com
Tel: ++ 86 23 68898289 (home)
           ++ 86 23 68806808 (office)

The Editor

Jon Sandifer
P.O. Box 69
Teddington
Middlesex TW11 9SH
United Kingdom

Email: jon@jonsandifer.com
Website: www.fengshui.co.uk
Tel: ++ 44 208 977 8988

Index

The Hexagrams

Upper Trigram → Lower Trigram ↓	Ch'ien	Chen	K'an	Ken	K'un	Sun	Li	Tui
Ch'ien	1	34	5	26	11	9	14	43
Chen	25	51	3	27	24	42	21	17
K'an	6	40	29	4	7	59	64	47
Ken	33	62	39	52	15	53	56	31
K'un	12	16	8	23	2	20	35	45
Sun	44	32	48	18	46	57	50	28
Li	13	55	63	22	36	37	30	49
Tui	10	54	60	41	19	61	38	58